TRENDS & ISSUES

IN POSTSECONDARY ENGLISH STUDIES

TRENDS AND ISSUES IN ENGLISH LANGUAGE ARTS

1999 EDITION

NATIONAL COUNCIL OF TEACHERS OF ENGLISH
1111 W. KENYON ROAD, URBANA, ILLINOIS 61801-1096

Staff Editor: Kurt Austin
Interior Design: Tom Kovacs for TGK Design; Carlton Bruett
Cover Design: Carlton Bruett

NCTE Stock Number: 55049-3050

TRENDS AND ISSUES IN ENGLISH LANGUAGE ARTS

Keeping track of the myriad issues in education can be a daunting task for those educators already stretched to get thirty hours into a twenty-four hour day. In an effort to inform and support English educators, the National Council of Teachers of English annually offers this volume featuring current trends and issues deemed vital to the professional conversation by our membership at large. Whether specialists or generalists, teachers know that no single "trend" or "issue" could touch the interest and concerns of all members of NCTE; with these books—one for each section of the Council: Elementary, Secondary, College—we aim to chronicle developments in the teaching and learning of English language arts.

The wealth of NCTE publications from which to draw the materials for *Trends and Issues* proves a double-edged sword. Publishing thirteen journals (bimonthly and quarterly) and twenty to twenty-five books annually provides ample content, yet what to include and what not? Of course, timeliness and pertinence to the issues of the day help shape the book, and, more important, we aim to meet our primary goal: Is this valuable to our members? This edition of *Trends and Issues*, we believe, offers readers a seat at the table, a chance to join the discussion. At the college level the trends and issues cited for this year are "Diverse Students, Diverse Teachers," "Ethics in Teaching, Research, and Publishing," and "Service Learning and Social Change." At the K–12 levels members cited "Multimedia in the Classroom," "Second Language Learners," and "How Politics Have Shaped Our Thinking and Our Classrooms" as those topics of current relevance to them as English language arts professionals.

We hope that you'll find this collection a valuable resource to be returned to often, one that facilitates professional development and reminds us that we all have a stake in the language arts profession.

NCTE invites you to send us those trends and issues in the English language arts that you feel are the most relevant to your teaching. Send your comments to our Web site at www.ncte.org (click on "Trends and Issues") or e-mail directly to John Kelley at jkelley@ncte.org.

Faith Schullstrom
Executive Director

CONTENTS

I. DIVERSE STUDENTS, DIVERSE TEACHERS

II. ETHICS IN TEACHING, RESEARCH, AND PUBLISHING

III. SERVICE LEARNING AND SOCIAL CHANGE

I Diverse Students, Diverse Teachers

Diversity has become a central theme in English Studies. Teachers and scholars alike have asked, "How do we teach a culturally, ethnically, and linguistically diverse student body? How do we represent and honor diversity in the curriculum and the classroom? How do we create and support a more diverse faculty in colleges and universities?" These questions are taken up in the essays in this section. In an article which won the 1998 Richard Braddock award, Arnetha Ball and Ted Lardner trace the implications of the 1975 "Ann Arbor Black English Case" in light of current debates about Ebonics. Ball and Lardner explore not only the legal ramifications of this case for educators, but also its pedagogical implications. They argue that the "Ann Arbor case suggests that the key to effective uses of language diversity in the classroom relates fundamentally to teachers' dispositions toward literacy—that is, depends upon teachers' affective stance toward themselves, their work environment, and especially their culturally diverse students." Ball and Lardner urge educators to pay closer attention to "teacher efficacy"—teachers' disposition, attitude, and expectations of students' knowledge and performance.

Building on the notion of "teacher constructs of knowledge," A. Suresh Canagarajah discusses "coping strategies of African American students." He illustrates how students from marginalized groups, in this case African American students, create "safe houses" in the academic environment—cultural or social places where they can safely use their home language and critique academic culture. Canagarajah provides examples from the classroom and from an electronic discussion, suggesting that "safe houses" are not only an important aspects of students' adjustment to a new environment, but can also serve as a pedagogical tool, illustrating such concepts as "cultures and counter-cultures" and the use of different rhetorical strategies.

In "A Good Gang: Thinking Small with Preservice Teachers in a Chicago Barrio," Todd DeStigter takes us into the heart of a Latino Youth Alternative High School in Chicago. He introduces us to the students who have enrolled in this small alternative school, pursuing what is often their last chance to complete a high school diploma. DeStigter introduces us to the teachers who work one-on-one with many of these students and details the benefits of including small school environments in teacher-training programs. Such environments bring teachers and students into close proximity, connect "caring and democracy," and challenge new teachers to see themselves as lifelong learners (although they can have, at times, unsettling effects—as in the case of the student who rejects the teacher by saying "I don't like white people; white people distract me"). In DeStigter's words, "for preservice teachers to participate in the relationships made possible by small schools and to understand negotiating these relationships as part of their never-ending process of 'becoming' as teachers is an essential part of any broader effort of school 'reform' worthy of the name."

Diversity plays a key role not only in the student body, but also among faculty members. In "On (Almost) Passing" we are introduced to a hearing-impaired professor who travels between the worlds of Deaf culture and Hearing culture. In a very personal and lively essay, Brenda Brueggemann narrates her experience as a "hard-of-hearing" student and teacher who only recently has decided to "come out" as a deaf person (having passed quite successfully in the hearing world for most of her life). She describes the research she conducted for her dissertation at Gallaudet University—the world's only liberal arts university for deaf and hard-of-hearing students—and her personal journey (and conflicts) that accompanied the research process and the "coming out" process, including her changing relations with students, colleagues, her husband and children.

1 Dispositions toward Language: Teacher Constructs of Knowledge and the Ann Arbor Black English Case

Arnetha Ball and Ted Lardner

So here's our hypothesis: what students learn about writing depends more than anything else on the context in which they write. . . . And if the linguists are right that the social context is the driving force behind literacy acquisition, then *the social context of your English/ language-arts classroom is the most powerful and important variable you can experiment with*. More important than what textbook or speller or dictionary to use; more important than what kinds of assignments to give; more important than how to set up cumulative writing folders; more important than the criteria by which you assign kids to peer response groups; more important than "teaching Graves" versus teaching Calkins or Hillocks. More important than anything.

—Steven Zemelman and Harvey Daniels (50–51)

Because composition has been organized as a field in terms of the classroom, the production, transmission, and assimilation of teacher knowledge continues to be a significant theoretical and practical concern. As John Schilb has recently pointed out, though many writing instructors attempt to separate pedagogy from theory, the "field identifies itself with pedagogy" (*Between* 30). In developing its discussion of pedagogical theory (as distinct from rhetorical theory), scholarship in composition studies has

Reprinted from *College Composition and Communication,* December 1997.

generated what we call constructs of teacher knowledge. In this essay we address competing constructs of teacher knowledge, analyzing them from a perspective which takes racially informed language attitudes and their effects on teaching and learning in culturally diverse classrooms as its central concern. In developing this analysis, our point of departure is the 1979 Ann Arbor "Black English" court case. This case focused on the language barriers created by teachers' unconscious negative attitudes toward students' uses of African American English and the negative effect these attitudes had on student learning.

In our reading, the Ann Arbor case is significant for composition studies for two reasons. First, it stands as a legal intervention into the educational process, disrupting business as usual by holding the school system responsible for the educational underachievement of Black students. It associated low educational achievement not with shortcomings within learners, but with inadequate, ineffective curricular and pedagogical routines. Second, in the Ann Arbor case the court held the school district and teachers responsible for rethinking pedagogy and curriculum in light of extant information about African American English. In so doing, it raised then and continues now to pose the question of how educators accomplish the necessary but complicated task of assimilating new knowledge about race and language in order to translate that knowledge into classroom practice. We believe that barriers similar to those identified in Ann Arbor still affect teaching and learning in many secondary-level and college writing classrooms. Similarly, the complex issues surrounding teacher education and changing teachers' attitudes and behaviors in the classroom remain to be explored in the scholarly dialogue of our field.

We begin here with a summary of the Ann Arbor case, highlighting its focus on teacher attitudes and the consequent issue of teacher knowledge and practice. Next, we argue that three distinct constructs of teacher knowledge are evident in writing studies today, each of which is differentially linked to the issue of race reflected in language attitudes raised in the Ann Arbor case. We conclude with some implications for composition as a field, arguing in particular that pedagogical theory in composition needs to more adequately address questions of language diversity and race in order to affect the climate in the writing classroom.

Background: The Court Decision

In 1979, a Federal District Court handed down a decision in favor of 11 African American children, residents of a scatter-site low-income housing project and students at Martin Luther King, Jr., Elementary School, holding the Ann Arbor School District Board responsible for failing to adequately prepare the King School teachers to teach children whose home language was African American English. The case drew national and international attention to the role of language variation in the education of Black children. Stating that a major goal of a school system is to teach reading, writing, speaking, and understanding standard English (Memorandum 1391), Judge Charles Joiner wrote that "when teachers fail to take into account the home language" (1380) of their students, "some children will turn off and not learn" (1381). Challenging a pedagogical ethos grounded in the presumption of universalities, Judge Joiner observed that the teachers involved in the case all testified that they treated the plaintiff students just as they treated other students. However, in so doing they may have created a barrier to learning (1379). In the Ann Arbor case, the Court ruled that the teachers' unconscious but evident attitudes toward the African American English used by the plaintiff children constituted a language barrier that impeded the students' educational progress (1381).

Like the recent Oakland School Board resolution on Ebonics, the Ann Arbor case stirred controversy. As in Oakland, the controversy was in part a result of inaccurate reporting in the media, some of which represented the Court as requiring teachers to teach African American English (see Smitherman, "What"). However, outside of the public furor and of much more substantive import, in ordering the defendant school board to invest time and money in a staff development program for King School teachers, the Court in the Ann Arbor case disrupted the institutional *status quo* by holding the school district accountable for the inadequate educational progress of the Black children involved. From this perspective, the Ann Arbor case can be viewed as a turning point in the history of educational justice for African American children, and the Court's Memorandum Opinion and Order signals this recognition:

> The problem posed by this case is one which the evidence indicates has been compounded by efforts on the part of society to fully integrate blacks into the mainstream of society by relying solely on simplistic devices such as scatter housing and busing of students. Full integration and equal opportunity require much more and one of the matters requiring more attention is the teaching of the young blacks to read standard English. (1381)

As much as the Court's decision can be viewed as an answer to "a cry for judicial help in opening the doors to the establishment" (1381), it must also be recognized that the overriding theme of the Court's ruling was to uphold existing linguistic, educational, and social arrangements. Many educators have viewed the Ann Arbor decision as a step forward on the same road leading from the *Brown v. Topeka* decision in 1954. Keith Gilyard, for example, calls the Ann Arbor decision a precedent-setting case which ought to have an officially established place within the educational environment (10). But while it is important to note such celebrating of the Ann Arbor case, it is also important to note that the elements of the decision which directly address language barriers and African American English have yet to be cited as a precedent in other cases aimed at school policy. Furthermore, the Court's final Memorandum Opinion and Order explicitly and unequivocally positions African American English in a subordinate relationship to the mainstream:

> Black English is not a language used by the mainstream of society—black or white. It is not an acceptable method of communication in the educational world, in the commercial community, in the community of the arts and science, or among professionals. (1378)

The Michigan Legal Services attorneys who mounted the case for the plaintiff children in Ann Arbor drew on the testimony of experts in sociolinguistics and education in order to establish two key propositions: that African American English is a rule-governed language system, and that the teachers' failure to recognize this linguistic fact led to negative attitudes toward the children who spoke it, that, in effect, their attitudes constituted a language barrier impeding students' educational progress. Establishing the first proposition, the expert testimony addressed the second by asserting that communicative interference can derive from either structural mismatches among dialects or from nonstructural phenomena. Nonstructural interference phenomena refers to differing attitudes and conflicting values about speech systems and the individuals who use them. Experts testified that negative linguistic attitudes shaped the institutional policies and practices that hindered the education of African American English speaking children. Then as now, research on language attitudes consistently indicates that teachers believe African American English speaking children are "nonverbal" and possess limited vocabularies. Speakers of African American English are often perceived to be slow learners or uneducable; their speech is often considered to be unsystematic and in need of constant correction and improvement.

In the Ann Arbor case, the Court identified teachers' language attitudes as a significant impediment to children's learning. Because the children failed to develop reading skills, they were thereby impeded from full participation in the educational program at King School. The Court enumerated multiple potential causes (absences from class, classroom misbehavior, learning disabilities, and emotional impairment and lack of reading role models [1391]) for their difficulties, but focused on one:

> Research indicates that the black dialect or vernacular used at home by black students in general makes it more difficult for such children to read because teachers' unconscious but evident attitudes toward the home language causes a psychological barrier to learning by the student. (1381)

The Court called for the Ann Arbor School District Board to develop a program to (1) help the teachers understand the problem, (2) provide them with knowledge about the children's use of African American English, and (3) suggest ways and means of using that knowledge in teaching the students to read (1381). In a court-ordered, 20-hour inservice program for the King School teachers, experts in reading and sociolinguistics furnished teachers with information on these topics. In spite of the wealth of information delivered to teachers, however, the school district's report of the results of this inservice program concludes that though teacher respondents "felt positively about all substantive issues, they were somewhat less positive about their understanding of the pedagogical issues" (Howard 17).

The nonstructural barriers resulting from negative attitudes were the focus of the Ann Arbor case, and they remain to challenge successful practice and our students' educational progress today. Survey results reported by Balester suggest that this was as true in 1992 as it was in 1979, the year of the Ann Arbor trial, or in the late 60s when scholarship in applied linguistics first took direct aim at many teachers' traditional, prescriptivist orientations. In 1994, Bowie and Bond found that teachers still continue to exhibit negative attitudes toward African American English, often stating that African American English has a faulty grammar system and that children who speak African American English are less capable than children who speak standard English.

Constructs of Teacher Knowledge

It is clear that the outcome of the Ann Arbor case left many questions unanswered, including the most pressing question of how teachers are to respond to the linguistic and cultural diversity of their students. At the heart of the Ann Arbor decision was the recognition of the need for teachers to become sensitive to students' uses of African American English, to move into a way of being in the classroom which is responsive to and informed by recognition of racial and linguistic difference. However, the unresolved pedagogical issues reflected in the King School teachers' responses to their inservice program remain at the center of our reading of the Ann Arbor case in relation to composition studies: How do teachers learn and transform new knowledge into classroom practice? We argue that three competing constructs of teacher knowledge offer divergent ways of responding to this question. The three constructs we wish to describe are the *teacher as technician, teacher knowledge as lore,* and *teacher efficacy.* We distinguish these constructs from one another in terms of their approaches to the underlying issue of racially informed language attitudes: How do they situate teachers in relation to confronting race as an element in classroom climate? How do they bring to the surface for teachers the awareness of unconscious negative language attitudes? How do they dispose teachers to be able to reflect on and move forward into alternative classroom practices?

Teacher as Technician

The teacher as technician is clearly the operative construct evident in the Ann Arbor case. This construct was a necessary feature of the "objectivist rhetoric" which made up the expert testimony in the trial, which was the dominant rhetoric in the Court's Memorandum Opinion and Order, and which continues to be the undergirding rhetoric of current scholarship on African American English in sociolinguistics, education, and literacy studies. Cy Knoblauch has identified "objectivist rhetoric" as empirical discourse which portrays knowledge as derived from unbiased observation and rigorous argumentative procedure. Because of this, the objectivist paradigm has served as a corrective to superstitions, emotional excesses, and prejudices (130). The Ann Arbor case demonstrates just this corrective potential.

One feature of objectivist rhetoric is its organization of knowledge in linear, cause-and-effect terms. A second feature, evident in the discourse of the case, is the trope of application. The Court acknowledged the necessary contributions of the King School teachers' "skill and empathy" (1391) to classroom success. But the chief significance of the trial lies in the way in which it focused on the need for teachers to apply in practice the findings of modern sociolinguistic scholarship. The process and outcome of the case reflects a technical construct of teacher knowledge in that it subordinates teachers' own reflective resources ("skill and empathy") to disciplinary (sociolinguistic) expertise. The case inscribes teachers as needy recipients of already-formed information which would, it was presumed, ameliorate their attitudes and which would (somehow) be translated into new, more effective teaching strategies.

The Final Evaluation of the results of the Ann Arbor inservice program stated that a great deal of information was available regarding such topics as the history and structure of African American English and the effect of teacher attitudes on student learning. But there was evidently little if any attention given at the time to the process of applying this knowledge in practice. Its application was apparently presumed to be automatic. Thomas Pietras, the Language Arts Coordinator for the Ann Arbor School District at the time of the King School trial, wrote that disseminating information to teachers about African American English "assumes that teacher knowledge will result in success in language arts" for speakers of African American English (qtd. in Howard et al. 59), but the results of the questionnaire that teachers filled out subsequent to the inservice speak to the disconnection between knowledge and application. The Final Evaluation distinguishes "substantive" issues from "pedagogical" issues, and the content of the inservice program itself virtually ignored questions of pedagogy, assuming perhaps that providing teachers with knowledge would lead by itself to improved student performance. How that improved student performance was (or is) to be achieved was never addressed; the teacher as technician construct doesn't ask that question, because it tends to bypass altogether the responsive decision-making that teachers must engage in.

The objectivist rhetoric exemplified in the Ann Arbor case in the testimony of experts served to move the Court to intervene in an ingrained, discriminatory institutional practice at King School. When William Labov, one of the leading expert witnesses to testify in Ann Arbor, wrote about the case saying that "negative attitudes can be changed by providing people with scientific evidence" (32), he expressed perfectly the objectivist view in which science serves as a corrective to prejudice. It also reflects a view of teachers as technicians and of pedagogy as the transparent process of translating "substantive" information in the classroom. Unfortunately, as the King School teachers' own evaluation of their training session indicates, introducing sociolinguistic information seems not to have led them to recognize avenues toward more effective classroom practice. Describing the limitations of objectivist rhetoric and the construct of teacher as technician we argue it entails, Knoblauch suggests that educators may speak of "advances" in "our knowledge of the processes of human learning, including the development of literacy" (130), and may thereby evince "a willingness to ground instruction in what we can observe about those processes" (130). However, Knoblauch goes on, "teachers and researchers accept the least advantageous assumptions of a positivist outlook . . . when they encourage [for example] the new knowledge of linguistics . . . to dictate instructional and learning agendas" (131). The practical (non-)consequences of this acceptance of a "positivist outlook" are evident in the King School teachers' responses. As much as they may have wished for it to be so, they seemed to recognize no clear way in which linguistic or sociolinguistic knowledge could "dictate" teaching and learning processes.

Teacher Knowledge as Lore

Such an impasse is perhaps what composition theorists who talk about teacher knowledge as lore might have predicted. Lore is a postmodern, "postdisciplinary" construct that rejects objectivist, linear, cause-and-effect discourse in favor of complex, multifaceted, and improvisational ways of understanding pedagogical interactions to explain how teachers know what to do.

We identify postdisciplinary views of teacher knowledge as lore with work which has emerged in composition in the last ten years—subsequent, that is, to the Ann Arbor case. Variously formulated by scholars ranging from Steven North to Louise Wetherbee Phelps and Patricia Harkin, this work has complicated the idea of disciplinary knowledge governing a teacher's practice in the classroom. In Harkin's formulation, lore is identified with teachers' informed intuitions about what works in the classroom. At the center of her discussion is the example of Mina Shaughnessy's *Errors and Expectations.* Harkin identifies Shaughnessy's book as exemplary of lore, and goes on to illustrate the disciplinary critique of lore by reference to critiques of Shaughnessy's work. Harkin writes that critics of teacher knowledge as lore see a danger in teachers who "are willfully ignorant of disciplinary knowledge," and who

> think they should be free . . . to ignore [for example] modern linguistic
> scholarship, free to invent their own programs as they go along . . .
> free to ignore evidence or theory, free to rely on their own insight,
> free, that is, to ignore facts. (130)

Harkin's reply is to turn aside the ethical implications (teachers ignore facts) and to deconstruct the idea of "facts" in itself: "Facts are only facts in the discipline which constitutes them," she asserts (130). Going on, she argues that because the complex scene of teaching cannot be reduced to the linear causality which disciplinary knowledge demands, teachers cannot be expected to obey disciplinary imperatives. Lore, with its improvisational logic, is the more appropriate interpretive framework with which to think about teaching, to think about how we know what to do in the classroom. The construct of teacher knowledge as lore thus turns us in the right direction as it asks directly about the process of discovery, application, and transformation of teacher knowledge in the classroom. Privileging teachers' direct experiences and reflective practice, lore draws our attention to the moment-to-moment process of observing, interpreting, and decision making that is characteristic of engaged teaching.

However, what the construct of teacher knowledge as lore works to resist—the apparent necessity for teachers to attune their practice to, for example, modern linguistic scholarship—lies at the heart of the Ann Arbor case and the intervention it represented into a discriminatory *status quo.* One unintended effect, then, of the construct of lore, of relying on teachers' informed intuitions, is to displace a direct confrontation with race as it may be manifested in students' strategic uses of African American English. In its effort to disrupt the disciplinary encroachment of, for example, sociolinguistics (we find Harkin's selection of "linguistics" as evidence quite telling), "postdisciplinary" theory substitutes for one problematic construct, the teacher as technician, an equally problematic construct of teacher knowledge as lore produced through "a process of informed intuition" when "practitioners do what works" (Harkin 134). In Ann Arbor, it took two years of legal action to force the school district to acknowledge that whatever its teachers' intuitions were, what was supposed to be working didn't work for a significant number of African American children. The case highlighted facts about language variation, race, language attitudes, and school performance which teachers ultimately were not free to ignore. Another effect of the postmodern construct of lore might thus be to undermine the strategic uses to which the objectivist discourses of the social sciences have been put. Since *Brown v. Topeka,* these discourses have been a chief weapon in the fight for educational justice for African American students. The familiar antifoundationalist critique that denies truth as a transcendent category could thus also deny access to the court of last appeal against racism in the quest for civil rights and educational equity. It is interesting to imagine but difficult to see how a postdisciplinary perspective might have carried the day in the Ann Arbor case.

The Ann Arbor case thus reveals possibilities and limitations of lore. We remain skeptical of the unintended effects of the antifoundationalism upon which lore is premised since this seems to rule out "appeals to truth, objectivity, ethics, and identity that social critics have traditionally made" (Schilb, "Cultural" 174). In terms of the issues of race and literacy highlighted by the Ann Arbor case and at play in composition classrooms today, postdisciplinarity and lore remain susceptible to such criticisms. Whereas scholars in other fields draw on postmodern theory to make race a prominent element in their analyses of cultural transactions (Cornel West, Patricia Williams), in many of composition's important discussions of postmodern theory, race is hardly mentioned. This is a striking oversight. What we are most concerned with, however, is to find ways to raise teachers' awareness of their own processes of pedagogical discovery and change, to help teachers recognize what their own habits of reflection make accessible to them, and what these habits of mind may leave out. The construct of lore moves us a long way toward the goal of seeing teachers' own reflective practice as the nexus of pedagogical theory. Our concern is that this construct does not put enough pressure on the question of "what works," thereby pushing teachers to confront the limitations of their practice—especially when for the majority of students everything seems to be running along smoothly, as was the case in Ann Arbor, where most of the students at King School were doing very well. In reference to issues of race which are raised in writing classes when students speak or draw on African American English in their writing, we see a need for teachers to avail themselves of facts which may seem external or peripheral to their experience of the classroom, but which may carry significance for some students. When lore does not confront practitioners with their own language biases, it works against change.

Teacher Efficacy

The third construct of teacher knowledge we wish to consider is teacher efficacy. It differs in one significant way from each of the first two constructs in so far as it draws attention to affect as an essential—perhaps the essential—component in teaching practice. In a field closely allied with composition, teacher educators such as Henry Giroux, Kenneth Zeichner, and Daniel Liston have offered a construct of teacher knowledge generated through reflective practice where teachers examine classroom routines in light of encompassing social and institutional pressures. We argue that the construct of teacher efficacy pushes beyond this enlarged view of reflective practice. By making affect a central issue in theorizing pedagogy, teacher efficacy moves closest to the largely unspoken dimensions of pedagogical experience when, let's say, white teachers in university writing courses attempt to mediate the discourse practices of African American English speaking students. Opening up these deeply felt but difficult to name dimensions of interaction, teacher efficacy speaks to the cumulative effect of teachers' knowledge and experience on their feelings about their students and their own ability to teach them.

This was what the Ann Arbor case was really about: the psychological barriers to learning that cause some students to dis-identify with school. Teacher efficacy as a construct of teacher knowledge places affect at the center and in so doing opens up and addresses questions of motivation and stance which are prior to and underlie curricular designs or pedagogical technique. When we speak of affect here, we refer to the emotional tone of classroom interactions. With reference to the Ann Arbor case, insofar as language variation is a factor in educational achievement, language as the medium of instruction is what counts. What is most relevant about Ann Arbor was how it drew attention to language as the medium of instruction and the interference generated by teachers' unconscious negative responses to their students' own language.

Defining affect in terms of "teachers' expectations, their empathy, and their own sense of self-efficacy" (370), Susan McLeod reminds us of the research which demonstrates the variable influence (positive or negative) of teacher affect on students' motivations for learning. Teacher efficacy refers to a teacher's beliefs about the power she or he has to produce a positive effect on students. McLeod points out that a teacher's emotional state or disposition forms one source of this sense of self-efficacy. Another source, and the most influential, is "the cultural beliefs that go to make up the macrosystem of American education," beliefs which inform teachers' common sense assumptions including "conceptions of the learner and the teacher and the role of education" (379). McLeod and others have shown that many variables contribute to teacher efficacy, including prior experience in multicultural settings, available resources, and teachers' visions of themselves as agents of social change. Teachers with high personal teaching efficacy believe that all students can be motivated and that it is their responsibility to explore with students the tasks that will hold their attention in the learning process. Valarie Pang and Velma Sablan propose that teacher efficacy is an especially important construct in the context of multicultural classrooms, and that teachers and teacher educators need to seriously examine what they believe about their ability to teach children from various cultural and linguistic backgrounds, particularly African American students. Pang and Sablan note that "when the overwhelming majority of the teaching force in this country is not from under-represented groups, the need to look at teacher misconceptions of African American culture, customs, history, and values is essential" (16).

Until the lawsuit, institutional custom invited the Ann Arbor School District to explain away African American student failure by attributing it to shortcomings in students rather than to shortcomings in the educational system or to the teachers' own lack of "skills or knowledge to help low achievers" (McLeod 380). Subsequent to the inservice program ordered by the Court, the King School teachers reflected low efficacy, that is, little confidence in their ability to adapt pedagogy to the various strengths and needs of speakers of African American English. Applied to the teaching of literacy that goes on in college writing courses, the question becomes, how do teachers become aware of unconscious negative attitudes (or even the dimly felt sense of unease resulting from lack of experience) they may bring with them to the learning environment? And, what steps can teachers take to communicate their sense of efficacy and high expectations to culturally diverse students?

Among the three constructs of teacher knowledge considered here, only that of teacher efficacy, grounded as it is in the consideration of affect in the classroom, makes these questions of felt sense, of emotional response, available for reflection. The Ann Arbor case focused on the language barrier which resulted from teachers' negative attitudes toward African American English. Racism—unconscious and institutional—was the clear subtext in the trial. Arthur Spears describes the problematic relationships among race, language variety, and school achievement. Citing dialect differences in other countries, Spears notes:

> Greater language differences are overcome elsewhere. Why can't they be overcome in American schools? The answer that comes through in a number of studies of the issue is that the real problems are attitudinal and social. All these problems can be related to the general problem of institutional racism . . . low teacher expectations and disrespect for the home language and culture of inner-city pupils. (53–54)

Though rarely acknowledged as such, racism in the sense reflected here still remains an issue in the current teaching of writing, surfacing in the classroom in a variety of often subtle, unconscious manifestations (see Delpit). Neither of the first two constructs of teacher knowledge described offer adequate approaches to this problem; neither offers a vocabulary within which to directly address teachers' effective responses—low expectations, disrespect—which are the chief means through which institutional racism is manifested. Neither the teacher as technician construct nor lore offers direct access to unconscious negative racial stereotypes as a central issue in pedagogical theory. Our conclusion is that while unconscious attitudes are indeed, as Labov points out, partly a problem of (lack of) knowledge *per se,* they are more urgently a matter of feeling, the affective domain of racialized classroom experience which neither the technician model nor lore explicitly engages.

Implications for Practice

The question remains, however: If our goal is to move urban youth in cities like Cleveland or Detroit into academic discourse communities, what stands in the way of that happening? In working toward building a sense of efficacy we need to give particular attention to staff development and writing programs in which teachers re-envision their capacity to function as catalysts of positive growth and development in students. In part, this improved sense of efficacy stems from an improved teacher knowledge base concerning the linguistic practices of diverse students. This can be accomplished by reviewing the literature diligently developed over the past four decades to provide a more complex, more complete linguistic profile of African American linguistic behavior. Characteristic features, discourse patterns, and rhetorical modes in African American English had been identified in the literature prior to the Ann Arbor case (Abrahams; Labov; Smitherman, *Talkin).* Research published since the conclusion of the case in 1979 has shed more light on distinctive discourse patterns and rhetorical modes. Much of this work has generated new knowledge of organizational patterns in the oral and written expository language of African American English speakers (Ball, "Expository"), the subtle ways that academically successful students strategically use African American English in their writing (Ball, "Cultural"), and on the assessment of writing produced by African American English speakers (Richardson). Research investigating the teaching practices of exemplary African American teachers working in community-based organizations has shown that these teachers build on the language practices of their African American students. They work explicitly to make students metacognitively aware of their oral and written uses of African American English and of alternative ways of expressing their ideas in academic and in technical, workplace English (Ball, Broussard, and Dinkins; Morgan; Ball, "Community").

Becoming informed about cultural discourse patterns and rhetorical modes is a significant resource that successful teachers can build on. Most interesting, however, is the impact of an awareness of cultural differences in discourse patterns on classroom interactions. The presence of varied patterns of discourse in classrooms can impact instruction in positive as well as in negative ways (Foster, "Effective"). Speech behavior is central to a full understanding of how a community expresses its realities, and research on teacher efficacy suggests that effective teachers develop strong human bonds with their students, have high expectations, focus on the total child, and are able to use communication styles familiar to their students. Exemplary African American teachers in community-based organizations are able to draw, to varying degrees, on primarily the rhetorical modes and discourse-level strategies of African American English in shaping interactive discourse as the medium of instruction with their students (Ball, Broussard, Dinkins; Foster "Educating"). Their practice in this regard stands as a model for other teachers to reflect on as they consider expanding their own pedagogical repertoires. We are not advocating that all teachers need to learn and teach Black English. We are arguing that the practices of exemplary African American teachers show us ways of focusing on participation patterns in interactive discourse as the medium of instruction in order to raise the awareness of teachers of the possible links between their own styles of communication and their students' responsiveness in classroom exchanges. Having high expectations and good intentions is not enough; these intentions and expectations need to be evident to students in observable or, we might say, audible behaviors in the classroom.

But as important as this knowledge base may be, it will not in and of itself activate teachers to change their practice. The cognitive internalization of information is not enough to increase teacher efficacy. The Ann Arbor case suggests that the key to effective uses of language diversity in the classroom relates fundamentally to teachers' dispositions toward literacy—that is, depends upon teachers' affective stance toward themselves, their work environment, and especially their culturally diverse students. More current research seems to confirm this. Addressing disposition as the most important variable, we have begun to push beyond internalization of knowledge about

African American English in the teacher-education programs we are involved in. In doing so, we have found ourselves observing the ways preservice teachers encounter and contextualize the pedagogical ramifications of language diversity. Our observations suggest that preservice teachers who attempt to address the complex issues relating to this topic may do so by examining personal experiences of crossing borders from one speech community to another. Given these observations, we have begun to consider occasions for knowledge-making that appear in "extra-professional" sites where teachers become aware of their own culturally influenced dispositions toward literacy. We have begun to explore ways of talking that help teachers connect to parts of their experience that conventional academic, theoretical frameworks seem to silence.

Implications for Pedagogical Theory

In 1991 Ann Dyson and Sarah Freedman challenged writing and composition professionals to take significant and positive steps toward building a more powerful theoretical framework for writing research and instruction by expanding our framework to

> include more analytic attention to how the complex of sociocultural experiences enter into literacy learning experiences that have roots in social class, ethnicity, language background, family, neighborhood, and gender. Without serious attention to the unfolding of this wider cultural frame in literacy learning, our vision of the whole remains partially obscured. (4)

This call addresses the ways we construct theory in our field, how we represent the relationships among literacy processes, pedagogy, interactions within the classroom, and cultural expectations which embed our institutions. The first two constructs—teacher as technician and teacher knowledge as lore—share a *curricular* view of the theory-practice relationship. Both of these views are consistent with extent models of pedagogical theory offered in composition studies (Brannon; Fulkerson). Each of the first two constructs we consider here analyzes the decisions teachers make in terms of the propositions of theory: a view of the writing process, the development of writing ability, the goal of writing and teaching, the ways knowledge is constructed. Each locates teacher authority within professional discourse, and assigns teachers a stable, centered, and professional subjectivity which is monologic, perhaps ungendered, and more to our point, unmarked by race. Both constructs are therefore, for teachers and the profession alike, discourses of control.

The third construct, teacher efficacy, reconfigures the representation of pedagogical theory. In particular, instead of seeing writing pedagogy as determined by a general theory of writing (in whatever versions this general theory might appear), the alternative we propose would place the teacher, the student, and the site of literacy instruction at the center, each exerting its influence on the others, each influencing an orientation toward the activity of the course, each in relationships with the others which are at best dialogical and, as some scholars have pointed out, often contradictory and conflictual (Lu). The construct of teacher efficacy does not subordinate pedagogy to a teacher's "substantive" knowledge, nor does it place teacher knowledge in dialogue with its situation, as the postdisciplinary view would have it. The construct of efficacy locates pedagogical theory in relation to three intersecting points of view: the institutional context of the writing course, the teacher's sense of herself as an actor within that institutional site, and the dialogizing, ambivalent, often resistant perspectives of students. The virtue of this model of pedagogical theory in composition is that by drawing attention to the "complex sociocultural experiences of literacy learning" Dyson and Freedman refer to, it sharpens the kinds of questions practitioners may ask about what works in and what works on the activity sponsored by the writing classroom.

Changing Dispositions

Disposition has two meanings which offer complementary views of the challenges surrounding literacy education in multicultural classrooms. The first meaning is "one's customary manner or emotional response; temperament." In its response to Oakland's Ebonics resolution, the American public's customary manner of emotional response toward African American English became front-page public news. The second meaning of disposition is "the power to control, direct, or dispose." These two meanings of disposition frame the interrelated issues surrounding the Ebonics controversy and the Ann Arbor "Black English" case, and the significance each holds for the field of composition. On the one hand, the Ann Arbor case came to focus on the language barrier which results from teachers' unconscious, negative attitudes toward African American English. On the other, ill-disposed toward their students' use of African American English, the Ann Arbor teachers expected less and their students not surprisingly lived down to these lowered expectations, evidence of the power of self-fulfilling prophecy.

More than 20 years ago, in response to the Ann Arbor case, the Black Caucus of NCTE and CCCC disseminated a carefully prepared "Commentary" regarding African American English. Recently reprinted in response to the Ebonics initiative, the purpose of the "Commentary" was to express the viewpoints of Black linguists and language arts educators on the topic. Briefly summarized, the "Commentary" asserts that the Black language system in and of itself is not a barrier to learning. The barrier is negative attitudes toward that language system, compounded by lack of information about the language system and inefficient techniques for teaching language skills, all of which is manifested in an unwillingness to adapt teaching styles to students' needs. Such barriers, in fact, reflect teachers', and the public's, dispositions toward literacy. In light of the public outcry over Ebonics, we ask: Have those dispositions changed today? The "Commentary" of the Black Caucus went on to say that the language of Black students is actually a strength on which teachers might draw in order to develop effective approaches to teaching. They concluded the statement with a call for thorough, unbiased research on the topic. However, based on the tone of the criticisms and emotional responses to the Ebonics issue, it became evident that society in general does not take such a detailed or objective view on the matter of the representations of diverse languages in the classroom.

After looking closely at the Ann Arbor case, it seems clear that for writing teachers today, many of the same barriers exist in the classroom that stood between the teachers at King School and their students. Because of cultural differences in patterns of language use, and because of differences in styles of interaction used to demonstrate knowledge, many students from diverse social and linguistic backgrounds are entering urban classrooms where teachers still have a difficult time recognizing and fully utilizing the wealth of language resources students use effectively outside school. These are resources that often go unrecognized and unrewarded within classroom settings. In spite of the considerable professional rhetoric over the past 20 years or so, recent research indicates that African Americans and other students of color are still faring very poorly in our nation's urban schools (Quality Education for Minorities Project). In light of the history of failure and miscommunication that marks the educational experiences of many African American English speakers, educators must continue to insist on seeking ways that the barriers created by diversity in language as the medium of instruction can become, instead, bridges between home language practices and academic registers teachers want students to learn. Making a significant place for affect within pedagogical theories is an important step toward this goal.

Acknowledgments

We would like to thank Ralph Stevens, Margaret Marshall, and Thomas Fox for their careful reading and suggestions on this article.

Works Cited

Abrahams, Roger. *Deep Down in the Jungle.* Chicago: Aldine, 1970.

Balester, Valerie. *Cultural Divide.* Portsmouth: Boynton, 1993.

Ball, Arnetha. "Community-Based Learning in Urban Settings as a Model for Educational Reform." *Applied Behavioral Science Review* 3 (1995): 127–46.

———. "Cultural Preference and the Expository Writing of African-American Adolescents." *Written Communication* 9 (1992): 501–32.

———. "Expository Writing Patterns of African-American Students." *English Journal* 85 (1996): 27–36.

Ball, Arnetha F., Kimberley C. Broussard and Delvin M. Dinkins. "Investigating Interactive Discourse Patterns of African American Females in Community-Based Organizations." American Educational Research Association. New Orleans, 1994.

Bowie, R. and C. Bond. "Influencing Future Teachers' Attitudes Toward Black English: Are We Making a Difference?" *Journal of Teacher Education* 45 (1994): 112–18.

Brannon, Lil. "Toward a Theory of Composition." *Perspectives on Research and Scholarship in Composition.* Ed. Ben McLelland and Timothy R. Donovan. New York: MLA, 1985. 6–25.

"Commentary." *Black Caucus Notes.* Urbana: NCTE. March, 1997.

Delpit, Lisa. "Education in a Multicultural Society: Our Future's Greatest Challenge." *Journal of Negro Education* 61 (1992): 237–49.

Dyson, A. H., and S. W. Freedman. *Critical Challenges for Research on Writing and Literacy: 1990–1995.* Technical Report No. 1–B. Berkeley, CA: Center for the Study of Writing, 1991.

Fulkerson, Richard. "Composition Theory in the Eighties: Axiological Consensus and Paradigmatic Diversity." *CCC* 41 (1990): 409–29.

Foster, Michelle. "Educating for Competence in Community and Culture: Exploring the Views of Exemplary African-American Teachers." *Urban Education* 27 (1993): 370–94.

———. "Effective Black Teachers: A Literature Review." *Teaching Diverse Populations Formulating a Knowledge Base.* Ed. Etta Hollins, Joyce King, and W. Hayman. Albany: State U of New York P, 1994. 225–42.

Gilyard, Keith. *Voices of the Self.* Detroit: Wayne State UP, 1992.

Giroux, Henry. *Teachers as Intellectuals Toward a Critical Pedagogy of Learning.* New York: Bergin, 1988.

Harkin, Patricia. "The Postdisciplinary Politics of Lore." *Contending With Words.* Ed. Patricia Harkin and John Schilb. New York: MLA, 1991. 124–38.

Howard, Harry, Lee H. Hansen and Thomas Pietras. *Final Evaluation: King Elementary School Vernacular Black English Inservice Program.* Ann Arbor: Ann Arbor Public Schools, 1980.

Knoblauch, C. H. "Rhetorical Constructions: Dialogue and Commitment." *College English* 50 (1988): 125–40.

Labov, William. "Recognizing Black English in the Classroom." *Black English Educational Equity and the Law.* Ed. John W. Chambers. Ann Arbor: Karoma, 1983. 29–55.

Lu, Min-zhan. "Conflict and Struggle: The Enemies or Preconditions of Basic Writing?" *College English* 54 (1992): 887–913.

McLeod, Susan H. "Pygmalion or Golem? Teacher Affect and Efficacy." *CCC* 46 (1995): 369–86.

Memorandum Opinion and Order. Martin Luther King Elementary School Children v. Ann Arbor School District Board. Civil Action No. 7-71861. 473 F. Supp. 1371 (1979).

Morgan, Marcyliena. "Indirectness and Interpretation in African American Women's Discourse." *Pragmatics* 1 (1991): 421–51.

North, Stephen. *The Making of Knowledge in Composition.* Portsmouth: Boynton, 1987.

Pang, Valerie O., and Velma Sablan. "Teacher Efficacy: Do Teachers Believe They Can Be Effective with African American Students?" American Educational Research Association. San Francisco: 1995.

Phelps, Louise Wetherbee. "Practical Wisdom and the Geography of Knowledge in Composition." *College English* 47 (1992): 338–56.

Quality Education for Minorities Project. *Education That Works: An Action Plan for the Education of Minorities.* Cambridge: MIT P, 1990.

Richardson, Elaine. *Where Did That Come From? Black Talk for Black Student Talking Texts.* MA Thesis. Cleveland State U, 1993.

Schilb, John. *Between the Lines Relating Composition Theory and Literary Theory.* Portsmouth: Boynton, 1996.

———. "Cultural Studies, Postmodernism, and Composition." *Contending With Words.* Ed. Patricia Harkin and John Schilb. New York: MLA, 1991. 173–88.

Shaughnessy, Mina. *Errors and Expectations.* New York: Oxford UP, 1977.

Smitherman, Geneva. *Talkin and Testifyin.* Detroit: Wayne State UP, 1977.

———. "'What Go Round Come Round': *King* in Perspective." *Harvard Educational Review* 51 (1981): 40–56.

Spears, A. K. "Are Black and White Vernaculars Diverging?" *American Speech* 62 (1987): 48–55, 71–72.

West, Cornel. *Race Matters.* Boston: Beacon, 1993.

Williams, Patricia J. *The Alchemy of Race and Rights.* Cambridge, MA: Harvard UP, 1991.

Zeichner, Kenneth M. "Alternative Paradigms in Teacher Education." *Journal of Teacher Education* 34 (1983): 3–9.

Zeichner, Kenneth, and Daniel Liston. "Teaching Student Teachers to Reflect." *Harvard Educational Review* 57 (1987): 23–48.

Zemelman, Steven, and Harvey Daniels. *A Community of Writers.* Portsmouth: Boynton, 1988.

2 Safe Houses in the Contact Zone: Coping Strategies of African-American Students in the Academy

A. Suresh Canagarajah

Minority communities possess traditions of cultural appropriation and resistance which have enabled them to engage in what Mary Louise Pratt calls the "literate arts of the contact zone." Inspired by the "extraordinary intercultural tour de force" of a 17th-century autoethnographic text from the non-literate Quechua community which expresses opposition against Spanish imperialism (34), Pratt celebrates the creative modes of text construction taking place in situations of cultural contact both inside and outside the academy. But, while acknowledging such fascinating examples of linguistic/literary resistance, we must remember that minority communities also inherit traditions of accommodation deriving from legacies of domination. Henry Giroux reminds us that "subordinate cultures are situated and recreated within relations of domination and resistance, and they bear the marks of both" (*Theory and Resistance* 229). How subordinate communities negotiate the conflicting impulses in their culture to engage in creative literacy practices needs careful exploration. Apart from this inner cultural struggle within the community, subordinate groups also need to cope with the power of the dominant codes and discourses out there in the contact zone where different communities interact. Although the inequalities of power stratifying the contact zone are acknowledged by contact zones theorists (see Pratt 34; Bizzell 166; R. Miller; Lu), we need more systematic and detailed observation of the complex ways in which subordinate groups negotiate power in intercultural communication. Minority students can

Reprinted from *College Composition and Communication*, May 1997.

experience similar sources of conflict as they develop literacy in the academic contact zone. It is important therefore to become sensitive to the conflicting tendencies in their culture, which can motivate them to engage variously with the stratification of power in the classroom, and critically interrogate their classroom discourses and learning strategies.

Pratt points out that the threatening atmosphere in the contact zone makes everyone (especially marginalized groups) appreciate the importance of *safe houses*—which she defines in passing as "social and intellectual spaces where groups can constitute themselves as horizontal, homogeneous, sovereign communities with high degrees of trust, shared understandings, and temporary protection from legacies of oppression" (40). In a special writing course for predominantly African-American students, I discovered the complex ways in which they constructed and used safe houses to resolve the conflicts they faced. While the challenges in dealing with institutional and discursive power in the academy made them hunger for safe houses, some of the communally mandated and historically developed cultural practices further encouraged this coping strategy. Although safe houses posed certain problems in developing academic literacy among minority students, critical reflection after the course convinced me that they also held immense pedagogical possibilities. In order to tap the hidden resources of this academic underground for the practice of contact zone literacy, we need more information on life in the safe houses than Pratt is able to provide in the single paragraph she has devoted to this subject. At least the following issues need to be clarified:

> What are the literate arts of safe houses? How do they relate to and compare with those of the contact zone?
>
> What is the location of safe houses in relation to the contact zone? Are they outside or inside, linked to or separated from the contact zone?
>
> What are the pedagogical and political implications of safe houses for the practice of contact zone literacy? Do they stifle/encourage, stymie/enhance such literate practices?

The Background

The writing course which I explore below was part of what is called the Preview Program at the University of Texas at Austin. This program is held each summer for first year ethnic minority students entering college the following fall. The idea motivating the program is the need to induct such students gradually into the "academic culture" in order to improve their retention rate. Usually, mandatory courses like composition and math are offered during this semester. Although these courses earn credit as in the regular courses, they are supposed to be conducted with a special sensitivity to the challenges confronting minority students. Besides taking classes, the students are expected to reside on campus and attend workshops conducted by the university to orientate them to academic culture. Of the twelve students in my class from this program, ten were African-American and two were Hispanic. Two Chinese-Americans (who stated that they spoke only English) and an Anglo-American student were also in the class to make up for failing a writing course in the previous semester. In order to develop a special analytical focus on the learning strategies of minority students, I observed and recorded the behavior and discourses of the African-American students in my class.[1] Since the course was organized primarily around argumentative academic writing, my discourse analysis focused on the strategies students displayed in oral and written communication at different levels of formality.

The safe houses of the African-American students were motivated by some of the peculiarities of the way my course (and research) was organized. Being a sizable body of students, they could develop a sense of "community" that was difficult for the students from other ethnicities in the class. Furthermore, though students could have constituted themselves in class or gender terms to form safe houses, the purpose of the Preview course and the curriculum I adopted heightened their ethnic consciousness at the cost of other identities. It is possible that as I set out to focus on African-American students, I may have overlooked the activity of safe houses defined according to other group affiliations. There is certainly nothing to preclude the formation of safe houses according to other social identities in a course organized along different lines, or with a different demography of students bringing into consciousness alternate senses of group affiliation.

The approach I adopted for my course called for a sensitivity to the vernacular discourses and communicative conventions minority students bring to the classroom, while enabling them to gradually cross discourse boundaries and get acquainted with the academic conventions. Although students are encouraged to employ their vernacular discourses in their own community (and possibly in informal contexts in the academy), they are expected to master academic discourse to communicate successfully in the college setting. Teaching in a networked classroom also helped me to conduct a student-centered, collaborative course. The many features for mailing, electronic conference, brainstorming, and revising offered by the computer program we used helped me construct a course that was less teacher-fronted than usual. Using the text *Critical Reading and Writing across the Disciplines* (Clegg), I encouraged students to explore the typical knowledge content and writing conventions of selected disciplines in order to understand how these differed from their own discourses, so they could then address the academic community as writers who could use the academic knowledge and conventions effectively.

Literate Arts of Safe Houses

I will first explore the communicative strategies students employed in the safe houses in contrast to those they used in the public sites of the contact zone. Such a consideration shows not only the rich linguistic competence of minority students, but also the complex strategies they adopt to negotiate the competing discourses of the academy and the vernacular community. Their discourses show the shifting identities and community membership they linguistically construct to manage the conflicts they experience in the academy. Even more important for our purposes is the manner in which students construct and use safe houses to negotiate the discursive and ideological challenges of the academic contact zone.

At the beginning of the semester, as in the case of most classes, the students were very formal and conscious of their behavior. They orientated themselves to the academic conventions quite scrupulously—as became evident in an online discussion on the second day of class on how writing under pressure exacerbates writer's block. The argumentative strategies students used here were quite different from those they would use later in their safe houses. Donnie Jones's comment that he "wrote better under pressure" challenged the position of the textbook and sparked off the debate. Dexter and David immediately offered their own positions, flagging their reasons with the discourse marker "because":[2]

> Dexter: i tend to agree with author on pressure and
>   disagree with Jones because i believe pressure
>   clouds your ability to think.
>
> David: I think that pressure is good for a person when he
>   or she is writing because I think it causes that
>   person to write better or put forward a better effort.

Andrew and Dexter are quite restrained as they move the argument to a balanced footing, stating that pressure could be good only under certain conditions (note their use of the discourse marker "but"):

> Andrew: pressure can be good, BUT it can also cause you
>   to overlook some important points.
>
> Dexter: did everone fail to read in the book the passage
>   that says pressure is good but also may earn you a
>   few D's.

Dexter cites the text as the authority for his standpoint. To contest this evidence, students like Rhonda cite personal experience:

> Rhonda: IT'S NOT THAT I DON'T HAVE THE TIME, I JUST
>   PUT IT OFF WHEN NOTHING GOOD COMES
>   TO MIND. SOMETIMES I PURPOSELY PUT
>   MYSELF THERE BECAUSE I KNOW SOMETHING
>   GOOD WILL COME OUT OF IT. IT HAD TO
>   BECUASE THAT'S MY GRADE!!

As the debate proceeds, others negotiate more qualified positions within the original terms of the argument in order to reconcile the divergent claims. Sonny synthesizes the claims made and consciously carves out a personal position in the conflict, taking into consideration the views expressed by Dexter and Andrew.

> Sonny: ON THE DEAL WITH PRESSURE; IT DOES HELP
>   ME TO FIND SOMETHING TO WRITE ABOUT,
>   BUT LIKE ANDY SAID, IT CAN CAUSE ONE TO
>   LEAVE OUT IMPOTANT PARTS OF THE PAPER,
>   AND LIKE DEXTER SAID, THAT CAN CAUSE A
>   FEW D'S.

In the end, the positions are reconciled in a useful manner by a couple of students as they modify their own initial positions to a healthy and pragmatic relativism. The students thus achieve a closure by acknowledging that each person has his or her own way of dealing with writer's block:

> Sonny: WRITING IS WRITING. WHATEVER YOU ARE
>   USED TO DOING KANE WILL PROBABLY
>   WORK. WHATEVER ALL OF YOU, KEEP DOING
>   IT SINCE IT GOT YOU THIS FAR. YOU ALL GOT

ACCEPTED AND MOST OF YOU ARE ON
SCHOLARSHIP! ! !

The claims of the students are carefully reasoned. They furnish clear
explanations and relevant evidence, and show the connections between
claims and evidence through subordinate sentences and discourse markers
of logical relationships. Such syntactic devices serve to decontextualize their
experience and foreground the reasoning with relevance to the argument.
Furthermore, the students display a disciplined focus on the words in the
text. Attending to the topic with much poise and detachment, they are able
to make sharply qualified claims and arbitrate between the different
positions expressed, sometimes self-critically. I will call such disputes *topic-
centered* arguments to distinguish them from other kinds of arguments we
will discuss below—those that are more implicit and context-bound (which I
will call *topic-associated*) or personal and agonistic (labeled *person-
centered*).

In these initial interactions the students all represent themselves in
academically favorable identities. They are smart, pragmatic, discerning,
reasonable, and balanced in the meticulous manner in which they debate
the topic. Moreover, in their fairly overt claims of having scored good grades
in writing and having won scholarships to come to the university, they are
presenting themselves as successful scholars. In analyzing the tricks they
consciously play with their minds and the unexpected consequences they
derive, they show themselves to be psychologically complex, self-analytical,
and self-aware. Students thus take measures to accommodate to the
dominant discourse of the context. But while they show the capacity to
recognize and use academic discourses, more important are their attitudes
towards this discourse. To adopt Chomskyan terminology, while students
display a general *competence* in academic discourses, their everyday social
interactions suggest a tension and inhibition experienced in *performance.*

Their attitude towards the academy was amply displayed in the identities
they adopted in the mailing system as the course progressed. Later messages
contradicted the positive images students had displayed to the others in the
contact zone. Contrary to the high sense of motivation and intellectual
curiosity expressed at the beginning of the semester, they often seemed
apathetic later. For instance, Diane openly discussed her boredom with the
rhetoric-based exercises from the textbook, exchanging personal messages
with Linda when both were supposed to be busy completing a task:

> Howdy doody doo. I am so bored and you are the only person who
> will laugh at my dumb jokes. I can see that you may need little

cheering up. I may be wrong, but I'm going to give you a little remedy. . . .

Students found many ways of distracting themselves, and among the topics usually discussed in the mail were romance, sex, music, friends, and family. Students were very playful as they quarreled over provocative messages, made up names for each other, or exchanged ritual insults.

There was also a heightened consciousness of their ethnic identity— which peaked in the final days of the course. This was caused by a gradual realization that academic writing involves "acting white." Before these messages, a student had been called "acting white" by her peers for having scored a better grade in her essay. In the ensuing discussion, most students protested against the label or feigned ignorance on what it meant. But then pithy messages like the following began to appear sporadically:

> Sonny: stay black, fight the power, support your people. PEACE HO!
>
> Dexter: TO STRONG . . . TO BLACK . . . TO STRONG . . . TO BLACK . . .
>
>   FFFFF
>
>   F
>
>   FF
>
>   F
>
>   F   IGHT THE POWER
>
> Sonny: everybody, it was great knowing you. hope to see you all in the fall. to the PREVIEW posse; stay close to each other. we are all gonna need help to get through, and i'd like to say all of us minorities make it. do it for your family, community, and culture, but most of all do it for yourself.
>
>   . . . good luck everyone
>
>   and remember, you on scholarshirp!!!!!
>
> Rhonda: Hello everyone, this is a reminder to everyone:
>
>   "STAY BLACK"
>
>   I LOVE YA'LL,
>
>   KELLI(MOOKY)

(The last two were farewell messages on the final day of classes.) These messages suggest a conception of the academy (or the public space of the contact zone) as an antagonistic site that threatens the identity of these students and their sense of community solidarity. The academy is presented as a locale where they have to struggle for success. The "stay Black" messages reveal students' awareness of the reproductive and hegemonic function of the academy. The mail forum served as a protected, trusted, safe house where they could express their frustrations, display resistance, and seek emotional sustenance and solidarity. In the midst of what was perceived to be an oppressive situation, students encouraged each other not to give up.

The safe house is, however, not an escape from pedagogical concerns. Even when students satirize or parody classroom matters, they are reframing these in their own terms with pedagogical value. For instance, a reading on male and female brain differences spawned a series of messages with claims to superiority based on physical or sexual prowess. The scientific research report was thus appropriated according to the values of street speech. Dexter formulated the sex chromosomes in mock-scientific terms: "XY > XX (except male feminists like Fab 5)." The parenthetical insult was aimed at Andrew, who insisted on advocating the equality of the sexes. Ironically, the interest in parodying pedagogical concerns demanded that they be attentive to classroom activities. Paradoxically, the safe house thus instilled a yet keener awareness of classroom concerns.

The mail system also functioned as a forum where students could engage in vernacular language/discourse forms to celebrate their ethnic solidarity and resist the hegemonic thrusts of academic discourses. Insult routines, playful verbal dueling, and "high siding" exchanges were frequently indulged in. These found more dramatic realization in face-to-face oral interactions in safe sites outside the networked classroom. It was evident that African-American students usually hung out together outside the classroom and rarely joined other student groups. Informal domains—such as residence halls, recreation centers, and student union rooms—functioned to build community solidarity among students. Consider, for example, how they argue as to who will win the boxing match between Tyson and Williams, which they were then watching on television in their dormitory:[4]

MM: Well, Tyson is finally gonna' get his ass kicked!

KN: Hell ya!!

DCW: What izs ye, ignant! Mike Tyson will kick tha fuck
        out of that fool.

DH: Now that's what I'm sayin'! Williams my boy and
        shit but goddamn he-

MB: Bullshit nigga! Williams gotta punch!

DH: Punch nigga? Tyson steady knockin' mothafuckas
        out, so don't come to me with that punch bullshit!

MB: You right about that, but who that nigga been
        fightin'? Spinks, Tubbs, Larry Holmes, why that
        ol'assfool come back anyway?

MM: For the money!

CZ: I heard that shit!

DCW: Hell yeah, for three million dollars I'd put my
        momma in the ring! I ain't bullshitin'!

Such agonistic interactions I term *person-centered* argumentation. They
tend to have very strong oral character and a distinct spoken idiom,
displayed by specifically Black English grammatical features: the use of
"steady" as an intensifier, deletion of the auxiliary, deletion of the copula,
and distinct phonological features such as deletion of word-final palatal
nasals. The argument above proceeds swiftly with assertions and
counterassertions on the main claim of whether Tyson or Williams will beat
the other. The focus is not on developing factual evidence to support the
claims, but subverting the opponent's claim in a rhetorically forceful manner.
The rhetoric thus dramatizes the "capping" sequences explained as typical of
vernacular discourse by Kochman (78), with the attempt of each speaker
being to perform a witty overturning (or rebuttal) of the opponent's claim.

Rhyme and rhythm are highly functional in this discourse. When IH
asserts that Williams can take Tyson's punch, as the argument proceeds,
DCW deals with this through a word play and rhyme—"Tyson fuck around /
stomp a round / hole in his ass!" Though the relevance of DCW's rebuttal to
IH's statement might be weak, what matters is the witty outsmarting of IH.
The crowning move is when CZ and DCW cap MB's claim that if the fight
goes on till the twelfth round Williams will win. DCW overturns MB's claim
by saying that Williams will be lucky to see the "second half of the first
round," while CZ improves that by saying "Yeah, he'll see the round from his
damn back!" The difference of this discourse from the topic-centered
interaction on writers' block is glaring. Students are not concerned here with
the academic practice of making balanced claims with valid evidence in a
detached tone to build a reasoned standpoint. They are instead switching to
vernacular discourse forms in the security of their safe house.

It didn't take long for students to also turn the electronic conference forum into a safe house for in-group interaction. Although at the beginning of the semester the conferences were quite formal, gradually the students discovered the scope it had for holding sub-conferences. Although others can eavesdrop, there is no compulsion for them to participate in these small-group discussions. In the following interaction, the African-American students are discussing a reading on recent revisions in history text books (see Clegg 406–412). Though the writer presents many details on the manner in which specific information and modes of presentation have been changed to correct the biases in previous texts, she doesn't favor these changes. The students dramatically appropriate the text to read their own themes and perspectives, thus eventually subverting the writer's message:

> David: I have noticed that in watchin tv that the indians are always considered the bad guys while the cowboys were considered the good guys.
>
> Sonny: Weren't most of the people who started civilization from Africa? Are not most Africans black? This is the biggest misconception of them all in my view. When I was young I thought that Cleopatra and all of the Pharoahs were white.
>
> Ray: That reminds me of the movie Moses, Sonny, that Pharoah was a Ramseses (the character that was played by Yuhl Brenner) He definitely wasn't black.
>
> Amos: i see too that they show all the egyptians as whites they do this because they won't get very vood reviews picturing them as they actually were "africans"
>
> David: Yea you know it is weird how the people who write most of the histroy books we read in school are white. Why is that? And why does it seem that the white man in those history books are portrayed as being the better of the races?
>
> Sonny: Exactly, Ray. Have you heard the song by BDP (I think) that talks about the black people of the Bible?
>
> Dexter: i feel the reason for the distortion is because whites want to portray themselves as doing the right thing to their children since they are the majority

Andrew: as in the book "1984", whoever controls the
present controls the past. Since the white man is in
power he can belittle the role of hte Indian and
black cowboys.

Ray: Yeah Sonny the Enemy is deep

Rhonda: History in school is very one-sided. It should be
called "white" history because that's basically all
that they talk about. They hardly ever mention
history of other races, and at my school they didn't
even offer a Black history class. I think one should
have the option to learn their own history. We
shouldn't be forced to learn only white history.

Donnie: Andy, keep your head out of them danm books

Ray: Like I said enough about BDP, PE is the one with
the serious messages.

David: I wonder if the white race would be in the same
shape that we are in if one of the minority races
became the majority.

Amos: it's kind of funny the only Blacks mentioned in the
history books are those that have been assasinated
by the white man (malcolm x, and martin luther
king jr.)

Sonny: I think minorities would write their history if they
could. How many companies want to publish
"History of the Negro(igga)"????

Linda: rhonda, do the people in your area recognize
Black history month? Some of the local churches
and elementary schools do in my hometown. I
agree with you about not learning enough of our
own cultural history, as well as other ethnic
groups. If it wasn't for the few Black people that do
recognize our history, I know that I certainly would
not have learned about it in high school.

Sonny: Ray PE does tell the stuff. That is why they are
looked at as militant-they tell the truth to the black
man.

Donnie: You know that most of the past inventions were
           invented by Black slaves. Like the cotton gin, Now
           come on people, do you honestly think that a
           white man is going to invent some thing to make a
           slaves life easier? He just took the claim because
           noone would have excepted that a slave invented it

Ray: FIGHT THE
           POWER!!

The *topic-associated* manner in which the students develop this argument is different from the topic-centered style of the academic discourse which they employed in the electronic conference cited earlier. This discourse does not have a tone of proving a point so much as exploring an issue collaboratively. The connection of their comments to the main issue being discussed is very much implied and might seem irrelevant at times. The narratives, anecdotes, and motifs from films, television, and rap music don't appear to be connected to the debate in a direct manner. But it is clearly implied that all these examples relate to racially distorted presentations of history and are, therefore, an indictment of the dominant groups and educational institutions. There is a strong sense of teamwork as the students interpret/amplify each other's statements, affirm each other's contributions, or ask for more information and opinions through knowing rhetorical questions. The students often used this topic-associated argumentation whenever they needed to take a common position against claims by opponents not directly present (authors of readings, famous theorists, or public figures), whereas the person-centered style we discussed above was employed for face-to-face arguments.

The difference in the sorts of evidence valued by the students further points to ideological differences from the academic community. For Andy, authority comes from published scholarship such as Orwell's book. This naturally invokes the insult of Donnie—"keep your head out of them damn books." But for the majority of the Black students much of their evidence came from rap music, films, television, and other sources of popular culture. Note the uses made above of the politically radical rap groups PE (Public Enemy) and BDP. Ray's invocation, "Fight the Power," is a popular but controversial recording by PE. It is significant that Sonny should say, "PE does tell the stuff. That is why they are looked at as militant- they tell the *truth* to the Black man" (emphasis added). Sonny thus reveals whom the students consider as their authorities in vernacular discourse.

Since the topic-associated argument of Black students is influenced by a different discourse from that of the academic community, it is not surprising that the students overturn the thesis of the writer in their interpretation of the academic text. While the writer criticizes the changes in the texts and wants to control the rewritings, the students encourage such revision, though their opposition to the author is not conveyed explicitly, but in their characteristic implicit fashion. Furthermore, the students amplify and explicate the text in their own terms: While the writer discusses biases only in general terms, the students discuss the subject specifically from the angle of racism against the African-American community. The students also make forays into the versions of history made available by vernacular texts (rap, films, etc.), embedding the author's text in a context relevant to their concerns.

Though their argument is context-bound and personal, this doesn't make their discussion static. The students explore many issues not raised by the reading and give additional depth to the subject. Starting from the what and how of distortions in history they go on to explore the why, and eventually probe the political-economy of textbook production that functions against minorities and sustains the hegemony of the majority group. The written word is thus creatively given new ramifications in reference to the larger social contexts and discourses of the students. Discussions such as this testify to the pedagogical richness and depth of the literate arts of the safe house. In enforcing linear, "objective," text-bound readings in the classroom, the academic contact zone sometimes loses a wealth of alternate readings and literacies brought by minority students. Such imposition can impoverish both the academy and the students.

Writing the Contact Zone

For their final writing project, I provided a subject that would enable students to reflect critically on their experience of the academy as a contact zone. They were asked to debate whether the academy is culturally biased against minority students, hampering their scholastic performance. In order to make the writing more relevant to their experience, I insisted that they include evidence other than the usual textual references: They were expected to interview two members of the ethnic group they were writing about and also to incorporate their own personal experiences and observations. The essays the students wrote allow us to explore how students treat a subject similar to that in the on-line conference above in an assigned writing for grading purposes.

Most students considered the topic in the light of their own experiences at the university. They articulated a clear sense of the academy as a site of social and ideological reproduction—as we can see from Donnie's essay below.

Culture Shock

The cultural orientation of the public school grew out of the anglicized social, political, and economic institutions established by the early colonists. One of the major social functions public schools acquired during the 1840's to the 1920's was acculturating the children of foreign-born parentage into the mainstream social political, economic institutions of society. But after a while the schools' social function became that of acculturating the young into an anglicized, middle-class conception of "Americanism" (Pizzillo, p 10). This acculturating continues even today not only in public schools but also in our colleges and universities. Minority groups confront a culture which is often in direct conflict with the culture of their homes and community. The culturally biased institutions could alienate Blacks and other minority students and affect their performance.

The criteria for being educated today is acceptance of the dominant middle-class culture of the school and rejection of those ways of seeing the world of feeling, valuing, and acting in the world that characterize the lower-class and/or minority group's personal and communal experiences (Pizzillo, p 10). Blacks must retire their culture so that they may be excepted by the majority. The most striking characteristic of the campuses to which minority students are now coming in is their essential whiteness. According to John Egerton, staff writer for the Race Relations Information Center, in both its makeup and its mindset, the whole of higher education is ". . . like a jug of milk—rich, white, and homogenized" (Altman, p 33).

Blacks are also having to remake the social and even physical environment that they left behind with their culture. They are having to work out their future in a curriculum which did not originally take them into account and which many white students find unsatisfactory even to themselves (Altman, p 50).

In order to survive, these students must band into their own social groups on the campus; thereby alienating themselves from the university which in turn looks upon these groups as outcasts to their society. Instead, universities should help build these support groups and assist the students within them. From my personal experience, I believe that most black families do not encourage their young to get a college education. They are satisfied that their children walked across a high school stage receiving their diploma. Lynell Tippen, a senior here at UT who has been here all four years, points out in an interview how most black parents never finished high school and would only expect their young to achieve just a little bit more than they did. Where as white families encourage their children to follow in their footsteps by attending college in order to succeed in life.

Two paragraphs follow here: one contains quotations from Altman on biases in the curriculum, the other discusses how students' native culture is affected.

Some people argue that Blacks alienate themselves from the rest of the community or even say that theses problems are too small to deal with on such a large scale. Lynell Tippen later in the interview states that most white people treat her better than then the Blacks around campus. Others could argue that it is not the schools that are biased but the Black students being bias against the school. Here again Lynell agrees. While these things are still being debated on today, I myself agree that this problem is too small to deal with but too large to ignore.

In comparison with the verbal disputes conducted in the safe houses, the argument in this and many other of the essays lacked conviction and force. Although students rightly shift to topic-centered argumentation in recognition of the demands of academic discourse, the development of their theses seemed to lack involvement. Their personal testimony was uneasily integrated into their essays. There is an unreconciled tension, for instance, between Donnie's personal statements and scholarly material. Curiously, in this, the most personal of all the essays written in the semester, the students seemed to hide behind their textual sources. In fact, they chose to speak about their own discrimination in institutions which they claim to have an Anglo-American bias through the very voices of middle-class white educators certified as authorities by the institution. The students readily quoted academic scholars who are supposed to carry the burden of proof for the claims made in their essays. For example, in his second paragraph, Donnie claims that Black students have to give up their culture in order to become educated. Rather than substantiating the cause-effect connection implicit behind this claim with support (perhaps from personal observation/ experience), Donnie merely provides us with the appropriate page numbers for Altman and Pizzillo. He goes on to claim that in order to cope with such problems Black students have to recreate social networks on campus for cultural and psychological support. Again, it is Altman who is supposed to do the explaining or provide the necessary data and warrants for this claim. We thus find an excessive dependence on scholarly authorities, in contrast to the electronic discussion above where students built their cases more thoughtfully and independently by marshaling evidence from rap music, films, and popular culture.

We must also examine the polemical strategies in Donnie's writing. He raises the counter-argument that Black students are to blame for their own biases against the institution and that it is inefficient to treat the problems of a few minority students when there are other problems to solve in a large institution. This does give Donnie's writing an objective and balanced footing. But his rebuttal is weak. He fails to answer the first criticism and tenders a hasty resolution for the second: "While these things are still being debated on today, I myself agree that this problem is too small to deal with but too large to ignore." Several other students failed to sustain the debate or rebut the opposing views forcefully, as they did in the person-centered arguments in the safe houses. Counter-arguments were instead introduced to give a perfunctory sense of balance in accordance with academic objectivity. Students who were experts of the "capping" speech act in oral interactions inside their safe house, allowed this rhetorical skill to become muted in their formal writing.

However, some other rhetorical strategies at work beneath the textual surface suggested a different reading of these essays. For example, while their writings displayed the stereotypical conventions of an academic essay, their content was radically anti-academic. Donnie is in unqualified agreement with the statement that the academic institutions are biased against minority students—especially Black students. The bland outer shell of the essay could lull us into overlooking the explosively radical content that is being developed. Since it is risky to articulate such an anti-institutional perspective in a graded essay, the deployment of the stereotypical conventions could have been intended as a concession to academic discourse or an attempt to provide a sense of balance and restraint to the writing. Thus, although some of the tensions in his writing may have resulted from a lack of confidence or uncertainty of direction, others seem to have been strategically employed for subtler communicative purposes.

There is a similar tension in the scholarly citations and the messages they are made to endorse. Donnie gets away with making some extreme accusations against the academy by carefully choosing his citations. Note the claims he contrives his authorities to make for him: "in both its makeup and its mindset, the whole of higher education is '. . . like a jug of milk— rich, white, and homogenized' (Altman, p 33)"; "the schools' social function became that of acculturating the young into an anglicized, middle-class conception of 'Americanism' (Pizzillo, p 10)." One can imagine Donnie chuckling to himself as he wrote these lines—since they are precisely the sort of pungent, expressive statements that vernacular discourse revels in. Perhaps in these instances Donnie was simply attempting to translate into the conventions and structures of academic discourse the claims he would like to make against the academy. But having to critique the academy by using its very rhetorical conventions and authorities creates some understandable uneasiness.

We should also not fail to hear the voices from the vernacular rhetorical tradition submerged in his text. The casual borrowing of sources and quotations in Donnie's writing, for example, resembles the "voice merging" that has been highlighted in the rhetoric of Martin Luther King (see Keith Miller). The oral community's practice of freely drawing from the communal stock of knowledge can sound plagiaristic when featured in the literate context. In the academic community, this communicative practice is considered a slavish dependence on others' views and words. However, there is a difference between masterful "voice merging"—which Howard calls "positive plagiarism" (796)—and non-imaginative, over-reliant pastiche. Donnie's writing may at moments fall short of rhetorically effective voice merging. But his struggle for an appropriate use of this vernacular practice may explain some of the tensions in the essay.

We might consider also whether the students' seemingly mechanical use of academic discourse conventions and identities could have served as a display of opposition through mimicry. What if their formulaic essays were a tongue-in-cheek parody of academic conventions? Parody requires a complex discursive competence. Students must understand the typical conventions of a discourse in order to mimic it. They must also be able to adopt an ideological distance from this discourse to resist it even as they use it. Parody can be a double-edged strategy that appears to satisfy the requirements of the instructors on the one hand while communicating to in-group members that the writer is simply indulging in play acting. A writer can indirectly say to his or her peers: "I have to indulge in this kind of writing because they expect us to do this for a grade; but you and I know that we don't believe in any of this—in fact, this is the silliest, blandest rhetoric on the face of the earth." Such a satiric attitude may function as an effective way for students to disarm the hegemonic thrusts of academic discourse. If these hidden messages can be found in Donnie's writing (and I will provide further ethnographic evidence to support it below) we might call this strategy a realization of the safe house phenomenon in the practice of academic writing. Not only can the safe house keep alive the vernacular or oppositional discourses that get encoded in the writing, it can also help develop certain complex strategies of negotiating competing discourses. Much as in safe houses students can express solidarity, retain vernacular discourses, and indulge in oppositional practices while outwardly conforming to the pedagogical requirements of the academy, in more formal writings they can also achieve a hidden textual space where they secretly communicate oppositional solidarity while "fronting" academic conventions.

The Art of Fronting

Thomas Kochman defines *fronting* as a seeming conformism that masks deeper oppositional tendencies, and argues that this practice has been historically developed by African-Americans in the face of pressure from mainstream society. Kochman describes fronting as "those anxious mental adjustments that are made in deference to the mode of oppression" (125). Ethnographer James Scott labels such forms of dissembling as the "weapons of the weak" (in his book of that title). Because overt and wholesale rebellion is often impractical, marginalized communities have often displayed surreptitious forms of everyday resistance through feigned ignorance, false compliance, foot dragging, and mimicry. Safe houses in the academic context allow minority students to practice similar forms of fronting. This strategy is calculated to having it both ways—on the one hand, students perfunctorily satisfy the academic requirements and vie for a good grade in the course by producing the typical academic communicative conventions; on the other hand, they oppose the academic culture and shield themselves from threats to their preferred identity, values, and group solidarity.

At the end of my course, in a highly charged discussion where everybody complained against the biases and injustices they experienced in college that semester, the students eventually rejected any interest in reforming the university or mobilizing collective actions of protest. At the climax of the discussion when I asked what should be done about the evils they perceived in the academy, the dominant response was neatly formulated by Sonny and Rhonda:

> Sonny: (. . .) our experience at the university is what we
>   make it, to a certain extent. We don't have to take
>   in everything, and believe it. Just remember it, put

it down as the correct answer, and go on with the good grade. Not everything that is heard has to be believed, just recalled for a good grade.

Rhonda: I really don't have much to say because I'm here and I know what it takes to make it. Things haven't changed and it's not likely that they will be soon, so instead of trying to fight the system, I'll just go along with it and perform as expected. It will make my college life a lot more peaceful and enjoyable. Suresh, imagine what kind of people and what kind of attitudes we would have if we went around holding grudges toward this university. Do you think they really care? They probably feel the fewer minorities, the better.

Certain paradoxical positions get articulated here. Although students are aware that the use of academic discourses would lead to deracination and domination, they are strongly motivated by academic success to still acknowledge the necessity of these discourses; although they are pessimistic about changes towards pluralism and equality in the academy and thus distance themselves from the academic community, they still choose to conform to its discursive practices (at least outwardly) in order to satisfy the requirements for educational success; although they confirm the oppositional attitudes towards the academy which we noted earlier, they also display a pragmatic recognition of the limits to which they can openly rebel against the academy. Fronting provides a temporary reconciliation for their conflict: nursing hidden forms of opposition, they go through the motions of college career, refraining from closer personal involvement in the learning process.

The practice of "fronting" offers further insight into the dynamics of safe house communication. Although they are supposed to be off limits to out-group members, including instructors, the fact that safe houses exist within the academy and often inside the same classroom provides certain indirect channels of access to others. The students in my class, for instance, were aware that in addition to the in-group, intended audience, there was an out-group, unintended audience that sometimes eavesdropped on their conversations. They therefore strategically exploited this additional level of communication to convey certain subtle messages to those outsiders—with their complaints about classroom boredom, protests against cultural alienation, and celebrations of socially stigmatized vernacular discourses. However, the students were also able to maintain the facade that these messages were not intended for out-group auditors. A similar strategy could be seen when under the guise of conforming to academic conventions students communicated oppositional perspectives in their writings. Through such safe houses students are able to challenge without retaliation, reject without punishment, resist without suppression.

Pedagogical Arts of Safe Houses

To say that the safe house can be a site of opposition to the academy is not to suggest that it influences students to turn their backs on learning. As we noted earlier, the safe house serves certain useful pedagogical functions. Paradoxically, in order to periodically gripe about curricular and pedagogical matters, students have to keep an eye on classroom happenings—perhaps more so than usual. Safe houses provide a parallel but safe site to respond to, reflect on, and comment about classroom concerns. The safety of this site, in fact, allows students to adopt alternate perspectives on classroom concerns, as they are able to reconsider classroom activities with a personal and community relevance. Robert Brooke, in his analysis of the "underlife" in writing classrooms, similarly brings out the pedagogical value of seemingly irrelevant and disruptive student behavior. Safe house activities can thus serve to develop meta-pedagogical awareness and reflective learning. The safe house is not a site of all play and no learning.

Safe houses provide a forum within the classroom where minority students can keep alive, practice, and develop their own vernacular discourse. To do so while acquiring academic discourses can generate spontaneous and ongoing comparisons between the two. The students in my course made partial but significant insights into a wide variety of discursive issues: contrasting rhetorical conventions, linguistic features, ideologies, socio-political ramifications, and implications for identity and group solidarity. Understanding such differences can help students develop greater appreciation of their own discourses and generate critical perspectives to reconstruct and further enrich the vernacular. In enabling minority students to keep alive their community-based discourses, knowledge, and values, safe houses can counteract the academy's history of suppressing minority discourses and reproducing dominant social relations and ideologies.

More relevant to the concerns of developing multivocal literacy is the function of safe houses as an experimental site where students can interrogate, negotiate, and appropriate new rhetorical and discursive forms without fear of institutional penalties. Ironically, in the safe houses of my class there was a more complex negotiation of discourses and mediation of cultures than in the public sites of the contact zone. In their discussion of biases in history textbooks, for example, students displayed subtle ways of appropriating readings to explore issues that concern them. They displayed the wise interpretive practice of situating the text in their own socio-cultural context to critique it, developed relevant themes in their own terms, and explored their own oral historical traditions to complement the text. The range of discourses in the safe houses was also dazzling. Moving from the academically preferred topic-centered argumentation of the first electronic conference cited, students moved to vernacular-based, person-centered and topic-associated modes in oral and written forms, showing an ability to negotiate a variety of discourses to suit the shifting topics, addressees, and contexts. The range of voices they were able to employ show immense creativity. Such linguistic creativity and heterogeneity are often absent in classrooms where minority students fear the imposition of a univocal discourse.

Considered from this perspective, safe houses make positive contributions for the process of knowledge construction in the academy. Safe houses ensure the survival and growth of alternate forms of knowledge that can challenge and redefine dominant discourses in the academy. They can reflect the situation of marginalized and emergent disciplinary groups, like the ethnic and women's studies circles. Such groups exist initially as alternate, informal bodies as they struggle for acceptance or dominance in the academy. From operating as small study circles and discussion groups inside or outside the institution, meeting on the members' own initiative in the beginning, they gradually move to direct confrontation and negotiation with hegemonic disciplinary groups. Safe houses can nurture such marginalized groups by providing a sanctuary for members of each community to interact among themselves and develop their discourses. Situated within the very institution they seek to change, safe houses can function as a strategic "underground" for conscientization, mobilization, and organization. But apart from enabling the often complicated and protracted stage of struggle for parity with other groups, in hosting alternative or oppositional discourses the safe houses also ensure the heterogeneity and diversity of the contact zone. They assure the healthy friction, challenge, and debate that can contribute to the vitality of academic discourses. A contact zone true to its definition—one that accommodates struggle between discourses and groups for ongoing negotiation of power and difference—will of necessity house safe sites, since no institution is so egalitarian as to permit equal status for all marginalized groups all the time. The success of the academy as a contact zone is, in other words, predicated on the existence of safe houses.

In the light of these larger considerations, what pedagogical functions would safe houses play in the development of academic literacy? A variety of thinkers ranging from poststructural discourse theorists (Foucault; Bakhtin), feminists (hooks; Gilligan), rhetoric scholars (Berthoff; Flower), educational theorists (Giroux; Grossberg) and, more relevant for our purposes, Black scholars (Gates; Ogbu, "Understanding") have articulated that simply acquiring the established academic/institutional discourses is not to speak but to be silenced. Safe houses can play a significant role in providing the critical distance, the oppositional stance, and the personal space needed to help students find a voice for themselves in academic discourse. The effects of the safe house are, for example, evident in Donnie's writing as he attempts various indirect strategies of finding an appropriate footing in this discourse. The hesitant, tentative, half-realized gestures he makes towards negotiating the dominant discourses to develop a voice need to be pedagogically encouraged and nurtured.

Towards the Pedagogical Arts of Contact Zones

But the positive potential of the safe houses needs to be transferred to the public sites of the contact zone before its promise gets fully realized. For this purpose, students must be encouraged to come out of the safe houses to negotiate the competing discourses in the academy. What teaching methods can we employ to help them make this transition? Richard Miller has recently argued, "The classroom does not . . . automatically function as a contact zone in the positive ways Pratt discovered in the Stanford course. . . . [There] is still a great deal of work to be done in constructing the 'pedagogical arts of the contact zone'" (399). However, while much attention has been given to matters of curriculum and teaching materials (see Bizzell), pedagogy has so far received insufficient consideration.

The pedagogical value of safe houses lies in the fact that teachers don't have to impose unilaterally developed or self-conceived teaching methods and tasks for students. The learning strategies, insights, skills, and discourses students spontaneously develop in the safe houses simply need to be tapped into. Safe houses show the steps students take to gain insights into the conventions and values of the academic discourse. Students critique the hegemonic and reproductive agenda of the dominant discourses. They negotiate the differences between the academic and vernacular modes of argumentation. They even go some way towards the construction of culturally appropriated, multivocal texts. Teachers can take advantage of the ground students themselves intuitively cover, to make these processes more conscious. After all, the secret of successful teaching is to make students more self-directed and autonomous in their learning by encouraging critical awareness, reflective learning, and strategic thinking. Encouraging the steps students themselves take in this direction in the safe houses can lead to a highly responsive, learner-centered pedagogy.

A way to promote such learning strategies is to use the texts constructed in the safe houses for discussion and analysis in the classroom. Transcripts of electronic conferences, verbal disputes in the mail, and drafts of essays can be used to non-threateningly analyze the ways in which the students' texts differ from the academic discourses, as well as the strengths and limitations of both discourses. Such strategies convey to students that their vernacular discourses are valued academically and that they don't have to be practiced in the secret of their safe houses. Similarly, the attempts students make to appropriate dominant discourses and construct hybrid texts is immensely useful. What students like Donnie might need is simply the encouragement to continue their experimentation with more confidence.

But it is of course dangerous simply to romanticize the texts and discourses of the students. As I noted earlier, students' behavior and discourses often show a mixture of oppositional and accommodative tendencies which need to be critically unpacked for their hidden values and implications. Students must be encouraged, therefore, to adopt a critical attitude not only towards the "alien" discourses, but towards their own—as we are reminded often by critical pedagogues (see Freire 30–35; Giroux, *Teachers* 183–185; *Border 29;* hooks 98–104; Willis). It is also important to show them how minority writers recognized in mainstream circles have themselves appropriated and vernacularized dominant discourses and used them with ideological clarity and linguistic creativity. Both literary figures like Toni Morrison and academic writers like bell hooks can be introduced to the students for the manner in which they masterfully grapple with the competing discourses to develop their voice.

We have to also consider how the safe house can itself be further utilized for pedagogical purposes. Realizing the "pedagogically safe and socially nurturing" atmosphere necessary for students "to cross ideological and political borders as a way of furthering the limits of their own understanding," Giroux urges us to provide what he calls "safe spaces" for students. Developing his own "border" pedagogy (which is motivated by principles not dissimilar from contact zones pedagogy), he articulates "the need to provide safe spaces for students to critically engage teachers, other students, as well as the limits of their own positions as border-crossers who do not have to put their identities on trial each time they address social and political issues" (*Border Crossings* 33). While networked classes like mine provide immense possibilities for students to develop safe houses by themselves, teachers can consider other ways to nurture such sites in their classrooms. Small group discussions, peer reviews and interactions, collaborative writing, and paired work assignments are simple ways in which safe houses can be constructed inside the classroom. Collaborative projects, guided fieldwork, and research activities (in libraries, dormitories, or outside the campus) can also help students set up and make use of safe houses outside classrooms. We must also become sensitive to what is typically regarded as disruptive behavior during class time—such as the ubiquitous whispers, secret notes, and digressive comments Brooke reports in his analysis of classroom underlife—for what they show about incipient oppositional discourses and critical learning strategies.

In order to understand and exploit safe houses for pedagogical purposes, then, teachers have to become ethnographers who are prepared to unravel the hidden cultures of their classrooms and students. This need compels teachers to creatively devise ways of participating in the different discursive interactions in their classrooms. Apart from the institutional boundaries and cultural borders we have to cross to discern the many literacies practiced in our classrooms, we have to also transcend ideological barriers to see apparently atypical forms of behavior as loaded with meaning and significance for students. To consider safe house or oppositional behavior as not educationally disruptive but pedagogically engaging requires ideological shifts in teachers' perspectives (see Giroux, *Border* 34–35). Safe houses therefore compel us as teachers to critically examine our own locations in the matrix of dominant and subordinate discourses in the society and the academy.

Safe houses also have significant implications for current debates on the place of sheltered courses for minority students. It is a testimony to the agency of our students that even if they are mainstreamed (as political and bureaucratic wisdom dictates these days) they will still construct safe houses within the existing structures of oppressive institutions to collaboratively work through the conflicts and challenges they face. It is certainly advisable for writing programs to provide institutional support for nurturing safe houses (without appropriating their subversive edge). But it is more important to remember that such sheltering is for the eventual purpose of negotiating with mainstream discourses and institutions for the empowerment of minority students and pluralization of dominant discourses, rather than being an end in itself.

We can now move to a more complex understanding of safe houses. Although safe houses can exist outside the contact zone for some time (as certain special interest groups, for example, have first mobilized outside the academy before moving with mustered strength for protracted engagement with it), they are typically situated *within* the contact zone and are linked to it. Thus while safe houses offer a measure of protection from the tense inter-cultural engagement of the contact zone, they are not cut off from it altogether. Furthermore, the safe house is not a passive site that simply provides psychological relief for marginalized groups; it is a radically active site that generates strategies and resources to transform the dominant discourses in the contact zone. It is not a politically-free or neutral site that helps marginalized groups take leave of struggles over power and difference; it is a subversive site that nurtures oppositional perspectives, demystifies dominant ideologies, and breeds constant friction with established discourses for their democratization. The safe house is integral to the contact zone—not only for its success as a site of multivocal text production and emergent discourses, but for its self-definition as a meeting point of heterogeneous cultures and ideologies. These two sites are then interactive and interdependent, while being antagonistic. Though each site influences life in the other, the influence of the dominant structures in the contact zone is hegemonic while that of safe houses is potentially resistant. Hence the pedagogical significance of safe houses. If knowledge construction in the academic contact zone is to be democratized/pluralized, then we need to visit the safe houses of our students to tap the resources, discourses, and strategies being developed there.

Notes

1. Among the subjects, seven were males. All students claimed to be from the middle or upper middle-class. Though it is possible to make a fine distinction between the discourse of middle-class and working-class Blacks, I am treating

both classes here as sharing many features of a common discourse (as also supported by Smitherman 114).

2. The data are cited with the spelling and grammatical errors as they originally appear. All names are pseudonyms, although students signed release forms to use all forms of their speech/writing during the course.

3. Since these data were transcribed by a student as the interaction occurred (when I was not present), it is stylized to some extent. The student also used the initials of the participants rather than the pseudonyms I used.

Works Cited

Bakhtin, M. M. *Speech Genres and Other Late Essays.* Trans. V. W. McGee. Austin: U of Texas Press, 1986.

Berthoff, Ann. *The Making of Meaning.* Upper Montclair, NJ: Boynton/Cook, 1983.

Bizzell, Patricia. "'Contact Zones' and English Studies." *College English* 56 (1994): 163–69.

Brooke, Robert. "Underlife and Writing Instruction." *CCC* 38 (1987): 141–53.

Clegg, Cyndia Susan. *Critical Reading and Writing Across the Disciplines.* New York: Holt, 1988.

Flower, Linda. *The Construction of Negotiated Meaning: A Social Cognitive Theory of Meaning.* Carbondale: Southern Illinois UP, 1994.

Foucault, Michel. "The Discourse on Language." *The Archeology of Knowledge.* Trans. A. M. Sheridan Smith. New York: Pantheon, 1972.

Freire, Paulo. *Pedagogy of the Oppressed.* New York: Herder, 1970.

Gates, Jr., Henry Louis. "Writing 'Race' and the Difference It Makes." *Race, Writing, and Difference.* Chicago: U of Chicago P, 1986. 1–15.

Gilligan, Carol. *In a Different Voice: Psychological Theory and Women's Development.* Cambridge, MA: Harvard UP, 1982.

Giroux, Henry A. *Theory and Resistance in Education: A Pedagogy for the Opposition.* South Hadley: Bergin, 1983.

———. *Teachers as Intellectuals: Toward a Critical Pedagogy of Learning.* New York: Bergin, 1988.

———. *Border Crossings: Cultural Workers and the Politics of Education.* New York: Routledge, 1992.

Grossberg, Lawrence. "Introduction: Bringin' It All Back Home—Pedagogy and Cultural Studies." *Between Borders: Pedagogy and the Politics of Cultural Studies.* Ed. Henry Giroux and Peter McLaren. New York: Routledge, 1994. 1–25.

hooks, bell. *Talking Back: Thinking Feminist, Thinking Black.* Boston: South End, 1989.

Howard, Rebecca Moore. "Plagiarisms, Authorships, and the Academic Death Penalty." *College English* 57 (1995): 788–806.

Kochman, Thomas. *Black and White Styles in Conflict.* Chicago: U of Illinois P, 1981.

Lu, Min-Zhan. "Professing Multiculturalism: The Politics of Style in the Contact Zone." *CCC* 45 (1994): 442–58.

Miller, Richard. "Fault Lines in the Contact Zone." *College English* 56 (1994): 389–408.

Miller, Keith D. *Voice of Deliverance: The Language of Martin Luther King, Jr and Its Sources.* New York: Free P, 1992.

Ogbu, John. "Class Stratification, Racial Stratification, and Schooling." *Race, Class and Schooling.* Ed. L. Weis. Buffalo: Comparative Education Center, 1986. 10–25.

———. "Understanding Cultural Diversity and Learning." *Educational Researcher* 21 (1992): 5–14.

Pratt, Mary Louise. "Arts of the Contact Zone." *Profession 91.* New York: MLA, 1991. 33–40.

Scott, James C. *Weapons of the Weak: Everyday Forms of Peasant Resistance.* New Haven: Yale UP, 1985.

Smitherman, Geneva. "Black Language as Power." *Language as Power.* Ed. C. Kramrae, M. Schulz, and W. M. O'Barr. Beverly Hills: Sage, 1984. 101–15.

Willis, P. *Learning to Labour: How Working Class Kids Get Working Class Jobs.* Manchester: Saxon, 1977.

3 A Good Gang: Thinking Small with Preservice Teachers in a Chicago Barrio

Todd DeStigter

> We cannot convince kids that we cherish them in settings in which we cannot stop to mourn or to celebrate. In our big-city high schools, numbness becomes our salvation, as it does for our children, and in the process we become passion- and compassion-impaired.
>
> Deborah Meier, 1995, p. 113

Making Histories

Sandra, a nineteen-year-old high school student, and I sat facing each other in a small office cluttered by four large desks and piles of books and loose papers. Traffic noise from an intersection just outside pushed into the room through an open window, and every few minutes, when a bus or truck hit a cavernous pothole in the pavement, the building trembled. As part of my work as an ethnographer among Latino students in Chicago, I had been eager to talk to Sandra for quite some time, especially now, since I had heard her reading of a poem entitled "I Am a Mexican Woman," which she had composed for a *Cinco de Mayo* celebration held in the pavilion of a local park. That day, Sandra had received a standing ovation from an audience of

Reprinted from *English Education,* October 1998.

about 200 people. In her poem, Sandra looks back at a "heritage" which she says "kindled pride from deep in my roots to the fire red blood that runs through my veins." She also looks ahead with hope, "to bear children one day so I could truly appreciate the preciousness of living." She speaks, too, of troubles and vulnerability, as she captures in this stanza:

> I am a Mexican woman who has experienced life.
> I pretend to be happy and make my good side shine.
> I feel like a failure, whose days are a waste of time.
> I touch the lives of others with my wisdom from the streets.
> I worry day and night what will become of me.
> I cry when I'm heartbroken like any other teen.

I asked Sandra about those days she calls "wasted," and she looked past me as she searched her memory of when she had dropped out of school. She pushed her black hair back over her shoulder, revealing a small, faded tattoo in the shape of a crown on the left side of her neck, an insignia identifying her as a member of the Latin Queens street gang: "Aw, Todd, back then I went crazy. There were times when I would really try to do good, but there were so many distractions. Fights, gangs, daytimes [parties], threats by other people."

These "distractions" led Sandra to leave school at age fourteen and to begin working, first in fast food restaurants and then in a factory that produces what Sandra describes as "little care packages for Christmas." The work, she recalls, was grueling:

> I was standing there ten hours on my feet, and I would have cuts all over my hands. I mean nasty. I really suffered working there, and only for like five bucks an hour. And I needed the money so I'd work over-time, fifteen hours on my feet, with only like ten minute breaks, you know? I was really tired, and my feet would hurt, and I was so hungry 'cause I really didn't have any money to buy any snacks. I was like, this is not the kind of life I want.

Though Sandra wanted to return to school, her gang involvement had created what initially seemed to her like insurmountable barriers. "At first I didn't know where to go," she said. "I'm like, my old school isn't going to take me back. I tried to go back there but they didn't want me." Attending other area schools, she explained, would simply have been too dangerous: "I couldn't go to any other school, 'cause those are my rival neighborhoods, and I'd get my ass whooped, if anything. But then my friend told me, 'Oh, I'm going to go apply to Latino Youth,' and that's when I came here."

The "here" Sandra refers to is Latino Youth Alternative High School, the educational unit of a social service agency housed in a converted four-story apartment building in the predominantly Mexican neighborhood of Chicago known as *La Villita,* or Little Village. The approximately eighty students who attend Latino Youth range in ages from sixteen to twenty-one and are there in that "alternative" setting because they have dropped out of or have been expelled from at least one of the scores of regular high schools in the Chicago public system, usually for reasons such as low academic achievement, teen pregnancy, gang involvement, drug abuse, or persistent "delinquency." For students like Sandra, Latino Youth offers a second chance, and often a third.

I will not for a moment romanticize the profound troubles that brood over this small place. I will not say that it is easy to sit, as I did recently in an English class, and listen to students brainstorm about themes of their experiences that they wished to develop into a play, themes that included domestic violence and gang-related homicide. I will not pretend that it is in any way delightful or exotic to see a ring of eight small white crosses stuck in the grass in front of the school in memory of friends and family who died prematurely in the past year. Nor will I dismiss the anguish I sensed in students as they left school early on a recent Friday afternoon on their way to the wake of a boy named Javier, whose graduation I attended in June of last year and who died in November, 1997, of a drug-induced heart attack.

Despite relentless and disheartening problems such as these, I have come to think of Latino Youth as the site of some of the most exciting and promising work being pursued in the English Education Program at the University of Illinois at Chicago (UIC). In January, 1997, in consultation with Latino Youth teachers and administrators, about a dozen UIC secondary English education students and I initiated the Latino Youth/UIC Tutoring Project, an enrichment opportunity in which university volunteers spend one or two periods per week serving as tutors and/or teacher aides in a Latino Youth classroom. The UIC students who participate in this program are still early in the English education course sequence; they have taken at least one methods class but have not yet begun their semesters of in-school observation or student teaching. Though most of the UIC students help out in English classes, some with broader interests and abilities work in other disciplines such as social studies, performing arts, or even math.

As I emphasize to the beginning teachers who participate in the program, we try to go to Latino Youth with no specific agenda other than to be useful in addressing the needs of Latino Youth teachers and students as they themselves define them. Sometimes we work with individual students generating ideas for papers or assisting with revisions in the computer lab. At other times, we are invited to lead small group discussions or even to teach a lesson to an entire class. This relationship seems to be useful to students from both schools: Latino Youth teachers have said that their students, whose average reading and writing skills are at a sixth-grade level, benefit from the one-on-one help from preservice teachers who have considerable interest and often some experience in working with high school–aged students. The UIC volunteers, on the other hand, have frequently mentioned to me how much they value the opportunity to work with "real students" as a way to complement and provide a context for the training they receive in their university methods classes.

What I wish to focus on here, however, is an aspect of this experience for the UIC students that is significant in ways that go beyond providing, as one of the tutors put it, "face time" with a group of students they might not otherwise encounter. Specifically, given the current discourse emphasizing the alleged need to reform our nation's schools by means of federally dictated learning outcomes and increased standardized testing, I will argue that it is important that beginning teachers receive at least part of their training in a small school like Latino Youth, for I believe that such settings encourage a sense of caring and genuine affection among students and teachers that brings encouragement and possibility to the lives of young people who have seen far too much loss and hopelessness. While the benefits of small schools in terms of student performance is well-documented in our professional literature (Bryk, Holland, and Lee, 1993; Toby, 1993; Lee and Smith, 1994; Bensman, 1994), my principal aim is to demonstrate what I see as the underlying, affective causes of these benefits and to urge English educators to include experiences in small schools as part of their teacher training programs. In my view, for preservice teachers to participate in the relationships made possible by small schools and to understand negotiating these relationships as part of their never-ending process of "becoming" as teachers is an essential part of any broader effort of school "reform" worthy of the name.

One way that I have found useful to think about this project is to understand it as a means of extending the *histories* of the UIC students as beginning teachers—a framework I borrow from early pragmatist writers, especially John Dewey and William James. As James T. Kloppenberg (1986) has noted, Dewey and James, in their search for pragmatic and provisional understanding, looked to immediate experience as the locus of knowledge.

Thus, in Dewey and James' view, the subject becomes, in a word, historical: She is embedded in socioeconomic and political contexts that historicize her consciousness and conceptions of knowledge; she can come to recognize, moreover, that her choices and actions make history, and that the truth of her beliefs and the correctness of her decisions are validated in concrete historical processes (p. 113). This is not to say that either Dewey or James denied that such decisions would be complicated by competing preferences or readings of history. Rather, it is to emphasize that to these writers history provides us with the best idea available of what we ought to do in any given set of circumstances. Dewey (1985/1916), in *Democracy and Education,* proclaimed as the first condition for determining "the criteria of good aims" that "the aim set up must be an outgrowth of existing conditions" (p. 111). Similarly, James, in "Humanism and Truth," wrote that "the only real guarantee we have against licentious thinking is the circumpressure of experience itself, which gets us sick of concrete errors" (p. 229). In Kloppenberg's words, this historical sensibility, which formed the roots of the political and ethical theories of social democracy and progressivism, "rests upon the belief that meaning is woven into the fiber of experience, that becoming rather than being is the mode of human life" (p. 4), and that people make rather than find their values and their understandings of what is good and useful. In sum, then, Dewey and James uncover in history an empirical foundation for judgment and critique.

To apply this framework to the English education program at UIC, one may view the tutors' experiences at Latino Youth as a way of extending their histories as beginning teachers to include working in a small, even intimate setting that demonstrates the value of close, empathetic teacher-student relationships. Typically, the histories of UIC education students are similar in that almost all of them are graduates of the large public high schools in and around Chicago. Also, upon entering the UIC education program, these beginning teachers will share the experience of having their observation and student teaching occur only in large schools. This policy of deliberately placing preservice teachers in large schools is justified by the UIC College of Education by reasoning that such placements prepare preservice teachers for work in the large schools in which they are most likely to find jobs. During the Spring semester of 1998, for instance, UIC secondary English student teachers were placed in Chicago public high schools like Farragut, with an enrollment of about 1,500; Benito Juarez, with approximately 2,000 students; and Lane Tech, which has a student population of over 4,000. Thus, despite the valuable mentorship often provided by teachers in large schools, it is likely that students earning certification from UIC will begin their careers with a knowledge only of educational settings where students are known more by the nine-digit numbers on their mandatory I.D. badges than they are by their names. As Deborah Meier (1995) has argued, whatever efficiency is gained by attempts to teach students within the structural constraints of such schools comes at the considerable cost of making it difficult for teachers to attend to students' unique intellectual and emotional dispositions. "Schooling is part of child rearing," Meier reminds us. "It's the place society formally expresses itself to young people on what matters. We forgot that when we built our schools to be huge factories" (p. 114).

Nonetheless, as I and the other UIC tutors have learned, alternatives do exist—alternatives that underscore the notion that, for many students, academic development and a sense of "belonging" are inseparable. In the course of more than a year of research carried out in conjunction with the tutoring project, I have interviewed several students concerning their views of the differences between their previous schools and Latino Youth, and each has spoken a familiar refrain. I invite you to listen to two of these voices. First, that of Maria:

> Before I came to Latino Youth I didn't really like school 'cause at my old school the teachers didn't pay attention to their students. I mean, they would give an assignment and the notes and that's it. And they would just be like, "Just do this and that," and that's it. And after I had my baby, I dropped out in my junior year two times. But here, I like it a lot. The teachers, you can tell that they really care about you. . . . And here you call them by their name, like Oh, Georgina, or Oh, Steve or Gloria, or whoever, and you talk to them like . . . how can I say—I don't know if you understand—like straight up. If I didn't like it here I wouldn't come. But I like it here. I love it here, actually.

Similarly, Raul, his head bobbing to the beat of Latin rap music during lunch time in the second-floor student lounge, said, "This place is different, man. Here, everybody's together. They help each other out. The teachers, too. Like this." Raul held up his hands at eye level, his fingers locked tightly together.

I believe that exposure to this type of environment described by Maria and Raul can have a profound and ameliorating effect on the visions that beginning teachers have regarding what schools should look like and how they should be with their students. For some preservice teachers, this transformative process begins as modestly as revisions in their expectations of what so-called "at risk" students are capable of, given sufficient guidance. A UIC student named Kevin told me, "I had somehow pictured these kids as being really uninterested in learning and having bad learning skills, bad study habits, or just being bad kids, but I didn't see that at all." In contrast, some of these revisions move in the opposite direction. Saralina, a UIC master's degree student and university composition instructor, admitted, "I'm still shocked by some of the students who can't get a sentence of writing onto paper; it's just a paralyzing thing for them. It's definitely something I'm going to have to adjust my teaching to."

As useful as it may be for the UIC students to adjust their notions about specific teaching practices in response to students' abilities, more important, I think, are those encounters that more deeply challenge assumptions teachers have about their sense of themselves and the nature of their relationships with students. Ruth Vinz (1997) has described such moments as "dis-positioning ourselves," as learning to "unknow" what we think our experiences have taught us about teaching and to "not know" with any kind of permanence or certainty how best to negotiate those relationships that are constantly being formed and reformed within the "alien, nonsensical, sometimes threatening, mostly unpredictable" contexts of classrooms (p. 139). Though teachers may yearn for the stability afforded by definiteness and order, Vinz argues that dis-positions of "unknowing" and "not-knowing" allow us to create spaces where we might critically interrogate the values, ideas, and assumptions we bring to our work and to understand the teaching life as a continuous, discordant process of "becoming" (p. 140).

One such unsettling experience at Latino Youth was described by a UIC tutor named Jalayna, who grew to "unknow" what she had previously suspected would be the factors influencing her interactions with students whose cultural and language histories differed from her own. Citing her unsatisfying experiences in multicultural education classes and her service in the military, which she described as "the only successful affirmative action program in the world," Jalayna had come to downplay the dynamics of culture and ethnicity that at times complicate our teaching relationships: "I had completely come up with an intellectual argument against focusing on things culturally, and I had put it to rest," she said. Jalayna added that she had assumed that her working class white family background would provide some basis for solidarity with Latino Youth students. However, during one of her first visits to Latino Youth, Jalayna was challenged to confront and reexamine those very issues she had been determined to disregard. While describing her attempts to help a student generate ideas for a story in journalism class, Jalayna recalls that the student alternately ignored and rebuffed her suggestions. Finally, the student turned to Jalayna and said, "I don't like white people; white people distract me." This was, Jalayna admitted, a painful experience, one made all the more personally disconcerting for her in that the student's distrust of "white people" did not seem to extend to the several Anglo members of the Latino Youth teaching staff. Nonetheless, reflecting on this encounter, Jalayna came to view it as an opportunity to revise—to "unknow"—those understandings of cross-cultural teaching and learning that she had constructed based upon her previous history:

> I had decided to stop thinking about how my whiteness might inter-fere with my ability to teach and to think "I've got a good heart; that's got to be enough." But I represent certain things to [Latino Youth stu-dents], and it's dealing with what I represent to these people that's a little harder than I thought. I get over there and I can't see how I can reject culturally sensitive teaching. I mean, it's about alienation, so I am going to have to come to terms with how I am as a teacher might alienate students.

As I think Jalayna's story suggests, the need to continually disposition ourselves as teachers arises from the fact that there is no way to separate individuals' identities as teachers and learners from their complex identities as human beings. Teaching is, after all, a relationship, a way of being with other people, and as such it is subject to all the wonderfully perplexing fluidity and instability that accompanies any other relationship we presume to establish. Such a view of teaching encourages us to understand education as an inherently ethical enterprise that is constantly subject to revision. As James asserted long ago, "There is no such thing as an ethical philosophy dogmatically made up in advance" (1969/1897, p. 169). Thus, whatever uncertainty accompanies conceiving of teaching as a relationship should not be viewed as a temporary deficiency to be solved once educators gain sufficient knowledge based on classroom experience or the study of pedagogical methods. Rather, to engage our students as human beings with desires and histories, goals and fears, should lead us to welcome this constant state of flux as a vital part of our vocation as teachers. As we have seen with Jalayna, to work in places like Latino Youth, places where such mutability is highlighted and embraced, may help beginning teachers recognize and name potential obstacles in their attempts to establish mutually constructive relationships with students. Further, I believe that to enrich teaching histories to include experiences in small settings like Latino Youth—settings that refuse to admit any artificial separation between students' academic and affective needs—is to encourage beginning teachers to view human solidarity as both an end in itself and a means of helping students achieve the confidence and motivation they need to open their lives to new possibilities.

This understanding of teaching as an evolving ethical relationship, and seeing that relationship as a way to make teaching and learning more productive and meaningful, is something Saralina added to her history as an educator as a result of her tutoring at Latino Youth. In the university methods class in which I had Saralina as a student, she had spoken frequently of her intention as a teacher to maintain high academic standards. While many of her classmates (and her instructor) applauded Saralina's resolve, our class's reading of Mike Rose's (1989) *Lives on the Boundary* helped us all more clearly understand that, for many students, "raising the bar" of academic standards requires that teachers offer not only pedagogical but also emotional support in order for students to clear that bar. In that well-known account of his own learning, Rose writes, "What mattered most . . . were the relationships [my teachers] established with me, the guidance they provided when I felt inadequate or threatened" (p. 235–236). Because of her involvement at Latino Youth, Saralina was able to experience firsthand this connection between a commitment to academic achievement and an attentiveness to the relationships with the students with whom she worked. She described one such learning moment this way:

> [I had worked with Jackie in journalism class.] At the end of the first session she had asked, "Are you coming back?" And I said, "Yes I'll be here every Friday." She missed the next week, but then I saw her the following week and said, "Hi Jackie, How you doing?" And she stopped and said, "You remembered my name." And I said "Yeah." And I think that moment of sort of warming up, that "Oh, you remember me," . . . I think that meant something to her.

By citing these examples, I do not mean to imply that demonstrations of the importance of teachers' and students' personal investment in each other do not occur in those larger schools where UIC preservice teachers are normally placed. To be sure, the commitment of teachers in these settings has often shown that such relationships can and do develop despite the institutional barriers that are (literally) built into the structure of large schools. However, my point is that these relationships tend to be more clearly a priority in small schools like Latino Youth and that experiences in such schools provide preservice teachers with an important part of the history they must use as a foundation for critiquing themselves and their work. Latino Youth is a place where teachers know when a student's child is in bed with the flu and how many hours a student works each day after school. It is a place where teachers and students share their lunches and conversations about their families. In sum, Latino Youth provides a model for beginning teachers of a space that consistently encourages those close relationships that enrich the lives of students and teachers alike—a place where human and humane connections are conspicuously foregrounded as the desirable nature of the school culture. Jennifer, another UIC tutor, expressed her growing understanding of the importance of such relationships in her comments regarding the sense of community she feels at Latino Youth:

> So many other kids I know in the city, they're alienated from their family, . . . then they go to high school, they're alienated there. . . . If I were in their shoes I'd be joining gangs left and right. Why not? 'Cause [in a gang] you're a part of something. These kids in the Latin Kings, I don't blame them at all, because the kids need some place to belong, and where everybody else has failed the gangs have suc-ceeded. You need to create your own little gang, and that's what Latino Youth has done. But it's a good gang.

I have to confess that I'm still trying to figure out how I feel about Jennifer's choice of metaphor—whether or not a "good gang" is a contradiction in terms. But I see her point, which I think suggests that she and the other tutors have begun to make connections between the caring relations they see at Latino Youth and the well-being of its students. I am encouraged by such comments, for I think they indicate that these young teachers are creating histories which include memories that are a vital part of their personal and professional development. As Nel Noddings (1984) has argued, it is only by recalling the memory of caring that we can learn to desire it further. Indeed, Noddings writes that an "engrossment" in and commitment to the other, an ethical, enabling sentiment of caring and being cared for, "occurs in response to a remembrance of the first" (p. 79). In my more optimistic moments, I think that by arguing that people must draw upon lived experiences of caring relationships in order to care deliberately, Noddings is describing the kinds of memories that are being created when high school and university students encounter each other at Latino Youth.

Latino Youth and Beyond: Toward a Connection Between Caring and Democracy

By now I hope it is clear that I see a great deal of potential value in placing beginning teachers in small schools for at least part of their preservice experience. As we listen to the voices of the UIC students cited above, we hear evidence that the relationships they have experienced at Latino Youth have encouraged them to revise assumptions they may have had about poor, ethnic minority students, to view social and emotional alienation as a hindrance to academic achievement, and to recognize the connection between caring and a humane ethic of teaching. What is less clear, however, is how these dispositions will be translated into classroom practices and how (or whether), in turn, these practices can be transferred into larger school settings. Indeed, is this account of young teachers' "histories" in a small school merely a nice story of their making friends with high school students whom they would be unlikely to meet in circumstances that are less contrived? Or, to put it another way, does this experience have specific consequences in terms of what the UIC tutors will chose to do in their own classrooms? This question is a fair one, I think, and difficult to answer without speculation because, as of this writing, the UIC tutors I have described have yet to move into large schools for their observation and student teaching.

An exception to this is a UIC tutor named Sue, who in the spring of 1998 moved from Latino Youth to a Chicago public high school of about 2,500 students, where in one semester she logged over eighty hours of observation and directed teaching. In what follows, I briefly draw upon two sources, an interview I conducted with Sue immediately after her work in a large school and a graduate seminar paper she wrote at the conclusion of her semester at Latino Youth, to explore what seem to me to be possible long-term consequences of her experience in a small, relatively intimate setting. As we shall see, Sue does not, at this point, have ready a slate of specific teaching practices derived from her experience in a small school that she intends to effect in a larger site as a student teacher. Rather, her assessment of her time at Latino Youth indicates that she sees the caring relationships encouraged by small schools as contributing to an ambitious vision of education that may be called "democratizing" in that it encourages students to recognize themselves as part of a community in which they can critique and act upon the world around them.

In order to clarify what I see as this connection between caring and democracy, I will follow Sue's example and rely principally on the work of Dewey, who highlights the role of localized relationships in creating a democratic society by insisting that democracy and community are inseparable: "Democracy is not an alternative to other principles of associated life," Dewey (1988/1927) writes. "It is the idea of community

itself" (p. 328). This vision of democracy and community as
interdependent—Dewey's notion that each, in effect, constitutes the other—
necessarily involves an affective dimension when we consider that, in
Dewey's view, if a society is to be transformed into a truly democratic
community, "there is no substitute for the vitality and depth of close and
direct intercourse and attachment" (p. 368). While other writers have
correctly emphasized the importance of making a provision in Dewey's
conception of community for plurality among members whose unique
functions complement one another (Harris, 1989; Trimbur, 1989; Fishman,
1993), I will join Sue in proposing a reading of Dewey that underscores the
notion that affective human relationships are essential to the "close and
direct intercourse and attachment" that he claims is necessary for
communities to negotiate this pluralism in productive and democratic ways.
Through such a reading, one can begin to see more clearly the personal
investment required by Dewey's notions of community—that such notions
imply that in working toward democracy, people must consciously and
deliberately seek to foster relationships that reflect what we have seen
Noddings describe as "caring," an "engrossment" in the other, a
commitment to "consider their natures, ways of life, needs, and desires"
(p. 17). Thus, Sue's reflections on her work at Latino Youth offer a glimpse of
how at least one UIC student has begun to develop habits of mind and ways
of reading sites of teaching and learning that will be useful to her regardless
of the type of setting in which she will begin her career as a full-time teacher.

Among the ways in which Sue views her experience at Latino Youth as
having been beneficial is that while there, she was able to work with
teachers who consistently strived to build a sense of community at the
school by fostering close relationships with their students. Sue
acknowledged that she had also met several "wonderful" teachers in the
large school where she was placed for her semester of observation.
However, the problem, she said, is that in contrast to Latino Youth, where the
small setting virtually compels teachers to establish close personal
relationships with their students, "at a big school, you see the gamut of
teachers. You see people who know their students well. But you also see
other teachers who are incredibly burnt out and just want to get the hell out
of there." For Sue, the increased likelihood of university education students'
being placed with "burnt out" or otherwise ineffective teachers represents a
considerable risk, in part because in such settings these education students,
most of whom at UIC are white and middle-class, will be denied positive
models for negotiating relationships with poor Latino students like those who

commonly attend the public schools on Chicago's southwest side. Sue emphasized the importance of mentor teachers' guidance in efforts to bridge cultural differences between students and teachers by telling this story illustrating how vast these differences can sometimes be:

> I remember distinctly still a conversation in a Latino Youth journalism class where a girl was writing a story about someone getting shot, and she was trying to figure out what kind of gun it was that shot them. And so these two kids had this conversation about the sounds that different kinds of guns make when they're shot. The fact that they knew the sounds that different kinds of guns make just blew me away. I can't understand that; I can't conceive of growing up with that kind of knowledge. I don't regret that, but every once in a while I get these flashes of like, how can I even talk to them? Our worlds are so different.

Faced with these dramatic distances between her own experiences and those of Latino Youth students, Sue recalled how she began to explore ways of reaching out across these sociocultural boundaries by observing how such connections were made possible by the environment of that small school. "My biggest sense all the time when I was at Latino Youth was that I was somewhere where the teachers cared about the students, and the students knew that." In this kind of setting, Sue said, teachers were able to become "familiar with each student's history and to share their stories." By following the model of Latino Youth teachers and sharing stories with the students there, Sue learned that, "[the students and I] know different things, and if we can exchange those with each other, that's the ideal." Moreover, from the vantage point of having worked at both Latino Youth and a large school, Sue noted that "at a bigger school, to some extent just because of numbers, that may not be possible."

Sue's claim that Latino Youth provided her with the chance to "share" stories with students and to "exchange" ideas and experiences with them offers an opportunity to understand more precisely the ways in which close relationships nurture the formation of democratic communities as Dewey defines them. Dewey (1985/1916) describes democracy as being characterized by two criteria: that it enable, first, "numerous and varied" interests shared by members within a society and second, "full and free . . . interplay with other forms of association" (p. 89). What Dewey is describing here is his own ideal of a way of being with other people and engaging with them in what he calls "associated activity." Early in his career, Dewey (1957/1891) wrote that assessing the "value" of these activities requires that they be viewed not as mere occurrences but as "conduct," which Dewey defines as implying "purpose, motive, and intent": "All action accomplishes something or brings about results, but conduct has the result *in view*" (p. 3, Dewey's italics). Among the elements that Dewey identifies as the "the various sides and factors of conduct" (p. 5) are "feelings," which he describes as the "moving or impelling cause to action" (p. 6). Dewey is quick to point out that "a mere feeling" in and of itself has no ethical value. However, "if it is directed upon an action, it gets a value at once; let the end, the act, be right, and [a feeling] becomes a name for a *moral* disposition—a tendency to *act* in a due way (p. 7) . Over thirty years later, Dewey (1930/1922) again asserted his argument that affect plays a crucial role in motivating human conduct. Using slightly different language, he argued that all "habits"—those dispositions which at once prompt and include certain types of activity—"are affections . . . all have projectile power . . . a predisposition formed by a number of specific acts is an immensely more intimate and fundamental part of ourselves than are vague general, conscious choices" (p. 25). Finally, Dewey (1935) wrote that the "scientific intelligence" that allows people to anticipate the consequences of various kinds of associated activity will not serve the interests of democracy unless human affect prompts people to act in ways that promote their own and each others' growth: "Intelligence does not generate action except as it is enkindled by feeling" (p. 51). Thus, in the context of Dewey's thought, interpersonal connections such as those described by Sue are important because, as Jim Garrison (1996) summarizes, affective feeling and emotion motivate action in the democratic communities Dewey envisions (p. 440). It may be that what I have been calling the connection between caring and democracy is often overlooked in Dewey's work because he does not write explicitly of the role of affective relationships in his definitions of democracy. However, if we situate Dewey's discussions of democratic communities within the context of what might be called his intellectual biography, we begin to see that the activities shared by members of a democratic community are not discovered and affected solely by reason; rather, such conduct is carried out due at least in part to affective relationships that inspire the "feeling" that prompts intelligence to action.

For many of the students at Latino Youth, the feeling they have of belonging, of being cared for by their teachers and by each other, leads them to pursue their education and the opportunities it helps make possible. Maria, we should recall, after speaking of the value she places on her relationships with her teachers, said "If I didn't like it here I wouldn't come." For Sue, the relationships she established with Latino Youth students inspired her toward a conviction that all students—even those who are often called "at risk"—are able to learn·

> I think something that's valuable about [working at Latino Youth] is
> that you get to see those kinds of kids that you might think of as the
> troublemakers or as the kids you don't want to deal with in the pub-
> lic school, you get to see that they are capable of learning. And
> instead of just brushing them off or instead of deciding that there are
> always going to be those kids who are unteachable, it will start to
> make you think of them as individuals. And even if you're at a big-
> ger school, it will start to make you think, now I know that there's a
> way to reach that kid because I saw people reaching those kids at
> Latino Youth, so I need to figure out what to do.

Though the relationships in which Sue participated at Latino Youth
underscored to her that all students are capable of learning, and though she
views this realization as a challenge to "figure out what to do" as a teacher
regardless of the setting in which she finds herself, Sue was careful to point
out that her Latino Youth experience did not provide her with a blueprint of
how she could facilitate such learning through specific teaching practices
that she could transport to other, larger schools. Indeed, Sue noted the irony
of the fact that, even in an "alternative" school like Latino Youth, the
language arts curriculum included studying canonical texts like *Of Mice and
Men*, "close readings of short stories and essays," and "writing out in prose
what [students] thought each stanza of a poem was saying and then
answering some general questions." In sum, Sue recalled that most of the
teaching she saw at Latino Youth was "fairly traditional." Perhaps I should be
more upset than I am that Sue is unable to identify any clear links between
the close student-teacher relationships at Latino Youth and the pedagogical
methods she observed there. After all, it would be eminently convenient for
her as a young teacher—and for me as an English educator—if she could be
assured that, by following a predetermined series of lesson plans, she could
create a classroom environment characterized by caring and by students'
sense that they truly belonged and wanted to be there. Still, while confirming
the importance and necessity of teachers' dispositions that strive to be
responsive to students' particular cultural circumstances and interests, I
believe that such dispositions are undermined if they are reduced merely to
questions of subject matter and methods. Rather, as I think Sue's reflections
suggest, there is no substitute for the time-consuming and often difficult
process of forming with students those relationships that will enable us to
continue "becoming" humane and effective teachers.

As we have seen, Sue seems to have gained from her time at Latino Youth
a genuine appreciation for the relationships she saw between teachers and
students there and for the positive effects these relationships had on students'

learning. Moreover, as I have been arguing, such relationships are the source of the affective "feelings" that Dewey describes as motivating the kinds of action necessary to establish and maintain democratic communities. Nonetheless, in the absence of teaching practices that can be easily defined and transferred from Latino Youth classrooms to larger settings, one may continue to ask with some justification whether Sue's conviction regarding the importance of close student-teacher relationships will amount to more than an affinity for relatively isolated encounters that are not likely to occur in schools that house scores of teachers and thousands of students. In my view, we can work toward answering this question more clearly by noting the way in which Sue wrote about Latino Youth in response to some of the texts she read in her university education classes. In her analyses of Latino Youth in light of writers like Dewey, Maxine Greene, and Paulo Freire, Sue further demonstrates that she has begun to make important connections between her observations at this small school and a broader vision of democratizing education.

Sue's interest in how pedagogy might at once reflect and encourage students' democratic participation in their schools and broader communities led her to ask the teacher with whom she worked at Latino Youth whether these democratic ideals influence her classroom practices. The teacher's response, Sue said, was that "she said that when she was in college, she read Freire and Maxine Greene and all those people, and she gave me exactly the same response that any teacher has given me when I talk to them about their teaching education, which is 'Oh, yeah, I read that stuff when I was in college, but I don't really think about it now that I'm out here in the field.'" Though Sue's Latino Youth mentor was unable to articulate any relationship between "that stuff" she read in college and her present work with her own students, Sue began to make these connections herself. In a paper entitled "The Community School and the School as Community: An Alternative School's Experiments in Freedom and Democratic Education," Sue appropriated the language and theoretical frameworks set forth by writers like Dewey and Greene to describe what she saw as examples of the ways in which Latino Youth students and teachers enact a vision of democratizing education by encouraging students to critique their world and act upon it.

As the title of her paper suggests, among Sue's objectives is to present Latino Youth as an example of what she understands to be Dewey's emphasis on the need to foster democracy through the face-to-face interactions of localized communities. Early in the essay, after citing Dewey's admonition that "Democracy must begin at home, and its home is the neighborly community" *(Public,* p. 368, in Weinstein, p. 1), Sue cites the goings-on in individual classrooms as evidence of teachers' encouraging what to Dewey are the mutually dependent aims of community and democracy. Although we have seen that Sue describes most of the teaching she observed at Latino Youth as "fairly traditional," in her essay she invokes Paulo Freire's language to make clear that Latino Youth teachers "walk the line" between traditional and "problem-posing education" depending on what they perceive to be the needs of their students (p. 5). In describing a literature classroom, for instance, Sue explains how the teacher avoided the "objectification" of students by encouraging dialogue that made room for their individual and original voices. Later, Sue cites Greene's notion of "defamiliarization" to describe how the teacher enhanced students' "critical awareness" during a classroom conversation that made "new possibilities open for reflection" (p. 131, in Weinstein, p. 6). Although Sue doesn't refer directly to Dewey in this section of her paper, the classroom practices she describes may be called "democratic" in the way Dewey uses the term in that they help students to develop their abilities to assess ideas and institutions, to name the obstacles and opportunities they encounter and/or create, and to act in ways that promote what they discover to be the common interests of themselves and their communities. Indeed, Dewey (1985/1916) argues that the principal aim of education should be to enable individuals to develop a "capacity for growth" that occurs through the freedom, creativity, and dialogue of a democratically constituted society (p. 107). This "democratic" society, Dewey (1988/1927) contends, "will have its consummation when free social inquiry is indissolubly wedded to the art of full and moving communication" (p. 350). Sue's descriptions and analyses of Latino Youth classrooms, in which—to use Sue's words—"students are encouraged to teach each other, to argue and disagree about interpretations of literature, and to produce writing which helps them work through authors' meanings and relate the readings to their own lives" (p. 4), suggest that she views the teaching practices she observed there as encouraging the "dialogue" and "free social inquiry" that Dewey claims are essential to democracy. Put another way, Sue seems to recognize that in these classrooms she has observed modest instances of what Dewey so emphatically sought: the ability of all members of a community to participate in and act upon consequential dialogue.

The kind of teaching Sue describes, which I think she correctly identifies as fostering students' democratic participation in their school community, is possible, she says, because of the caring Latino Youth students receive from their teachers. To underscore this point, Sue refers to a conversation she had with a Latino Youth student named Lisa, who is the mother of two children:

> Lisa says the support she receives from the teachers at Latino Youth is a change from the negativity she has always heard on the streets, from people in her neighborhood, or "the cops," or "the ones who have jobs." She says these people say, "You're not going to do nothing 'cause you're just another Mexican having more kids; you don't go to school; you don't have no education." In contrast, Lisa said that her teachers "think we're going to be somebody, or they *know* we're going to be somebody." (p. 17, Weinstein's italics)

While emphasizing the ways in which caring promotes a feeling of solidarity among Latino Youth students and, in turn, a willingness to participate in their school community, Sue does not downplay Dewey's claim that democratic communities must accommodate the "numerous and varied" interests of their members. Indeed, at several points in her essay Sue affirms the diversity among Latino Youth students in terms of their backgrounds and aspirations. Some of these students, she points out, want a better job; others want to pursue goals such as law and other forms of activism to change the social, economic, and judicial systems that they see as oppressive. But while acknowledging that students bring to their school different histories and that they aspire to different futures, Sue argues, with Dewey, that they are participating in the fostering of a democratic community in the sense that they have, "in partnership with the school and the staff, created a community in the present as well, one in which the consequences of combined action are perceived and become an object of desire and effort" (p. 16). Specifically, Sue notes that while many other schools in Chicago also have large Latino populations, what sets Latino Youth apart "may be the fact that teachers and students are embarked on the kind of shared project which Dewey describes as essential to community building—students don't enter the school already part of a community simply on the basis of a shared race, but they leave as members of a community because of the work they have done together" (p. 4). Central to this democratic project, she writes, are the relationships teachers have with their students: "Teachers may be teaching things very similar to what was taught in [students' previous] schools, but two things make a difference: agency and caring" (p. 16).

In what I see as a particularly astute reading of the interactions among Latino Youth's students and teachers and of how caring promotes agency that at once reflects and fosters democracy, Sue further applies her reading of

Dewey to Latino Youth by suggesting that education can only be democratic if it is in a vital relationship to the world outside of school:

> Latino Youth Alternative High School is a democratic project in this sense; it is constantly breathing its neighborhood in through sound, through the mixed Spanish and English of the students which is also the language of the surrounding streets, through the Mexican lady who stands with her cart in the hallway at lunchtime selling tamales, and of course through the students themselves, who are members of both the school community and the larger neighborhood of which it is a part. (p. 2)

In addition to the symbiotic relationship that Latino Youth has with its cultural surroundings, Sue argues that this school community is connected to the broader society in that the agency students learn in Latino Youth classrooms makes it possible for them to participate in communities that extend beyond the school itself. Recalling Dewey's claim that democratic communities must accommodate "full and free . . . interplay with other forms of association," Sue sees Latino Youth as a democratic enterprise in that "we can view Latino youth students as individuals who are making the attempt to move into new groups of associated activity, different from the ones they are coming from, which have become too limiting for a variety of reasons which they have identified" (p. 14). Thus, while claiming that Latino Youth is, in one sense, "a community in and of itself which is created by the interaction and shared projects of its students and staff" (p. 15), Sue argues that Latino Youth is also a space where students learn modes of thought and conduct that enable them to participate in other communities they see as serving their interests.

For Lisa, the young mother introduced above, her aspirations to attend college and to work as a computer programmer mean that these varied communities will include those formed through academic and professional association. In the case of a Latino Youth student named Pedro, however, the agency he learned in the context of relationships with teachers who he says "click with us" has led him to participate in communities whose primary objective is social activism. Concerned with the possibility of reductions in financial support for Latino Youth, Pedro attended a meeting that included representatives from organizations (including the Chicago Public School Board) that provide funding to alternative schools. He described his participation at the meeting in this way:

> I heard the Board of Education is trying to take away fundings from alternative education, and I disagree with that 'cause these schools

have been helping out a lot of people. I didn't have the chance to be on the panel of students who were answering the questions. But we need the funds, so I wrote down some notes, and when the funders stopped asking questions, I stepped up to them, especially this one lady. And I went up to her and told her, "You know what, I have a lot of comments and a lot of experiences in that kind of question you were asking." She was asking a lot of questions about teen pregnancy, and she was saying, "If you have responsibility, why are you all having kids." And I was like, "Well, we made mistakes maybe, but sometimes we have personal problems that make it hard for us to stay in school." And she kinda, like, got it, and she was like, "Well, I like your comments; let me get your number."

Pedro's activism in public spheres outside of school has not been limited to this single meeting. He also recalled, for instance, attending with several other Latino Youth students and staff members a protest against the Chicago Police Department's brutality toward the city's Latino community: "We were down at that protest, and one of our students got interviewed, so it helped out. I mean, Latino Youth was right there making a difference." While I grant that these kinds of public activism can and do include students who attend large schools, it is important to remember that, prior to attending Latino Youth, Pedro was disenfranchised at his previous school to a point where he dropped out. In the context of the caring relationships at Latino Youth, however, Pedro has developed the ability and the desire to move beyond his school and into forums where he hopes to influence educational and other forms of public policy. Similarly, as we have seen, Lisa, encouraged by teachers who "know" she is "somebody," anticipates joining communities that she believes will enable her to build a brighter future for herself and her children. These students' stories, viewed in light of Sue's observation that Latino Youth students "are making the attempt to move into new groups of associated activity," capture what I think Dewey (1988/1927) means when he claims that democratic communities, while created and nurtured by "vital, steady, and deep relationships," will not be isolated, but will be "responsive to the complex and world-wide scene in which it is enmeshed" (p. 369).

Thus, though we cannot say that Sue has benefited from her work at Latino Youth in terms of specific, day-to-day activities that she will be able to use in her own classroom, her spoken and written reflections suggest that she has taken from her time there something even more enduring and valuable, and that is a history that has been enriched by the experience of seeing the vital place that close, local student-teacher relationships occupy within the context of a broader vision of democracy in school and society.

Downsizing as Reform

It is, in some ways, ironic that I write of the importance of local, affective connections in teaching and learning and of the role that such connections can play in young teachers' developing their own visions of democratizing education from Chicago, a city that in recent years has been at the center of the national debate over school reform because of the broad institutional changes being effected here. In December of 1988, responding to mounting public pressure to improve the school system that the then Secretary of Education William Bennett had described as "the worst in the nation," the Illinois legislature passed the Chicago School Reform Act. This bill changed the structure of school governance in Chicago, removing a considerable amount of decision-making authority from the notoriously inefficient and unresponsive bureaucracy of the system's central administration and placing it in the hands of Local School Councils—elected bodies made up of principals, teachers, parents, community members, and students for each of the city's nearly 600 schools. The Reform Act also included a provision that allowed Mayor Daley to place the Chicago school system under the direction of a Chief Executive Officer, whose principal effort has been to increase educators' accountability for student performance as measured by standardized test scores. Schools that fall short of district-wide goals are put on probation, a designation that may lead, as it did for nine high schools last year, to a "restructuring" in which allegedly inept teachers and administrators are replaced. President Clinton, promoting his campaign for national standards testing, visited Chicago in November of 1997 and proclaimed its school system a model for those in other large metropolitan areas. Michael Katz (1995), too, is optimistic about the prospects for effective school reform in Chicago, describing it as a "daring, exciting, and unprecedented adventure" (p. 138).

To debate the merits of such reform efforts is not my purpose here. Rather, I am suggesting that whatever broad structural changes are made to our educational institutions, they will ultimately fail if they ignore and do not seek to emulate the truly significant changes brought about by teachers and students who are working together to build and maintain relationships in local spaces like Latino Youth. Indeed, Latino Youth students previously attended (and left) schools that have been sites of citywide reforms, which have now been in process for nearly a decade. These students have been in classrooms under local school councils, and many of them have seen—from a distance—their principals being replaced. The Latino Youth students I've spoken with, however, have remained largely oblivious to these reforms. When I ask about local school councils, for instance, a typical response is the one I got from a student named Raphael, who shrugged his shoulders and said, "A local school council? What's that?" Raphael, an accomplished musician and a former dropout now on the verge of graduating, doesn't know what a local school council is, but he does know that a sure way of getting himself into trouble at Latino Youth is to fail to notify his teachers of an upcoming gig by his Andean musical group so that at least a couple of them can attend. To Raphael, the Chicago reforms, at least in terms of his immediate experience influencing his decision to remain in school (or not), have not yet mattered. What has mattered is that his teachers have supported and even participated in his passion for music. Similarly, as we have seen, what has mattered to Maria is that Latino Youth is a place where "the teachers really care about you." What has mattered to Raul is that teachers and students are "together," like fingers intertwined.

If those of us who teach teachers believe that fostering such relationships is an important aspect of what I have been arguing is truly consequential education reform, I believe we can help the new generation of teachers share in this vision by including as at least a part of their preservice preparation the opportunity to observe and/or student teach in a small school. Recently, Cathy Fleischer (1998) has argued that in this era of school reform, it is essential that teachers "begin to think about their roles a bit differently: to see themselves as advocates, not just for students, but for their teaching practices" (p. 80). Though Fleischer's principal argument is that educators should enlist the help of parents in these forms of advocacy, to this I would add that teacher educators can assist beginning teachers in their role as advocates by exposing them to the small schools that I believe facilitate sound and humane teaching practices. As I mentioned earlier, Dewey and James view people's histories as providing them with a foundation for judgment and critique. In the case of English education students like Jalayna, Jennifer, and Sue, their histories, which now include having worked at Latino Youth, enable these beginning teachers to draw from their own experience in order to advocate more effectively and urgently for small schools and the benefits they afford. Moreover, though it is delicate to say so, if we teacher educators fail to seek out alternatives to large schools, I think we need to ask ourselves hard questions about our own complicity in the consequences of continuing to place young teachers only in settings that are often dysfunctional in terms of their inability to encourage close and productive relationships among students and teachers.

For Sandra, the poet introduced at the beginning of this essay, the relationships she has had with her teachers have been crucial to her continued success in school. For although she admits that pursuing her education has often been difficult due to family and personal troubles, she continues to attend Latino Youth, she says, in large part because of the caring and encouragement she receives from her teachers. Close to graduating, Sandra plans to be a teacher:

> My teachers here helped turn me around to what I am now. I'm not saying, Oh, I'm such a genius, but I think that I'm a lot better than what I was three or four years ago. And that's why I wanna be a teacher. It would make me so proud, for me to turn a person that was like me and just completely turn them around to a person that actually knows where they're going in life, that actually has goals. That would make me real proud.

A UIC preservice teacher named Franz recently stopped by my office to tell me that he had been assigned to student teach the following semester in a high school of about 2,000 students. Franz had visited the school earlier that day, and his impressions had been favorable. He liked the ethnically diverse student body and said that his mentor teacher seemed knowledgeable and friendly. Soon, though, he began to reminisce about his tutoring at Latino Youth, which was drawing to a close. He spoke fondly of individual students with whom he had worked and of the teachers he had observed and assisted. "Man," he said, shaking his head and staring vacantly out the window toward the city's west side, "I'm gonna miss that place." I am confident that Franz, a bright and committed beginning teacher, will have a positive student teaching experience in that large school. Still, when the UIC preservice teachers I have described eventually take jobs—as they usually do—in schools where they wade through hallways awash in thousands of unfamiliar faces, I hope that they, with Franz, miss their time at Latino Youth. I hope they miss the murals on classroom walls depicting Mexican landscapes and Aztec goddesses painted and signed by students they know; I hope they miss the building's slightly musty but curiously pleasant smell that stays in the lining of one's jacket; I hope they miss sights like that of Tina, the young principal, scooping into her arms a student's toddler son, giving the child a kiss on the cheek, and carrying him off to her office for a graham cracker. I hope, in short, that these beginning teachers remember and miss the smallness of Latino Youth, of this place where there is no anonymity to absolve students or teachers from the joy of their responsibilities to each other as human beings. For I am convinced that it is by creating and then drawing from these memories, these histories, that the teachers we teach will desire that schools be more exciting and humane places, and then devote themselves and their careers to making them so.

Works Cited

Bensman, D. (1994). *The graduates of Central Park East Elementary School: Where have they gone? What did they really learn?* New York: NCREST.

Bryk, A., Holland, P., and Lee, V. (1993). *Catholic schools and the common good.* Cambridge: Harvard University Press.

Dewey, J. (1930/1922). *Human nature and conduct: An introduction to social psychology.* New York: The Modern Library.

Dewey, J. (1935). *Liberalism and social action.* New York: G. P. Putnam's Sons.

Dewey, J. (1957/1891). *Outline of a critical theory of ethics.* New York: Hillary House.

Dewey, J. (1985/1916). *Democracy and education.* In J. Boydston (Ed.), *John Dewey: The middle works, Vol. 9: 1899–1924.* Carbondale and Edwardsville: Southern Illinois University Press.

Dewey, J. (1988/1927). *The public and its problems.* In J. Boydston (Ed.), *John Dewey: The later works, 1925–1953, Vol. 2: 1925–1927* (pp. 235–372). Carbondale and Edwardsville: Southern Illinois University Press.

Fishman, S. M. (1993). Explicating our tacit tradition: John Dewey and composition studies. *College Composition and Communication, 44,* 315–330.

Fleischer, C. (1998). Advocating for change: A new education for new teachers. *English Education, 30:2,* 78–100.

Garrison, J. (1996). A Deweyan theory of democratic listening. *Educational Theory, 46,* 429–451.

Greene, M. (1991). In search of a critical pedagogy. In M. Okazawa-Rey, J. Anderson, and R. Traver (Eds.), *Teachers, teaching, and teacher education.* Cambridge: Harvard Educational Review, 239–252.

Harris, J. (1989). The idea of community in the study of writing. *College Composition and Communication, 40,* 11–22.

James, W. (1917). Humanism and truth. *Selected papers on philosophy.* New York: E. P. Dutton, 218–244.

James, W. (1969/1897). The moral philosopher and the moral life. In J. Roth (Ed.), *The moral philosophy of William James.* New York: Thomas Y. Crowell, 169–191.

Katz, M. (1995). *Improving poor people: The welfare state, the "underclass," and urban schools as history.* Princeton: Princeton University Press.

Kloppenberg, J. (1986). *Uncertain victory: Social democracy and progressivism in European and American thought, 1870–1920.* New York: Oxford University Press.

Lee, V. and Smith, J. (1994). High school restructuring and school achievement: A new study finds strong links. *Issues in restructuring schools.* Madison: Center on Organization and Restructuring of Schools.

Meier, D. (1995). *The power of their ideas: Lessons for America from a small school in Harlem.* Boston: Beacon Press.

Noddings, N. (1984). *Caring: A feminist approach to ethics and moral education.* Stanford: Stanford University Press.

Rose, M. (1993). *Lives on the boundary.* New York: Penguin Press.

Toby, J. (1993). Everyday school violence: How disorder fuels it. *American Educator,* 46–62.

Trimbur, J. (1989). Consensus and difference in collaborative learning. *College English, 51,* 602–616.

Vinz, R. (1997). Capturing a moving form: "Becoming" as teachers. *English Education, 29* (2), 137–146.

Weinstein, S. (1997). The community school and the school as community: An alternative school's experiments in freedom and democratic education. English 554, University of Illinois at Chicago.

4 On (Almost) Passing

Brenda Jo Brueggemann

It was not until I had embarked upon my "coming out" as a deaf person that I considered my rites of passage, and dwelled on my acts, both deliberate and unconscious, both past and present, of passing. Because my "coming out" was a mid-life event, I had much to reflect back on and much, too, to illuminate ahead of me. This "passing" through an identity crisis, as it were, and the rites of passage then involved in uncovering the paths of my lifelong passing as "hearing," took place in a hall of mirrors. (Later I would come to know this place as the art and act of rhetoric.)

I first saw myself mirrored in several students I met at Gallaudet University (the world's only liberal arts university for deaf and hard-of-hearing students). I was thirty-two and finishing my PhD, writing a dissertation—that quintessential act of literate passing. What's more, I was finishing it by doing an ethnographic sort of study on deaf student writers at Gallaudet University; thus I was using the guise of an academic grant and a PhD-producing project as a professional foil to make a personal journey to the center of Deaf culture.

I was always good at finding a way to pass into places I shouldn't "normally" be.

So, there I was, doing time as a teacher and researcher at Gallaudet, collecting data for my study, taking a sign language class, living with a Deaf woman and faculty member at Gallaudet, going to Deaf gatherings, tutoring some of the students. Mostly, I was trying to pass in ways that were both familiar and unfamiliar to me: to pass (unfamiliarly) as D/deaf—and doing a lousy job of it—and to pass (more familiarly) as H/hearing and thereby through this last of major academic hoops. The differences between "Deaf"

Reprinted from *College English*, October 1997.

and "deaf," between "Hearing" and "hearing" concerned me far more
personally and powerfully than just as markers distinguishing cultural
deafness (with an upper-case "D") from medical/audiological hearing loss
(with a lower-case "d"). At any one moment, I might be labeled as any one
of those four possibilities; at any one moment, I was trying to pass as any and
all of them.

In this passing, I spent a good deal of time watching—an act I had, as a
hard-of-hearing person, lifelong experience and impeccable credentials at—
watching myself, watching the students I was doing case studies of, watching
everything in the ethnographic scene of Deaf culture before me. I kept
seeing myself in and through students I worked with in the "basic English"
classrooms. They were the mirror in my ears; and they were so, too, in all the
distorting, cacophonous ways that this mirror metaphor doesn't "fit" the
notion we have of what mirrors usually do (allow us to see ourselves, to
look—not to listen and hear ourselves). These Students often had volatile, if
not violent, histories of passing—especially academically. Most of them, by
virtue of finding themselves "stuck" (there is a powerful sign for that—two
fingers jammed into the throat, a desperate look on the face) in English 050,
were still floundering mightily, struggling violently, to pass at basic English
literacy. Having negotiated that passage rather adeptly, I now, oddly enough,
found myself struggling to squeeze through another doorway as I myself
engaged in a mighty, violent struggle to pass in basic "D/deaf" literacy.

I don't think I ever got it right. Almost, but not quite. I couldn't be "deaf,"
any more than I could be "hearing." I was "hard-of-hearing"; and I was as
confused and displaced, in either "Deaf" or "Hearing" culture, as this
multiply hyphenated term indicates.

The mirror in my ears threw back odd images—distorted, illuminating,
disturbing, fantastic, funny—but all somehow reflecting part of me. It put my
passing in various perspectives: perspectives of tense and time (past, present,
future); perspectives of repeated situations and relationships in my personal
and academic life; and perspectives on the ways that stories are told,
identities forged, arguments made. These are but some of the things I saw as I
passed through, by, on.

For some twenty-five years of my life, from age five on, I went to the
movies. And while I always more or less got the plot, I missed everything in
the dialogue. For twenty-five years I sat, passing time with a Three
Musketeers candy bar, some popcorn, a coke. I sat with my sisters as a grade
school child on weeknights when my mom had to work and my dad was
running the film from up in the little booth (both my parents had two jobs).
To be sure, we often didn't sit so much as we crawled the aisles, playing hide

and seek quietly in an always near-empty theater; sometimes, more sensibly, I went to the lobby to do some homework. Through some films—the Disney classics and the cartoons that opened and closed each feature film—I did, though, try to sit, to listen and watch. I don't think I had a conscious knowledge of it at the time, but now I know that I really heard nothing, that I was a pro at passing even back then.

I got better, too, with age and the social agility that becomes most junior high and high school girls. On weekends in my very small, very rural western Kansas town the theater was the only place to go, the only thing to do. Past the Friday night football or basketball game, the movies beckoned; we'd often go to the same film both Saturday and Sunday night. Going to the movies was the only date possible in Tribune, Kansas.

I dated. My dates took me to countless movies, and I never heard a word. What's more, in the dark of the movie theater, with no hope of reading my date's lips as they struck up conversations with me, I nodded and feigned attention, agreement, acceptance all the more.

Now it all seems ludicrous, if not painful. For years I have listened to my friends—especially my academic friends—rave about movies, past and present. For years I have shifted back and forth on my feet at parties, smiling, nodding, looking genuinely interested in the discussion of this film or that. Not that I felt left out. I just felt somehow disoriented, out of step—not quite passing—in their discussions. Like many deaf people, I not only saw films, but enjoyed them. What I didn't know in all those years of adolescent pretense is that I tend to enjoy films differently from a hearing audience. I came to know that while others were concentrating on clues to solve the mystery, say, in the dialogue between characters, my eyes, a little more attuned than theirs, would see in the background the weapon of death or notice the facial tension and odd mannerisms of the guilty party.

Take one example: in my early years of graduate school, the last years I still let dates take me to movies, I saw David Lynch's *Blue Velvet*. Recently I had a conversation with my husband about that movie; it was a conversation based on memory, of course, and on memory in different contexts since we had not seen the film together or even in the same place. What I remembered, what I talked about, were vivid visual details: the ear lying in the grass that opens the movie, the color of Isabella Rosellini's lips and the way they pouted and quivered, the tension in her body, the vivid surreal scenes splashed like canvases in a museum of modern art. And while he himself pointed out how visual the movie was, what my husband remembered most clearly were the conversations. He knew that the severed ear in the grass belonged to Rosellini's husband, that the husband had been kidnapped, and that her actions throughout the movie were done as ransom to keep her husband alive (plenty of reason for body tension and quivering lips). My husband knew this, of course, because they talk about it in the movie.

But I didn't know this. I thought the ear was a symbol of all the scenes of eavesdropping in the film, or that the severed ear and the blue velvet forged some artistic link to Van Gogh. This was the sense I made with one sense missing. (The severed ear now seems a metaphor for my own disconnection from the movie's soundtrack.)

So, when the pieces began to fit together and I began, late in my twenties, to understand that I understood precious little of movies beyond the roar of the dinosaurs in *Jurassic Park* or the catchy little tunes of the latest animated Disney "classic," I just stopped going. I had better things to do with my time than hog down a Three Musketeers and bad popcorn. There were other options for dates—especially since my dates now preferred to actually talk about the movie after it was over, trying out their latest readings in critical theory on the poor, defenseless film over coffee, a drink, dessert. I couldn't hold up my end of the conversation, so I let it stop before it could begin.

I could not always stop conversations before they began, though. (If the genie were ever to grant me three wishes, this would definitely be one of them.) And more times than enough, I found myself pressured into passing and then greatly pressured by my passing. Some days I could pass; some days I could *almost* pass; some other days the "almost" got yanked out from under me.

My first high school sweetheart was, now that I look back, a real sweetheart; when he could have yanked, he didn't. He let me pass, and he let me do so with grace, saving my hidden deaf face, as it were.

Paradoxically enough, what first attracted me to him was his gentle manner, his quiet, soft-spoken demeanor. It was that demeanor, of course, that doomed our relationship. He was a senior, I only a sophomore—and although I felt enormously comfortable around him (maybe because he didn't talk much, so I didn't have to listen much?), I wanted greatly to impress him. Apparently I did so because soon we were dragging main (the only option besides "parking"—which only bad girls or long-since steadies did—or going to the movies in Tribune, Kansas) and Steve asked me to go steady with him, to wear his gigantic Senior class ring. Actually, he asked three times. I didn't hear a one of them. But by the third time (which I didn't even know was the third time)—even across the cavernous distance of his big Buick front seat in the dark of a December night—I could *see* that he was saying something, trying *hard* to say something.

So I said the words that are surely the most common in my vocabulary: "What? Hmmmmm? Pardon me?" (I don't recall which variation it was.)

Now Steve could have been mighty frustrated, out and out angry (and I would not have been surprised, since this response is all too common when we are asked to repeat something)—but instead he smiled in his gentle way, the way that had attracted me to him in the first place. He pulled the car over to the curb on Main Street right then and there, and he shut it off. He turned to face me directly, and I could read his lips now. "I said," he still barely whispered, "would you wear my class ring?"

It was bitter cold, a blustery, snowy December night on the western Kansas plains. But I was hot, my face burning. Shamed. And shamed not so much at having not heard the question the first three times, as at having myself, my deafness, so thoroughly unmasked. It felt as if someone were holding a mirror up to the sun with the reflected sunlight piercing through me. The mirror in my ears hurt. And it hurt even more because in that one fleeting instant in that big Buick at the mere age of fifteen, I realized, too, how *deaf* I was. And I knew I would have to say "no" to soft-spoken Steve, his gentle ways, his giant class ring. I was not hearing enough; he was not deaf enough. And although I couldn't voice it at the time, I knew even then that this was more than just a sheet of glass between us, more than a barrier we could "talk" to each other through.

And I think—in fact, I'm sure—that he knew this, too. But still, instead of saying "never mind" or "oh, nothing" to my "What?" (another frequent response), he let the moment play through, let me have the benefit of the words I had missed. He let me play at passing, let me play it as if it could really be, our going steady, our promise as a couple. He could have ridiculed me with taunts of "gee, you just don't hear *anything*," or worse, in its "innocent" ignorance, "what's wrong, are you *deaf*?" Those, too, are all too common responses to my requests for repetitions.

So the moment passed. Steve and I didn't go steady. Nearly a decade later, when he and I were both married (to different persons, of course), we recounted this scene for our spouses in mutual company; we laughed, they laughed. For a moment, Steve and I locked eyes—and I read it all there: he had known then, as he knew now, that I was indeed deaf. But neither he nor I, then or at the present moment, would say the word. We let it pass. The conversation went on elsewhere.

When I began talking and working with deaf students at Gallaudet University as part of my dissertation research project, the conversation always went directly here: how I, how they, how we, coped with our deafness in personal relationships and especially in relationships with lovers

and significant others. We were trying out our mirrors on each other, trying
to see if these multiple mirrors would help us negotiate the difficult passages
we always encountered in relationships.

One student, David, an older non-traditional student, had mentioned
several times in the course of his interview with me that his wife was far
more "deaf" (in strict audiological terms) than he. It came up most strongly
when I asked him directly about how much time he spent with hearing
people and in "Hearing culture" as opposed to with deaf people and in
"Deaf culture." His answer hinged on his relationship with his wife:

> I have a little bit of a struggle with my wife over this issue. She isn't
> comfortable socializing with hearing people she doesn't know or with
> my hearing friends who don't sign. So I would end up having to inter-
> pret for her or stay right with her to keep her company. So I would
> either go alone, or go with her with a group of deaf people. I didn't
> have problems with either group [deaf or hearing], but she did have
> a problem with the hearing group.

I mentioned, smiling, that my husband might say some of the same. We
left the issue at that, and I went on to other questions. But at the end of the
interview, when the videotape was off and the interpreter we used had left
the room, David turned directly to me and in both spoken English and sign
language asked, "I'm curious. You said that you and your husband have
similar communication problems in hearing situations since you are hard-of-
hearing and he isn't. How," David paused, with genuine pain on his face,
"do you work around this?" I could see that this was a sore spot, a blemish
on both our mirrors. And unfortunately, I didn't have any particularly
inspiring answers—no secret passageways that might help us both solve this
mystery more neatly, more quickly.

We were (and are) both stumbling and groping, looking for light switches
in the often dark hallways of our deafness within relationships.

I too had looked in the past to others more "deaf," than I was to help
illuminate my way through the relationship with my new husband. When I
first came to Gallaudet, at the age of thirty-two in 1991, I became good
friends with a woman some ten years older than I. She had gradually
become late-deafened (her deafness was genetic and the result of an
auditory nerve degeneration). Her intellect, acumen, wit, and passion
amazed me; she liked simple food and good beer and wine; she was the
heroic single mother of four teenagers; and she thoroughly enjoyed the
company of men. Like adopted children who often feel as if they never quite
"fit" with their own parents, in this time of substantial identity shifting (I was

trying to "come out" in my deafness) I fantasized her as a potential role model, a mentor, a long-lost mother—or maybe sister—of sorts.

What I watched most carefully in that mirror was my own just-married relationship with a hearing man and the various reflections of my new-found friend, Lynn (not her real name), in her relationships with men, both deaf and hearing, past and present. It was not always a pretty sight. What I saw in watching Lynn, and in sharing many conversations with her about the dilemmas of life with a hearing man or life with a deaf man, was as inspiring as it was often scary. Either way, the spectre of dependence always lurked: to marry a deaf man meant she (we) would be the one(s) that might be most depended upon (especially because as late-deafened and exquisitely literate persons we had skills and experience well worth depending upon)—and this, then, would leave us little room for our own sometimes necessary dependence; but on the flip side (the magnified side of that mirror?), marrying a hearing man might well mean we would come to be too dependent and would, therefore, risk our chances of passing on our own, as our own.

When the woman is deaf, in a culture where the woman is still seen as typically more "dependent" in the male-female relationship, her further dependence on a hearing partner can dangerously diminish her autonomy. Yet at the same time men typically depend on women in certain specialized areas; as Bonnie Tucker points out in her controversial recent autobiography *The Feel of Silence,* men expect their female partners to carry out an array of social functions that demand precisely the kind of communicative competence that is challenging for the deaf. Women generally mediate between the home and the world in arranging the social obligations and daily domestic duties of (heterosexual) coupled and family life. This calls for speaking with many people, a high proportion of them strangers, both in person and by telephone (in stores, offices, schools . . .), in contexts where the conversations can't be carefully anticipated or controlled. Discussing her own earlier marriage to a hearing man, Tucker sees the disruption of these cultural norms in the social parameters of male-female relationships as largely responsible for the fact that successful relationships between hearing men and deaf women are few and far between.

Within Deaf culture, there is much at stake beyond the bounds of the intimate relationship: to marry either deaf or hearing marks one, proffers one a pass, in the eyes of Deaf culture. Simply put, to marry deaf is to be Deaf; to marry hearing is to be Hearing. And over 68 percent of deaf people do marry endogamously, with 86 percent expressing a desire to do so (Schein and Delk).

To marry one or the other, then, is to pass as one or the other. Yet another reason, then, that I have *almost,* but not quite, passed: when Deaf culture seeks to identify me, they hold up the mirror and see my husband, a hearing man. He is a gentle man, a generally soft-spoken man—like the Steve I didn't go steady with. And yes, I must often depend on him in ways I'd much rather not—asking him to make phone calls for me, asking him to interpret or relay bits of conversation I've missed in social settings, asking him to repeat what one of our own children has said, asking him to help me bow out of uncomfortable social situations, asking him to order for me at restaurants, asking him to pronounce with exaggeration words I'm not sure of, and often, most difficult of all, asking him intuitively to know when I want to pass on my own and when I want to depend upon him.

It isn't easy. Sometimes I feel like shattering the mirror: it shows me as "crippled," as "disabled" in my dependence.

It was a young woman, a new and struggling student, whom I met at Gallaudet when I first went there and was so engrossed in my own coming out, so obsessed with my own identity, who first showed me and let me feel the shards of that mirror. She had been a student in the English 050 class I was a teaching assistant in; I had also tutored her individually and she had served as one of my in-depth case studies, meeting with me weekly for interviews and videotapes of her in the process of writing. We had come to know each other well. And although she looked, figuratively or literally, nothing like the older deaf woman I now know I fetishized, I think the mirror drew us to each other—in the way most of us can hardly resist glimpsing ourselves, turning to stare at ourselves, when we pass by a mirror or reflective glass. This younger woman (whose pseudonym, interestingly or conveniently enough, I had also assigned as "Lynne"—with the added "e") turned to me as her model and mentor—me, the mainstreamed, academically and somewhat socially successful woman who had married a hearing man and got along, so it seemed, rather well in the Hearing world.

I hadn't realized how much she had turned to see me in her mirror (and I, as we do when the mirror flatters us, had not only let her, but probably encouraged her)—I hadn't realized until I received several desperate long distance phone calls from her mother in Nebraska toward the end of the semester. Lynne was not doing well at Gallaudet. It wasn't just her grades. No, those were bad enough, to be sure. (Lynne was one of the products of mainstreaming—now quite abundant at Gallaudet—who came there as a college freshman with few sign language skills and found herself immersed, even drowning, in Deaf culture and the precedence of sign language—yet another language now, in addition to English, that she didn't quite get.) Lynne was failing miserably in the Gallaudet social arena; she was lonely, depressed, even cast out. She just didn't fit. And her mother suffered for her, with her.

Back home, it turns out, Lynne had a hearing boyfriend. In righteous anger, her mother wanted her out of the "meanness" of Gallaudet, and so she had begun calling me to seek my counsel on both the "meanness" and on getting Lynne out. Even the fact that Lynne's mother took it for granted that she could speak with me on the phone—as she did with Lynne—is a telling one. Deafness is rarely the absolute audiological deficit many without hearing loss tend to imagine it as, and plenty who are deaf/hard-of-hearing can (and do) talk on the phone if necessary. Yet even those who can *talk* on the phone, as I can, have a great deal of difficulty *hearing* phone conversations well. We tend to do far better with familiar voices and with those from whom we know we can safely ask for repeats without risking the judgments that often come with that asking. Lynne's mother, like all of us who understand labels mostly from our own experiences with them, codes "hearing loss" as a category that can still include phone conversations.

She wanted me to talk to Lynne and encourage her to abandon her long dream of studying at Gallaudet. Understandably, she wanted Lynne back in the hearing world. It was mean there, too—but I think her mother had forgotten about that for now. What's more, she wanted Lynne married to a hearing man.

In a bit of conversation that jarred my very bones, her mother asked me if I was married. "Yes," I replied tentatively, not sure why this question had come up.

"Is he hearing?" she probed further. And here, then, I knew just why the question had come up and where it was headed.

"Yes, he is," I confirmed.

"Are you happy—married to him?"

I sputtered a little, I remember, not quite comfortable with the suddenly personal tack this conversation with a stranger some thousand miles away had taken. But I didn't know how to turn back or away. "Yes," I answered simply.

"Well, good—then there's hope for Lynne, too. Would you tell her that? Could you tell her that she could be married—and happy—with a hearing man?"

I don't know what I said then. Stories and memories are selective, and, as Benedict Anderson wrote, "all profound changes in consciousness, by their very nature, bring with them characteristic amnesias" (204); mirrors simply cannot say and show it all. But I do know that I felt deeply the pain of a shattered mirror—that I felt deeply the pain of trying to be Lynne's inspiration, her role model, her fetish, her whatever. I could barely get it right for myself, could barely pass as either clearly and securely "D/deaf" or "H/hearing"—how could I ever show someone like Lynne which, if any of those, to be?

I felt nailed to the threshold.

When I get to feeling this way—trapped, nailed, stuck inbetween overwhelming options—I tend to become frantic, nervously energized, even mean. And my will to pass, to get through and beyond at all costs, kicks in ferociously. Some animals freeze in fear, shut down in fright; I run—harder, faster, longer. I run until I pass—until I pass on, or out.

And that running always seems to lead me to stories. I have always been a storyteller, a writer, a talker. These "talents" pass me off as "hearing" even as they connect me to "the Deaf way." "The Deaf way" revolves around narrative, around sharing stories—and the narration itself is, in Deaf culture, far more than incidental to the experience. Using sign language, Deaf culture prides itself on its "oral" and "narrative" nature. And for the Deaf, who tells the story and how they tell it is every bit as important as what the story is. The narrator, then, is in control of the experience instead of vice versa.

I tend to control conversations. This is not something I am proud of, but it is the experience I present, the face I show in the mirror. I can talk a lot. I ramble, I chatter—especially on the phone and in one-on-one conversations. It is safer this way: if I don't shut up, if I keep talking, then *voilà,* I don't have to listen. And if I don't have to listen, I don't have to struggle, don't have to ask for repeats, don't have to appear in any of the guises I and other deaf/hard-of-hearing people often appear in—stupid, aloof, disapproving, suspicious. If I keep talking, I pass. I thrive and survive in perpetual animation.

But in situations where animation affords me no control—in social settings with more than two in the conversation, for example, or as a student in the classroom—I resort quite rhetorically to another strategy: I disappear. (My mother and sisters called it "Brenda's La-La Land.") I just fade away, withdraw from the conversation. Here it is safer not to speak at all. For if I do, I am sure to be off-topic, three steps behind, completely out of synchronization with the others. Or even worse, if I speak, someone might ask me a question—a question I would struggle to hear, would have to ask for a repetition of (probably more than once), would fail then to answer with wit, intelligence, clarity, quickness. Passing is treacherous going here, so I usually choose not even to venture out, not to cross over the mythical yellow line that marks the "center" between D/deaf and H/hearing.

When I do venture out or across, I've been trapped more than once—have talked myself right back into the deaf corner. You see, when I talk, people sometimes wonder.

"Where are you from? You have quite an accent," I have been asked too many times to count—and usually by near strangers. The question is, I suppose, innocent enough. For many years I used to pass myself off as German; it was easy enough since my grandparents were quite German and I, as the child of an army family in the '50s, was born in Germany. Of course, having grandparents who once spoke the language and having lived there, as part of the US Army, for only the first four years of my life didn't really qualify me as a native speaker, complete with an accent. But my interlocutors didn't need to know any of that; when I said "German," they were satisfied. "Oh yes," they nodded, completely in understanding now.

But some years ago, as another act of "coming out," I stopped answering "German." First I tried out a simple, direct "I'm deaf." But the result was too startling—it rendered my audience deaf and dumb. They sputtered, they stared at me speechlessly, they went away—fast. It quite unhinged them.

So I have softened the effect a bit and begun to respond, "I'm quite hard-of-hearing." For this one I get a split response—they will smile and nod an affirmative, "oh yes, I understand now" (although I know that they really don't understand the connections between hearing loss and having an "accent"), and they will also back away rather quickly, still reluctant to continue a conversation under these circumstances.

I didn't like passing as German, but I'm never sure I like their response to my "real" answer any better. When I see the fright in their eyes, the "oh-my-god-what-should-I-say-now?" look that freezes into that patronizing smile, I feel cornered again. I feel scared, too, for the way it reflects back on the way I saw myself for many years. I wish I had just stayed mute.

For all it scares me, though, when I get cornered and I see my scared, caught between the hyphens, hard-of-hearing face in the mirror, something comes of it. The first and most significant time this happened to me was at my first successful academic conference. I had just finished my first year of graduate school and had journeyed to Wyoming that summer to give a paper at the Wyoming Conference on English. I had been to this conference the summer before as well, but in my silently passing mode. This year, however,

I was animated by everything, from a very positive response to my own paper on the first day to a headful of theory-stuff mixed near-explosively with my first year of teaching college freshmen. I was primed. I was talking a lot.

On the third day of the conference we were having a picnic lunch up in the mountains and I was at a table with one of the conference's biggest stars, feeling lit up, I guess by the glitter he was sprinkling on me with genuine interest in my own projects and things I had said in earlier sessions. I was telling stories about growing up in western Kansas. The table full of people was listening, engaged, laughing.

Then a woman across the table, slightly to the left of me, wearing a tag from some small place in Louisiana, I remember, asked me, point-blank, "So, how long have you been *deaf?*" (And that word, especially, went echoing off the mountain walls, I swear.) The question did not fall on deaf ears. The table, full of some sixteen people, went silent—awfully, awesomely silent. They waited.

"A-a-all my life." Silence again. Eons of silence. Echoes of silence.

"Wow," said the star, and he touched my arm—a genuine touch, a caring touch, a you-don't-have-to-feel-bad touch.

But I felt plenty bad. I excused myself under pretense of wanting some more potato salad. Instead I went behind a giant pine tree on the other side of the chow table and tried to breathe, tried to think of how I could make it past those people, to my car, out of here, out of here, out of here.

I know that in this telling it may all sound quite melodramatic. But in that moment, I learned, if nothing else and quite melodramatically, that I am the narrator of my experience. I learned that there was a price for passing, that the ticket cost more than just a pretty penny, that the perpetual fear of being "found out" at any moment was far worse than telling at the outset. (Like telling a lie and having to remember who you told it to, who you didn't.)

And what was I so afraid of in the first place?

That moment in Wyoming, at the dawn of my academic career, shortly before I entered my thirties, was I think the first time I asked myself that question. And when I began asking it, I also began taking charge of narrating my own experience and identity. I began "coming out," as it were. At the age of thirty, I took my first sign language class (and cried mightily on the first night at the sheer thrill of not having to sit in the chair at the front and center of the classroom so I could "hear" the instructor—cried for the simple freedom of choosing my own seat). I also dreamed up a dissertation project, rhetorician that I was, that would take me into "deafness"—my own and others'—and take me to Gallaudet University, to the heart of Deaf culture.

If nothing else, I could always write about it, read about it. I had been doing literacy, and doing it well, all my life as yet another supremely successful act of passing. In all those classrooms I disappeared from as I drifted off, when my ability to attend carefully was used up and I wafted away to Brenda's La-La Land, I made up for my absence by reading and writing on my own. If nothing else, I could always write about it, read about it.

At Grandma's family gatherings for the holidays, Brenda was always in the other room, away from the crowds, reading. Nine times out of ten, when Brenda's high school friends went out for lunch and to drag main, Brenda went to the high school library and read (or wrote one of her crummy poems). The summer before she was to start college, Brenda spent her lifeguard breaks at the noisy pool in the corner of the basket room, plowing through a used introductory psychology textbook she'd gotten from an older friend already at college. As it turns out, this plowing was what saved her when that fall she found herself in the cavernous "intro to psychology" lecture hall with some three hundred other students—thankful that her name alphabetically allowed her to sit near the front, but still yearning to be an "A" so she could optimize the lecture from the choicest chair.

And she read. She bought or checked out a dozen more texts on psychology, biology, the skills of writing an essay. She took copious notes from each of them, recorded and memorized key vocabulary, read those notes and her own in-class lecture notes (which she didn't trust) over carefully each week, adding notes on top of those notes.

She spent most of her freshman year in the all-girls dorm holed up in her room, writing, reading, taking notes, passing. She went swimming—a silent, individual sport—for a "social" life. After that first frightful year it got better. The initial fear of failing, of being found out, subsided. She even skipped class now and then, forgot to study scrupulously for each and every test. She still passed quite well. She took a job—a safe one—lifeguarding in a tall, antisocial chair at the university pool on nights and weekends. She kept writing and reading, but now found her interests went far beyond college textbooks and careful notes; outside of her homework, she started working her way through Russian literature (don't ask me why) and writing short stories. She avoided bars and parties— sooner or later a young man would come slosh a beer on her, ask her something, and not having heard him, but not wanting to appear any of those dreaded things, she would just nod "yes." It was not always the answer she meant to give.

Books were far easier to control. When she didn't understand a text, it didn't seem to mind her asking for a repeat. She could stare hard, be aloof, acquiesce without embarrassing consequences, speak out of turn, and question a book again and again. It didn't seem to mind. She wasn't deaf when she was reading or writing. In fact, she came to realize that we are all quite deaf when we read or write—engaged in a signing system that is not oral/aural and that is removed from the present.

How many times must she have written—to herself or to someone else— "it's easier for me to write this than it is to say it; I find the words easier on paper." On paper she didn't sound deaf, she could be someone other than herself—an artificer (thus fulfilling Plato's worst nightmare about the rhetorical potential in writing). On paper she passed.

Through the years, although I've become more confident at public speaking and far more willing to unmask myself, my deafness, before others have a chance to, I've always been better at writing and reading than I have at speaking. In graduate school, I was given a prestigious fellowship— principally for my writing skills—and thus my colleagues, both the faculty and other graduate students, expected me to be a class leader, to speak often and well. I didn't. In fact, I later came to know that many interpreted my silence in the classroom as showing I'd neglected the reading, or just arrogant indifference. Neglecting reading was never a crime I was guilty of, although I might own up to some indifference. (How could it be otherwise when only two of my graduate school professors spoke loudly and clearly enough for me to understand more than half of their mumbled, head-down, eyes-stuck-on-the-page lectures?)

Mostly I was still afraid of myself—still scared of what I saw when I stood in front of the mirror and spoke. As long as I had a written text—something I had worked on and rehearsed in order to smooth out my odd "accent," my tendency to fast talk and non-logical progression, and my tonal infelicities—I could be comfortable speaking from and through it. But to speak well extemperaneously—this was risking breaking the mirror, seven years' bad luck. Writing smoothed the blemishes, softened the sharp edges.

Even when I teach, I teach from and with writing, thereby maintaining control. I avoid at all costs leading large group discussions where students might speak from the back of the room—from the places where even my hearing aids on the highest setting won't go. I put students in small groups for discussion and then I walk around, lean over their shoulders, sit down with a group for a short time. Then I bring one group to the front of the class to help me lead the whole class through discussion, branching out from what they were talking about in their smaller groups. In this way, the students take charge of receiving the questions and become interpreters for me and one another. I like to argue that they gain in this process a new kind of responsibility and learning that they might not have had before; but I know, truth be told, that it's mostly just a matter of getting *me* past some of the more difficult parts of teaching.

My premier pedagogy for passing is, of course, writing. My students, even in the more literature-based classes, write a lot. They always keep journals; they always write too many papers (or so it seems when I'm reading and responding to all of them). And my students, for fourteen years now, are always amazed at how much I write in responding to their journals and papers (they tell me so in evaluations). For here is a place where I can have a conversation, unthreatened and unstressed by my listening limitations. They write and I write back. Writing is my passageway; writing is my pass; through writing, I pass.

Works Cited

Anderson, Benedict. *Imagined Communities.* London: Verso, 1983.

Schein, Jerome D., and Marcus T. Welk. *The Deaf Population of the United States.* Silver Spring: National Association of the Deaf, 1974.

Tucker, Bonnie Poitras. *The Feel of Silence.* Philadelphia: Temple UP, 1994.

II Ethics in Teaching, Research, and Publishing

Discussions of ethics have emerged as another central theme in English Studies. Once considered "old-fashioned" and "too traditional" (as Wayne Booth explains in his essay), ethics has made a comeback of sorts in the study of language, literature, and writing. But this return to ethics is different: it does not presuppose universal norms or binary oppositions to establish standards for what is "good and bad" or "ethical and unethical." Rather, new notions of ethics are attuned to the diversity in social contexts, backgrounds, ethnicities, and worldviews. This grouping of articles on ethics touches on the full spectrum of work in English Studies: the ethics of teaching and responding to student writing; the ethics of the teaching of literature; the ethics of designing and conducting person-based research; and the ethics of publishing.

Dan Morgan raises issues all too familiar to many writing teachers who assign personal essays: how to respond when students reveal personal details of their lives, when they confess to illicit or illegal activities, when they describe a personal crisis that calls for response, or when they reveal abusive or violent relationships. Morgan does not offer any simple solutions to addressing the ethical dilemmas of students' personal writing; rather, he suggests that students' topic choices reflect their experiences (and our society), and that as teachers, we can remind students to consider audience, purpose, and goal when they compose personal essays.

In "The Ethics of Teaching Literature," Wayne Booth traces the rise and fall of "ethics" as a topic of professional conversation and argues for renewed attention to this key concept in the teaching of literature. Booth's article carries the lively tone and examples he included when he first presented this essay as a keynote address to the College Section Forum at the 1997 NCTE Annual Convention. He concludes his article with six practical—and challenging—suggestions for teachers of literature, all of them intended to encourage more teachers to "devote themselves to the pursuit of some version of the ethical aims of education."

Ethical considerations have also emerged as a key focus of inquiry in conducting case study and ethnographic research. Paul Anderson traces the history of Institutional Review Boards (IRBs) at colleges and universities, boards whose purpose it is to monitor and approve research involving human subjects. Anderson argues that these boards, designed with medical and sociological research in mind, are not always able to address the ethical dilemmas educators are likely to face. He describes some of the special ethical considerations literacy scholars need to take into account, such as when they take on the role of teacher-researcher and study their own classrooms. Anderson cautions that such practices—quite common today in composition studies and English education—need to be examined critically: How do we ensure that students do not feel coerced to participate in our studies? That they are neither silenced nor embarrassed by our research studies? Anderson concludes by suggesting that the profession focus its attention on ethical issues in human-based research and more carefully guide new scholars through the thickets of ethical dilemmas.

Peter Mortensen tackles another topic with ethical implications: publishing for audiences beyond the academic community. He argues for the importance—indeed, the ethical obligation—of scholars to engage in public discourse because that discourse shapes public perception and representation of the people we study and thereby can determine educational, legislative, and fiscal policies that affect them. Mortensen does not argue that all scholars should become "public intellectuals," but he suggests that scholars need to learn how to address the communities in which they study, work, and live.

5 Ethical Issues Raised by Students' Personal Writing

Dan Morgan

A couple of years ago, very early in the semester, one of my first-semester composition students wrote a personal narrative in which he confessed to murder. In "Life on the City Streets" he described receiving instructions over the phone and then proceeding to kill a nameless victim in cold blood. The paper disturbingly lacked remorse; the student explained to me later that it was intended to show what he had had to do to survive on the streets. It was way short of the assigned length and very poorly written. Of course I had questions about the authenticity of the narrative. Also, I confess that in the first, dismaying, how-do-I-respond-to-*this* moments after I read this paper, the thought crossed my mind—as indeed it may be crossing your minds right now—that it is perfectly possible to go through an entire career without having to confront a paper such as this . . .

Some weeks later, when I shared this paper at a professional meeting with colleagues across my college district, almost all of them thought that the narrative was "real," not fiction, though personally I have doubts to this day. Some advised various approaches one could take to get at "the truth," while at least a couple pointed out that as an "officer of the college" I was obligated to turn the whole matter over to the college deans and to the police. But, leaving aside that I had never thought of myself in quite that way, there was really not enough evidence to take such a step. Instead, I asked the student to see me in conference, and when he finally kept his appointment, we discussed the paper in more detail. He repeated several times that the murder had really happened, and we negotiated a revision which would expand the narrative, clarify the thesis, define some terms, and provide the

Reprinted from *College English,* March 1998.

indispensable details of context. Then we set up another conference where he would bring in a draft of the revision. But, although he completed one other assignment in the course, the student continued to attend class only rarely, never came to a second conference, never wrote the revision, and vanished from school less than halfway through the semester. There is no tidy resolution to this incident.

Maybe the issues are clear-cut: if a student confesses to a crime, the teacher must contact the authorities. But as this example shows, the issues may *not* be clear-cut, and so a few questions arise. Is it part of the teacher's role to act as a detective in such cases? Get a fuller, usable confession? Then shouldn't teachers also report to the authorities students who relate personal involvement in lesser crimes or illegal activities, from vandalism and drug dealing to underage drinking or passing bad checks? Granted, murder is much more serious, as are assaults and other crimes of violence, but where and how are the lines drawn? I think of an essay by Lad Tobin on the personal narratives of adolescent males, where he discusses at length a student's gameplaying pattern of shoplifting (159–65). The *teacher* must make the determination whether a crime is serious enough to make it reportable? Moreover, are student essays always in the public domain? I often use workshopping activities in composition classes, and often rely on student essays, but I also inform students that their papers might be discussed publicly unless they request otherwise on individual assignments. In his influential essay "Fault Lines in the Contact Zone," Richard Miller suggests that teachers might turn student papers to public discourse, so that, say, essays containing hate speech can become "teachable objects" (395). But can we also turn personal crises, traumas, or past suffering into teachable objects, or should we perhaps try instead to prevent or strongly discourage such self-disclosing papers from being submitted in the first place?

It might seem equally clear-cut that if a student writes about emotional distress, potential suicide, or major psychological problems, the teacher must intervene and refer the student—sometimes even taking that student by the arm—to appropriate counseling services, on the assumption, of course, that all institutions have adequate resources in this area. What to do, how to respond, in these and other "rescue" situations, is outlined very usefully in an article by Marilyn Valentino in the December 1996 issue of *Teaching English in the Two-Year College* (274–83)—an article which I think should be required reading in teacher-training programs.

For the sake of argument, let's pretend that in the disclosure of criminal activities or in the case of personal distress or risk, a teacher's response and course of action *are* unambiguous, especially if there happen to be clearly stated institutional policies and guidelines. I suspect that in reality such policies and guidelines are seldom clear or comprehensive enough, or may not exist at all, and that for the most part, in most institutions, teachers are on their own when it comes to such issues. But let me simply put out a call to college administrators to create detailed and responsible institutional policies and provide adequate resources before I zero in on another aspect of this issue of teacher response to students' self-disclosure. Here what to do is even more troublesome than in the examples I've already discussed.

Last year, one of my students wrote a persuasion essay in which she explained in disturbing detail her involvement with an abusive man who was on crack. In my view, this woman (who is waiting for the man to come out of prison in five years because, after all, he is the father of their child, and, she believes, is bound to be changed for the better by the prison experience) revealed far more about herself than she may have considered, and really needs to re-examine *her* decisions. I even think that how she will conduct her life and how she will raise the child are more important issues than how well she wrote this one paper. The paper was weak, the ostensible thesis (that crack is bad) obvious and seemingly tacked on, the narrative repetitive, the sentences often ungrammatical, and the details badly in need of more judicious editing. As a reader, my main concern was with the student's own lifestyle, values, and prospects. As a teacher, how do I negotiate my written responses? To address writing issues seems cold, and, frankly, even irrelevant at a certain level. And I have some misgivings about the ethical appropriateness of issuing an unsolicited referral to counseling. So, to paraphrase Miller, do I work to help this student write a *better* paper about how a person should continue staying in a relationship with an abusive crack addict?

A rare and extreme example, you say? Here is another. In a paper entitled "Have We Gone Too Far?" a student writes about her alcoholic father throwing her across the room when she was three and a half years old, whipping her with a belt, and kicking her for twenty minutes. Her brother took her into the bathroom to help her clean up, and they sat there for an hour as he applied ice to her face . . . until the father said it was time to go to church. A pattern of physical and mental abuse characterized her childhood. And what is the point of her paper? She is concerned that kids, especially teenagers, don't get enough discipline, and that parents have been denied the means to administer needed discipline these days. "Even though my father abused me, I still respect him," she writes in her closing paragraph, going on to state that social workers today are far too quick to involve themselves in family affairs.

Now of course this paper could be discussed openly in class and its perspective on child abuse debated publicly, but *would* it be helpful to the student to know that many people find her respect-the-father-no-matter-what conclusion appalling when so much of her life seems to be anchored on that conclusion? And this student, now an adult, does not appear to be in crisis or asking, even indirectly, for intervention or rescue. Is it appropriate for an *English teacher* to nudge a student toward rethinking the traumas of her life? Or should the teacher focus on writing issues such as paragraph unity and sentence structure—issues this writer certainly needed to address? What *is* the nature of our "contract" with students, exactly? (My college uses the term "customers," but that's another essay . . .)

Two semesters ago, in a paper entitled "Do You Trust Me?" a student wrote about date rape. Since she did not request confidentiality, should we use this paper in a general class discussion, so that the student can write a better paper about her naïveté and personally experienced sexual abuse? And speaking of extreme examples, another student wrote about running away from home—at age twelve—with her boyfriend, who was twenty-four. The drugs came later, as did two brutal rapes within a span of ten hours. And another student wrote about a fifth-month abortion—at age fourteen—and I've had personal narratives dealing with a parent's violent suicide (the student discovered the body), dire poverty, serious eating disorders, living in a cardboard box on the streets of Chicago, gang participation, and more. If we encourage students to write about what they know, what are our responsibilities when they do, especially if, as Miller says, "it is of paramount importance to begin where students are, rather than where one thinks they should be" (405)? And, again, let me emphasize that many of these examples—and others like them—do not involve a student's illegal activities or a direct "cry for help," but, rather, blunt disclosure of personal experiences, and personal conclusions about those often astonishing experiences.

Underlying all these issues are some basic questions: Why would students turn in such deeply personal essays, especially when personal revelations are unsolicited? Why would they disclose matters that would ordinarily seem to be too private or not appropriate to a classroom environment? And what, then, are a teacher's responsibilities? Valentino suggests that "the intimate nature of writing itself may serve as both a stimulus and a catharsis for past experiences. When these feelings are expressed, albeit unsolicited and unforeseen, the teacher cannot avoid or dismiss them. To do so would be negligent" (278). Yet she also describes what most of us have encountered when we question students about their expectations following self-disclosure: to the teacher's question, "What would you like me to do?" the answer is often "Nothing." The students just want someone to listen (279). To me, the inescapable conclusion is that the very nature of teaching itself has changed, especially in a field such as composition, where "content" is most often the students' own writing. With all the safeguards possible—legal, ethical, professional—our interaction with students, our responses to their work have become more personal.

A teacher's responsibilities always did entail more than content expertise and classroom management, always did include listening, encouraging, mentoring, and even, occasionally, some degree of informal counseling. But we now live in a time when many more college students have "special needs," when we see a much higher proportion of students who have led nontraditional lives, a larger number of what I call "broken wing" students. And so, our roles have of necessity become even more time-consuming and challenging.

What to do? Valentino provides indispensable advice in her article, from using reflective statements ("This must have been horrible for you"), through specific ways of keeping one's professional distance and setting limits, to networking actively with the school's support service specialists. I want to take a broader view and list a few additional, common sense and immediate measures—with their attendant difficulties.

- Emphasize audience and purpose much more thoroughly than ever before. Highlight this aspect of writing early and often, thus driving home to students the need to consider these crucial matters *every* time and evaluate appropriateness with *every* writing task. However, the fact is that most teachers already do plenty of work on audience and purpose. And furthermore—prepare to be shocked now—students don't always follow directions fully, no matter how much time is spent on them: they tend to write about what they want to write about. For example, in the second-semester composition course, after many weeks of discussing argumentative writing and many illustrations, I use an argument assignment based on a seventy-item list of *Harper's* Index Facts. Last fall, one of my students turned in a paper that was not even marginally connected to any one of these items. Instead of an argument, he wrote a personal narrative in which he talked about falling in with the wrong crowd, smoking a lot of marijuana, doing petty crimes to sustain his habit, and dabbling with Satanism, which eventually led to not one but two suicide attempts, which he survived only because God was watching over him. The paper was heartfelt and fairly well written, but had nothing directly to do with the specific argument assignment or the specific (and generous) list of possible topics. Responding to such a paper, rather than simply returning it as a do-over, was a moral obligation nonetheless, I felt, and a challenge as well, because there was more at stake than fulfilling an assignment or earning a grade. In addition to written comments, mostly of the reflective kind suggested by Valentino, I spent a good deal of time talking to this student. Without delving into additional and probably painful details of the personal experiences themselves, I tried to steer him back toward argumentation. And I also talked to him about the strengths of his writing, and about his staying in college despite the challenges he was still facing. The interaction was formal but decidedly personal.

So yes, students will write about what they want to write about, but now in any early-semester discussion of audience and purpose I do bring up scenarios involving self-disclosing essays, whether based on hypothetical examples or on older essays whose writers have given me permission to use their work (anonymously) in class.

I have also begun to specify to students that I prefer not to see papers dealing with past or present illegal activities.

- Or how about this: Insist on tightly assigned topics, which always require prior approval in individual conferences, thereby eliminating the option for students to "stray" in the direction of possibly inappropriate subjects that may be too personal and self-disclosing. And, to reinforce the initial, required conference, schedule additional required conferences for draft evaluation and updates. This may indeed be a sound approach in theory, but it is not a practical solution from a purely logistical point of view. Extensive, concentrated individual attention is best, I am convinced, but many of us with heavy teaching loads read and evaluate over eight *hundred* essays per semester already, and don't work in private offices. Thus, my reality is that I can hold required conferences for *all* my writing students only once, to discuss, approve, and help with term paper topics.

Instead—and this is a solution driven by necessity—more than ever before I encourage and occasionally require revisions, preceded by conferences. This puts more responsibility on the students themselves—and enables me to give more attention to those who seem to need it more. Thus, I still can't prevent a student from writing about how she was dumped by her boyfriend the minute he found out she was pregnant (though they had used precautions—most of the time), and how this led her to go all alone to have an abortion over which she grieves to this day, and how she never told *anyone* about it, not even her parents; but I can respond first by acknowledging the (startling) trust she showed in writing this paper, and eventually by discussing how such deeply personal material can be shaped to communicate usefully to a larger audience, if not for this one essay (the student chose not to revise), then for future writing. Similarly, when a student writes a tearstained paper about her lifelong struggles in dealing with her alcoholic father, the teacher must respond with compassion and empathy, *and* do the best he or she can to help the writer improve her writing. It is often a delicate balance, for the interaction is unmistakably personal.

In my day, none of this was covered in graduate school symposia . . .

- Here is a more radical solution, seriously contemplated by one of my colleagues: eliminate the personal narrative altogether. I cannot support this idea at all, but I will say that it would be most helpful if the model essays used in the anthologies that cross my desk were more in touch with the kind of writing students actually tend to do, reflecting the actual concerns in their lives. The students I work with do not write about multicultural encounters or issues of ethnicity; nor do they relate much to shooting elephants or going to the lake, much as those wonderful essays have to offer. For that matter, they also don't write about proving themselves in the Big Game. They *do* write about family relationships and the impact of divorce, teenage parenting, rehab programs, the bureaucracy of social agencies, and the failures of the education system personally felt. Rather than eliminating personal narratives, we—and the anthologies we use—should rely on models that enable students to reflect upon and understand their experiences in a larger social context.

- Or this: Whenever a student writes about a personal crisis past or present, refer him or her to counseling (the Ann Landers solution). I've already talked about limited resources and the questions I have about the ethics of such unsolicited referrals. But there are additional problems. In my experience, hardly any students have ever welcomed referrals to counseling—or agreed to them. Some students are already in counseling, or have completed a round of counseling. A colleague told me of a student who wanted to write about her harrowing experiences being stalked by a violent ex-boyfriend. "Are you sure that's a good idea?" my colleague asked this student in conference, trying hard to dissuade her; "It might be too painful." But the woman assured her that she had had counseling and that writing about this issue would be helpful and good for her. She was adamant that she would write on this topic and no other, despite my colleague's efforts to steer her in a different direction. Should my colleague have been equally adamant in refusing to accept this topic? Should she have insisted on contacting the counselor personally before approving the topic? Made the student sign a waiver? Again, how far do the responsibilities of a teacher extend, exactly? As it turned out, the process of writing this paper contributed to sending the student over the edge to a nervous breakdown and hospitalization. Plainly, the send-them-to-counseling solution has its limits. (And here I might add that my town's local newspaper recently carried a front-page story about the severe shortage of adequate counseling services in area schools.)

Perhaps the examples I have detailed seem extreme, but let me assure you that every class in every semester produces a few "extreme" examples. These are our students. For, finally, I think there is a deeper truth here: *these students' topics and concerns, and their life experiences and points of view, reflect what has been occurring in our society at large.* Our students write about violence and substance abuse and broken families because they're writing about what they have lived and witnessed firsthand, what they care most deeply about. Their crises, past or present, mirror the condition of our society, reflect what has become more and more ordinary. And writing about profoundly personal issues comes easily to our students because we live in a pervasive culture of public self-disclosure, as talk shows, tabloids, daily newspapers, books, and movies will attest. In our popular culture, private issues are no longer private, and public self-disclosure seems to have become a means toward personal validation.

When I first started teaching, many, many years ago, I would often hear students asking me if I was *sure* it was OK to write in the first person: in all their previous writing classes they had always been told that they should never use the pronoun "I." As I smiled benignly and gave them the go-ahead, it was a liberating experience for all of us. (Then, while I was on a roll, I even suggested they could start sentences with the word "and," if they didn't overdo it: another major empowerment!) It seems to me that the pendulum has swung to the other extreme in the intervening years. And while I certainly don't advocate a return to inhibiting the personal voice in writing, I do think we must give much more attention to the increasing complexities of our roles as teachers—living and working in a broken society—to the complicated and thoroughly nontraditional lives led by most of our students. regardless of age or background, to the unavoidably and increasingly personal interaction that takes place with our students, to issues of trust and ethical responsibilities.

Works Cited

Miller, Richard E. "Fault I ines in the Contact Zone." *College English* 56 (1994): 389–408

Tobin, Lad. "Car Wrecks, Baseball Caps, and Man-to-Man Defense: The Personal Narratives of Adolescent Males." *College English* 58 (1996): 158–75.

Valentino, Marilyn J. "Responding When a Life Depends on It: What to Write in the Margins When Students Self-Disclose." *Teaching English in the Two-Year College* 23 (1996): 274–83.

6 Simple Gifts: Ethical Issues in the Conduct of Person-Based Composition Research

Paul V. Anderson

Since the 1970s, much major work in composition has been driven by moral purpose. Beginning at least as early as Mina Shaughnessy's *Errors and Expectations*, Richard Ohman's *English in America*, and Ira Shor's *Critical Teaching and Everyday Life*, researchers have striven to develop theories and practices that further social justice, combat harmful stereotypes, correct imbalances of power in society and the classroom, and provide effective, respectful, and caring instruction to all students—regardless of gender, ethnicity, class, or sexual orientation. Yet, curiously, our moral gaze has almost completely overlooked one crucial area of our personal and disciplinary responsibility, namely our ethical obligations to the persons whose words and actions we transform into the "data" of our research.

I'm not thinking of our *text-based* studies. When incorporating, building on, or contending with the likes of Aristotle, Bakhtin, Elbow, or Lunsford, we have several ethical guides. We are aided not only by our individual sense of courtesy, but also by the strictures of copyright law, the taboos and institutional policies against plagiarism, and socially enforced customs concerning acknowledgment and citation. We have, however, no comparable guides to the ethical treatment of the individuals on whom we rely in our *person-based* research. In addition to quantitative and qualitative studies, our person-based research includes the publications and presentations in which we describe people we've encountered in the normal course of our professional and personal lives, outside of formally planned

Reprinted from *College Composition and Communication*, February 1998.

investigations. It also includes studies in which we quote the unpublished words of these individuals. Most often, the persons we use in these ways are students, but we also use colleagues, family members, and even strangers in similar fashion.

There are good reasons, I believe, for us to become more reflective about the ethical issues involved with person-based research. First, this type of research constitutes a substantial portion of our contemporary literature. More than half of the 71 articles that *CCC* published in volumes 43 through 45 (1993–95) contain at least some person-based material. Fifteen of these articles (20 percent) involve formally designed quantitative or qualitative studies, and in 22 others (31 percent) the researchers quote someone else's unpublished writing, quote or paraphrase spoken words, or otherwise incorporate "data" they obtained through interaction with other individuals. Moreover, *CCC* isn't alone in publishing substantial amounts of person-based research. During 1993–95, *College English* carried 23 such articles, *JAC* 24, *Research in the Teaching of English* 36, and *Written Communication* 30. Thus, during the brief period of three years, these five journals alone published 150 articles incorporating person-based material.[1] Numerous additional person-based studies were reported in other composition publications, including books, or were presented at professional conferences like CCCC.

A second reason for us to become more reflective about the ethics of person-based research is that the issues involved are complex. Many, if not all, of us would benefit from the resource that a discipline-wide discourse would offer as we endeavor to deal ethically with the people who contribute to our own person-based projects. One cause of this complexity is that our studies often rely on individuals who may be especially vulnerable to (unintentional) infringement of their rights, dignity, and privacy. For example, in quantitative and qualitative studies we sometimes use our own students as research participants, either by observing their "natural" behavior in classrooms, conferences, or other venues or by asking them to engage in special research activities for the sake of our projects. Students may be doubly vulnerable to us because of the trusting relationship they have with us as their teachers and because of the power our position as teachers gives us over them. How can we assure ourselves as individual researchers and as a research field that we are treating our student-participants ethically? That we are not exploiting privileged access to their writing and personal disclosures for our own ends? That we are not abusing our power as teachers to coerce them into participating in our studies? And how should we address

the many other ethical issues that arise when our person-based studies
involve faculty colleagues, university administrators, or members of the
many other groups studied in composition research?

We might respond by declaring that responsibility for answering these
and similar questions belongs to each individual researcher. In part, I agree.
We should allow nothing to diminish our personal sense of ethical
obligation to the people on whom we depend in our research. I also believe,
however, that we should assume collective responsibility for addressing such
questions. As members of a knowledge-constructing field, we have an
ethical obligation to see that the knowledge with which we work—the
knowledge created in our collective name—is generated only through
ethical means. Recognizing their corporate responsibility for the ethical
treatment of participants in their research, other disciplines have developed
formal codes of research ethics. For example, psychology has had one since
the 1960s, sociology since 1971, and anthropology since 1973.
Additionally, researchers in these fields have devoted entire books to
research ethics, as well as articles appearing in their fields' major journals.
As we've adopted research methods from these disciplines, we've gained a
great deal of knowledge about how to employ the methods as we study
writers, writing, and its teaching. However, we haven't simultaneously
developed our understanding of the measures we must take when using
these methods to assure that we treat our research participants ethically.

This oversight is particularly striking because moral commitment is so
evident in other aspects of our research. There are, I believe, two reasons for
it. First, as we've forayed into the social sciences, we've retained our
powerful sense of the ethical practices salient in our institutional home, the
humanities. Continuing to adhere scrupulously to what copyright law and
courtesy require when drawing on the published work of others, we haven't
realized that our newly acquired research methods might require new
ethical guidelines. Moreover, the social sciences' extensive discourse on
research ethics is so deeply embedded in those fields that it constitutes a
form of tacit knowledge. As such, its very existence can easily go unnoticed
by outsiders. For example, knowledge of the *APA Ethics Code* is so pervasive
in psychology that most books on psychology research methods don't even
mention it. Composition's pioneering introductions to social science
research methods (Kirsch and Sullivan; Lauer and Asher) resemble similar
books written by social scientists because they discuss techniques only—but
differ because they are not set in a context that includes a rich, disciplinary
discussion of the techniques' ethical dimensions.

Fortunately, during the past few years several events in composition studies have prepared a foundation for composition's own discourse on research ethics. In 1992 the Modern Language Association issued a "Statement of Professional Ethics" with provisions that touch briefly but importantly on the use of student writing and of students as research participants. In 1993 Sandra Stotsky, as editor of *Research in the Teaching of English*, advertised her interest in receiving manuscripts dealing with research ethics, and the next year her entry in the *Encyclopedia of English Studies and Language Arts* identified several research ethics issues that composition should begin to address. In 1994, as editor of *CCC*, Joseph Harris announced a policy regarding quotation from student work, and in 1996 NCTE published a book edited by Gesa Kirsch and Peter Mortenson, *Ethics and Representation in Qualitative Studies of Literacy*, which contains essays mapping several issues in research ethics. Also, within the past five years, NCTE began requiring authors to obtain written releases from students and other persons who served as research-participants if their writing is quoted substantially. At approximately the same time, MLA began requiring authors to obtain written permission from persons whose unpublished writing the authors quote or who served as research participants in the studies the authors describe.[2]

My primary goal in this article is to encourage us to build on this foundation, to widen and deepen our discussion of the ethical issues involved with person-based research. I will begin by discussing an enormously important discourse about research ethics with direct relevance to composition studies. As yet, it has gone almost entirely unnoticed by us. I will also discuss several specific issues in research ethics as a way of illustrating how this discourse can provide us with new, productive ways of thinking about what we must do individually and collectively to treat our research participants ethically.

A National and International Discourse on Research Ethics

December 9, 1996. At the end of the afternoon, I squeezed into the driver's seat of my aging Honda hatchback, started the engine, turned on the radio, and pulled slowly out of my parking spot in the lot next to the English department's red-brick building. On the seat beside me were a set of papers and the latest issue of *CCC*, my reading for the evening. From National Public Radio I heard the following words, delivered in a solemn, yet urgent, voice:

Between September 1939 and April 1945, all of the defendants
herein unlawfully, willfully and knowingly committed crimes against
humanity in that they were principals in, accessories to, ordered,
abetted, took a consenting part in and were connected with plans
and enterprises involving medical experiments without the subject's
consent . . . in the course of which . . . the defendants committed
murders, brutalities, cruelties, tortures, atrocities and other inhumane
acts. (National Public Radio)

As NPR correspondent Linda Werthheimer then explained, it was the 50th
anniversary of one of the most important of the Nuremberg War Crimes
Trials. I had just heard a recording of the prosecution s opening statement.
Twenty Nazi physicians and three other members of the Third Reich were
accused of killing, maiming, and torturing Jews, Gypsies, and other persons
in a variety of cruel "scientific experiments." Some victims were exposed to
contagious diseases, some injected with poison or gasoline, some placed in
chambers where the air pressure was reduced to the point where their lungs
and skulls ruptured and they died.

As I drove through the serene, tree-lined streets of Oxford, Ohio, I seemed
to be almost a universe away from Nuremberg, the former center of Nazi
war production, reduced largely to rubble by intensive Allied bombing,
where the 23 defendants faced an international tribunal in 1946. Yet,
through a nearly direct historical path, one action of the judges at the so-
called "Doctors' Trial" provides composition researchers with a rich ethical
legacy whose value we have not yet begun to realize even half a century
later. To defend themselves, the Nazi doctors argued that their cruelties were
actually justifiable medical research. In response, the judges drafted the
Nuremberg Code, a ten-point statement of the conditions under which
humans can be used as "subjects" or participants in research. Around the
world, the *Code* formed the basis for extensive discussions of the ethical
issues in human-participant research, and in many countries it provided the
foundation for newly developed government policies designed to ensure that
the human participants in research are treated ethically. The United States
adopted such a federal regulation in 1974.

This regulation has the special distinction of being accompanied by a
government-sponsored declaration of the ethical principles that pertain to
the domain of activity it covers. At the same time this regulation was
adopted, Congress also created the National Commission for the Protection
of Human Subjects of Biomedical and Behavioral Research. This
commission was charged to review several areas of research in order to
recommend refinements for the regulation and also to identify the ethical

principles that guided their deliberations. In 1979, it articulated these principles in the *Belmont Report*, which remains a powerfully influential force in the design and implementation of the federal policy governing human participant research (National Commission).

In this article, I will show how we can use the ethical discourse embodied in the *Nuremberg Code*, the federal regulation, and the *Belmont Report* to shed new light on the ethical issues associated with our person-based research. In doing so, I don't mean to suggest that there is even the remotest resemblance between the atrocities committed by the Nazi doctors and the activities of composition researchers. I want, instead, to focus on the positive legacy of the Nuremberg judges, whose ten-point code prompted a worldwide discussion of the ethical treatment of human participants in *any* research, even the most benign.

I begin with the *Belmont Report*. Of its three ethical principles, the most broadly relevant to composition research is Respect for Persons, which asserts that "individuals should be treated as autonomous agents" (4), whose freedom to deliberate about their own goals and act in accordance with their decisions must be protected unless their actions are clearly detrimental to others. This principle, the *Belmont Report* explains, means that investigators should involve others in their research only if these individuals have given their informed consent—that is, only if they freely volunteer to participate after being fully informed about the nature of the study and its possible consequences for them. In emphasizing "informed consent," the *Belmont Report* echoes the *Nuremberg Code*, whose first and cardinal tenet is that it is "absolutely essential" to obtain a person's informed consent before involving him or her as a research participant (*Trials* 181). The *Belmont Report's* other two principles are Beneficence (researchers should do nothing they know will harm participants and should strive to minimize the risk of harm to them) and Justice (among other things, researchers should avoid systematically recruiting participants from classes of people such as welfare patients and persons confined to institutions simply because they are easily available or readily manipulated).

In the federal regulation, these three principles are elaborated into procedures and lists of criteria to be applied when evaluating proposed research projects (Federal Policy). This evaluation is conducted by committees, called Institutional Review Boards (IRBs), that will approve the studies only if the researchers have met all of the regulation's requirements for the protection of research participants. If researchers were to conduct a study covered by the regulation but didn't submit it for IRB review or didn't follow all requirements stipulated by the IRB, they would place both themselves and their institutions at risk. The researchers and their institutions could both lose current federal research funds and eligibility for future funding.

It's important to note that the provisions of this regulation apply not only to research supported by federal agencies but also to much that is not. The regulation requires that before they can begin their first federally supported research project involving human participants, institutions must adopt an institutional policy that covers all human-participant research, even that not under federal sponsorship. Most colleges and universities adopt the federal policy as their institutional policy. From 1993 through 1995, the five journals named above (*CCC, CE, JAC, RTE,* and *WC*) published 84 articles describing formally planned quantitative and qualitative studies involving human participants. Of the 129 authors and co-authors, 118 identified affiliations with colleges and universities in the United States (a total of 108). All but three identified institutions that have an IRB or similar committee.[3]

How Composition Should Respond to the Federal Regulation

Although the federal regulation has applied for nearly 25 years to much of the qualitative and quantitative research conducted in composition, it still remains unknown to some in our field, including persons who undertake these very kinds of study. Some prominent composition researchers have told me that they were unaware that such a policy exists. Moreover, new members of our field are not necessarily being taught about it. Through an informal survey of several graduate programs in composition, I learned that some do not teach about the regulation, not even in their research methods courses. In all composition literature, I know of only one mention of the regulation—by myself, and in a book published within the past two years (Anderson).

Accordingly, as we formulate our agenda for addressing ethical issues in person-based research, I believe our first business should be to make the regulation more widely known. One obvious strategy would be to publicize it in our journals, perhaps in the advice to authors usually published in every issue. Another would be to urge all graduate programs to discuss the regulation with students. This would not only help students treat the participants in their graduate research ethically, but also enable them to avoid difficulties they could encounter in their careers if they were to proceed in ignorance of the regulation. At least twice in the last few years, speakers at CCCC have had to tell their audiences that they were unable to present their papers because they had, in ignorance, conducted studies without first obtaining IRB approval. When the IRBs learned this, they prohibited the presenters from disseminating the results. Circumstances like this add considerable urgency to our efforts to broadcast information about the regulation to graduate students and colleagues. Some IRBs grant approval to studies already begun if the researchers' reason for not obtaining approval was ignorance of the policy and if they immediately bring the studies into conformity with the regulation. By alerting researchers immediately of their obligations under the regulation we may help some who have unapproved studies underway to contact their IRBs in a timely fashion, perhaps preserving studies that could turn into lost work if we don't act quickly and determinedly.

In publicizing the regulation, we might emphasize that the federal Office for Protection from Research Risks (OPRR), which implements the regulation on behalf of the U.S. Department of Health and Human Services, has recently issued a directive changing the way the regulation is implemented at some colleges and universities.[4] Since 1981, certain kinds of studies have been exempted from its provisions. These include one type that is widely employed in composition: studies "conducted in established or commonly accepted educational settings, involving normal education practices" (Federal Policy 28012). Other exempted studies include certain kinds of survey and interview research. Some colleges and universities have long required researchers to submit for IRB review even studies they thought to be exempt (so that the IRB could certify the studies' qualification for exemption). However, other institutions have allowed researchers simply to bypass the IRB review process altogether if they felt their projects fell into an exempt category. But in May 1995, the Director of the Office for Protection from Research Risks instructed IRBs that they should no longer allow researchers to declare unilaterally that their own studies are exempt, so some composition researchers who previously (and correctly) thought that they did not need to obtain IRB approval for their studies must now do so. Although IRBs have been notified of this change, they may not have conveyed news of it to all individual researchers at their institutions.

In addition to publicizing the regulation, we might also consider moving (temperately) to the position that we will publish only studies in which the researchers have followed federal and institutional requirements for the protection of their research participants. In fact, NCTE has already taken a step toward a somewhat analogous position. In 1994, it began requiring

authors to obtain written agreement from research participants, and it had its
attorneys prepare permission forms that researchers may use for this purpose
if the researchers have not already obtained this permission using a form
approved at their own institutions. Unfortunately, the forms are at least partly
at odds with the federal regulation. One asks participants to grant permission
for NCTE to publish the results of a study in which they "participated"—
using the past tense. (See Appendix A.) This means that NCTE would
apparently be willing to publish research for which the participants gave
only retroactive permission, even though the federal policy requires *advance*
consent. NCTE's second form is designed for researchers to use to obtain
advance consent, but it contains the following statement: "I hereby
irrevocably consent to participate in this research study." (See Appendix B.)
Such a statement is contrary to the federal regulation, which insists that
research participants be free to withdraw from a study at any time and that
they must be told this in advance. Moreover, neither of the NCTE forms
could substitute for the written acknowledgment of informed consent
required by the federal regulation because the regulation stipulates that these
acknowledgments must contain many elements not present in the NCTE
forms. And even if the NCTE forms did precisely mirror the federal
requirements, they could not substitute for IRB review. Whatever protection
these forms may provide to NCTE from lawsuits by persons disgruntled by
the publication of studies in which they were involved, the forms do not
meet the federal regulation's standards for the protection of research
participants.

It would be more sensible for NCTE to require authors of formally
planned quantitative and qualitative studies to submit along with their
manuscripts a copy of the authorization they received from their Institutional
Review Boards or similar committees. Other composition publishers might
do the same. Researchers working at the small minority of institutions that
don't have IRBs or similar committees could substitute a letter affirming that
fact. In this way, NCTE and these other publications can assure themselves
that the research participants have been treated in compliance with the
federal regulation. If such a policy were adopted by NCTE and other
publishers, it could be prominently stated in the journals' instructions to
authors and prominently announced in multiple forums when first adopted.
It would be desirable that the policy be adopted jointly and simultaneously
by all publishers of composition research, including both professional
organizations like NCTE and independent publishers. We should also
consider adopting a similar policy for our professional meetings. We now tell

speakers at CCCC, for instance, not to bring us presentations that contain sexist and discriminatory language. It might be reasonable for us to be equally insistent that no one present the results of person-based research in which the researcher did not comply with the federal regulation for the protection of the research participants.

As we consider the possibility of adopting such policies, we should also consider how to address researchers who have, in good conscience, conducted studies without knowing that a federal or institutional policy applied to them. Their ignorance of the regulation is quite understandable. The regulation received its broadest publicity when it was originally being developed and debated in the early 1970s. At that time, composition was just beginning to explore the use of social science research methods, and the few compositionists involved would not have had occasion to read the journals where the debate over the regulation was being conducted. Also, publicity about the regulation has focused over the years on biomedical research, and knowledge of the regulation has been slow to spread throughout some fields using social science research methods. Anthropology is an example. Even though anthropology adopted its own statement on research ethics in the early 1970s, a major anthropological journal as recently as three years ago published an article intended to disseminate knowledge of the regulation more broadly in that field (Fluehr-Lobban). I feel particularly sympathetic to researchers who are just learning about the regulation. I became aware of it only several years ago, long after completing and publishing the results of a study that I should have checked with my own IRB.

My sympathy for researchers who don't yet know about the federal regulation, combined with my belief that our only responsible course of action as a discipline is to insist on compliance, leads me to believe that we should begin publicizing the regulation immediately and vigorously.

If we chose to emphasize compliance as I am suggesting, we might appear to be substituting blind adherence to a bureaucratically administered government policy for our own effort to develop ethical standards for our knowledge community. It's easy to imagine that we would frame our ethical principles at least somewhat differently than did the *Belmont Report* and that we would devise at least somewhat different means of enforcing them than are used by the federal regulation. Nevertheless, it seems to me that it would be highly undesirable for us to encourage composition researchers to ignore a federal regulation that is designed to protect the students, colleagues, family members, and other participants in the research that is conducted in

our collective name. Section 6.08 of the *APA Ethics Code* asserts that
"Psychologists plan and conduct research in a manner consistent with
federal and state law and regulations . . . particularly those standards
governing research with human participants" (American Psychological
Assoc. 1608). I am unable to imagine us taking a contrary position.
Moreover, adherence to the regulation scarcely obviates the need for
discussion of ethical issues in composition research. We still have much to
talk about, as I will demonstrate in the next sections of this article.

Beyond the Federal Regulation

Although the federal regulation provides important guidance in key areas of
research ethics, it doesn't specifically address some of the common concerns
that arise in our field. The same is true in other fields as well, of course. After
all, the regulation is framed to cover an extraordinary range of research
designs occurring in both biomedical science and social science. It could
not possibly address the "local" ethical questions that are peculiar to specific
research designs employed in particular disciplines. Other fields such as
psychology and sociology fill these gaps with their own disciplinary codes of
research ethics, something we might consider doing. Even if we don't create
such a code, however, we should at least begin discussing research ethics
more extensively than we have so that researchers can refer to our
conversation as they design their studies.

    As examples of issues we should address, I've chosen several involved
with the recruitment of research participants. In the *Nuremberg Code,*
Belmont Report, and the federal regulation, the core ethical principle
governing recruitment is informed consent. This complex principle involves
several concepts, all intended to ensure that people can freely decide
whether to volunteer after fully understanding what the research entails for
them. Prospective participants must be told, usually in writing, such things as
the purpose of the study, what they will be asked to do, any risks they might
encounter if they volunteer, and the length of time required. Prospective
participants must also be assured that if they decline to participate or decide
to withdraw after the study commences, they will not lose any rights or
benefits to which they would otherwise be entitled. To ensure that
prospective participants can consider this information freely and freely
decide whether to volunteer, the policy also requires that participants must
be able to deliberate about volunteering without any coercion or undue
influence.[5]

This last point has special relevance to much composition research. The *Belmont Report* and the federal regulation emphasize the need to protect persons who might appear to be volunteers but aren't truly because their circumstances exert an undue influence that diminishes their ability to deliberate freely. I first realized the danger of such undue influence when, as a conscientious objector during the Vietnam War, I investigated the experiences of COs during previous wars. I learned that many WWII COs volunteered for experiments conducted under the auspices of the US Office of Scientific Research and the Surgeon General's Office. For example, at the University of Chicago Medical School, Stanford, and Massachusetts General Hospital, COs allowed themselves to be infected with malaria so that doctors could experiment with medications that might substitute for quinine, which was in short supply because its sources were behind Japanese lines. In studies conducted by the University of Pennsylvania and Yale University to determine how hepatitis is transmitted and might be treated, groups of 30 to 60 COs allowed themselves to be inoculated with plasma thought to be infectious, drank contaminated water, and swallowed nose and throat washings and body wastes of infected patients (Keim 75–79).

I was (and still am) filled with admiration for the bravery of these men, who for the sake of conscience not only took a very unpopular course during an extremely popular war, but also placed their own health at jeopardy to advance medical knowledge. But I thought also about the circumstances under which they volunteered. Assigned to Civilian Public Service Camps, usually in rural areas distant from their homes, the COs worked under complete governmental control, most at manual labor. Although more than one-third had dependents, they received no pay—not even the 80 cents per day the Germans paid American prisoners of war (Keim 97). To what extent, I wondered, were these men exploited by researchers who felt confident that the COs, hoping for some change, some improvement in their situation, would volunteer for medical experiments much more readily than would the non-conscripted population in the cities that were home to these esteemed universities and research centers?

Reflecting a similar awareness that a person's circumstances may curtail his or her freedom to decide, the federal policy instructs IRBs to protect the rights and welfare of persons who might be especially vulnerable to coercion or undue influence when recruited for a study. Examples of such individuals, according to OPRR's *Guidebook* for IRB members, include prisoners, impoverished persons, and medical patients. The *Guidebook* also alerts IRB members that a possibly vulnerable population is the one most often recruited for composition research: students. Of the 84 formally planned, person-based studies that I examined, 76 (90 percent) involved students either as the sole participants or as one part of a larger group that also included teachers, parents, tutors, or other individuals. The number of students involved in a single study ranged from one (Prior) to 3,927 (Pritchard and Marshall).

In their codes of research ethics, both the American Psychological Association and the American Sociological Association specifically address the use of students as research participants. Because research in our field so frequently involves student participants, it would be appropriate for us to develop our own discourse to supplement the protections IRBs might offer and to supply guidance to researchers conducting studies that are exempt from the federal regulation. In fact, this is one area in which we in composition should be able to be especially perceptive and resourceful. In developing our pedagogical theory and practice, we have been very sensitive to ways the hierarchical relationship between teacher and students can operate to students' detriment. Numerous strategies have been suggested for decentering the classroom, democratizing it, and empowering students in a space where they traditionally have very little power. We should, I believe, explore with equal energy and creativity the ways the imbalance of power between teacher and student can create ethical problems when instructors, standing in front of their classes, request volunteers to participate in a research project they or their colleagues are conducting. We might, for example, weigh the value of urging composition researchers, where possible, to seek participants outside their own classrooms. Such a practice should not hinder our ability to study most issues of interest to us because we could answer the majority of our research questions about first-year composition, for instance, with the help of any of the hundreds or thousands of students taking that course at our institutions, not just those in our own sections. On the other hand, there are studies where it is crucial that the participants be a researcher's own students. Perhaps we could collectively construct guidelines for ethical research in these situations. For example, we might consider whether to suggest that the researcher collaborate with a colleague in a study design that prevents each from knowing which of his or her own students have volunteered. In this design, each researcher might recruit in the partner's classroom when the partner is not present, might interview students at a remote site so that the partner does not know who is being interviewed, and might postpone data sharing until the end of the term, after grades are turned in.

We might think also about what happens when a student desires to withdraw from participation. As mandated in the federal policy, an essential element of "informed consent" is the volunteer participant's right to withdraw from a study whenever she or he wishes, without suffering loss of any benefit to which he or she would otherwise have been entitled. Thus, students who initially volunteered for a study but subsequently desire to withdraw must be able to do so without asking permission or needing to give any explanation. And they need to be told this as part of the initial informed-consent procedure. However, it's easy to imagine students being reluctant to withdraw from a study conducted by their teacher for fear of losing favor with the person who will assign their grade at the end of the term—or they may be reluctant to disappoint a person with whom they have not only the relationship of participant-to-researcher but also that of student-to-teacher. Here, we might also consider recommending a practice observed by some historians working on oral history projects. Prior to an interview, these historians will go over the informed consent form with the person being interviewed. However, they won't ask the person to decide whether to sign the form until after the interview, in case the interviewee has said things that he or she decides, upon reflection, not to make public. We might consider the value of suggesting that researchers using their own students as participants request a confirming consent after the end of the term. Although the NCTE forms and the *CCC* policy, all of which seem to allow for retroactive informed consent, cannot substitute for prior review by an IRB, in modified form they could constitute a similar, post-study confirmation.

As this discussion of informed consent illustrates, some of the special features of person-based composition research raise ethical concerns that are not expressly addressed by the federal policy and may not be perceived by individual IRBs. Consequently, we cannot fulfill our ethical responsibilities as a discipline simply by notifying our colleagues about the federal policy and urging them to comply with it. Insofar as we are an ethically committed discipline, we must also explore these additional concerns to develop our own disciplinary understanding of what it means to treat the participants in our research ethically.

Privacy and Confidentiality of Information Obtained Outside of Formally Planned Studies

My remarks so far have focused on research that investigators plan in advance, deciding at least in a general way what their research questions will be, who they will ask to volunteer as research participants, what they will ask the participants to do, and so on. If the researchers include other people's unpublished words or personal information in these studies, they do so because they have gathered this material through investigative methods they planned before initiating their investigations. However, people's unpublished words and personal information often find their way into composition research by an alternative route.

In these instances, a researcher encounters someone's writing, hears someone speak, or otherwise gains information about a person in the course of the researcher's ordinary professional or personal life. Only after this encounter does the researcher realize its significance and incorporate something from it in a research project. The most familiar examples are those in which a composition specialist writes about a student he or she taught during a previous term or quotes a student paper or journal turned in as a regular assignment in a course that was not the subject of a formally planned research project. Because the federal policy applies only to formally planned research, it does not cover such situations. Yet here, too, ethical issues abound, most of which we have not, as a field, taken up. I will discuss two sets, treating them separately because they lend themselves to somewhat different (although overlapping) analyses. The first set of issues arises when researchers desire to include information about specific students that they have obtained outside formally planned research, and the second occurs when researchers wish to quote or paraphrase students' unpublished words encountered under the same circumstances.

Privacy and Confidentiality

What kinds of things and under what conditions can we report about someone else in our research? Such questions can be addressed from many perspectives, and the value of bringing these various perspectives to bear is one of the major reasons that a discipline-wide discussion of research ethics can be so worthwhile. As a way of starting the conversation, consider the issue from the standpoint of privacy, a central concern of the federal regulation and also of the Social Sciences and Humanities Research Council of Canada, which has its own policies for human-participant research. The Canadian Council says the following:

> The right to privacy extends to all information on a person's physi-
> cal and mental condition, personal circumstances and social rela-
> tionships which is not in the public domain. It gives to the individual
> or collective the freedom to decide when, where, and in what cir-

cumstances and to what extent their personal attitudes, opinions, habits, eccentricities, doubts and fears are to be published. (Canadian Council 4; see also Office for Protection from Research Risks 3–27)

If privacy is defined in this way, we can see that composition teachers often make excursions into the realm of the private. Sometimes we are invited there; in their papers and conferences with us, students sometimes spontaneously reveal things about themselves that they consider to be highly personal. Additionally, in many composition courses, teachers invite—and even expect—students to write and speak about their family backgrounds, experiences, beliefs, and other personal matters that the students might not choose to discuss with a teacher or a roomful of other students if they had not been directed to do so by a person with authority over them. Research ethics can make no judgment concerning the propriety of these instructional strategies, many of which seem to me to be fully justified on pedagogical grounds. However, when teachers change roles to become researchers who wish to incorporate the students' personal information in an article, book, conference paper, e-mail posting, or other communication addressed to people outside the classroom, then we need to consider the extent to which research ethics would require the teacher/researcher to treat the students' disclosures as confidential.

In this inquiry, we might begin with the definition of confidentiality provided in the OPRR *Guidebook*:

> Confidentiality pertains to the treatment of information that an individual has disclosed in a relationship of trust and with the expectation that it will not be divulged to others in ways that are inconsistent with the understanding of the original disclosure without permission. (Office for Protection from Research Risks 3–27; see also Canadian Council 5)

This definition decenters us as researchers from the ethical equation. Framed from the standpoint of the person making the disclosure—in our case, the student—it says that any assumptions we might make about our "right" to divulge personal information about our students don't matter. We can share information about students only if we have their permission or if the students communicated this information fully expecting that we might disclose it to other people. Although I have no empirical evidence on the matter, my tentative assumption is that students do not come to our classes and our offices with this expectation. If I'm correct and if we accept this line of ethical reasoning, we need the students' permission to quote their language (either written or spoken), no matter how difficult it might be to obtain.

Note, by the way, that the issue of privacy is quite distinct from questions of harm. Sometimes I have heard composition specialists argue that if a student won't be harmed, there can't be anything wrong with talking about the student's attitudes, opinions, habits, eccentricities, doubts, fears, or other personal attributes in conference papers and publications. To support their belief that the student couldn't be harmed by such disclosures, these compositionists adduce such things as their use of pseudonyms, their commitment to portraying the students respectfully, and the fact that neither the student nor anyone who knows the student is likely to read the article. When viewed from the ethical perspective of privacy, as defined by OPRR and the Canadian Council, these considerations are irrelevant. Even when no harm is imaginable, we cannot disseminate information students have shared within the student-teacher relationship unless we have their permission.

If we follow this line of ethical reasoning, we may want to consider extending the *CCC* policy on the use of unpublished writing. This policy requires researchers to obtain written permission from the authors—including students—of the unpublished material even if it will be cited anonymously (see Appendix C). *CCC* editor Joseph Harris has urged also that when researchers seek this permission from students, they show the students the passages in which the quotations would appear. This would enable the students to see not only what would be quoted but also how it would be discussed. In the spirit of the OPRR and Canadian constructions of privacy and confidentiality, we might also say that when researchers plan to discuss or describe individual students in any way, they ought to show the students what would be said about them so the students can judge for themselves whether their privacy has been violated.

At the beginning of this discussion of the ethical issues that arise when researchers wish to use information encountered outside of formally planned studies, I noted that these issues can be approached from many perspectives. To illustrate this point, consider an approach to privacy and confidentiality that differs substantially from the one described in the preceding paragraphs, which would prohibit researchers from creating any representation, no matter how complimentary, of a student (or anyone else) without that person's authorization. Like teachers, psychologists obtain much personal information in the normal course of their professional practice. Section 5.08 of the *APA Code of Ethics* allows psychologists to discuss this information in articles, professional presentations, and other places provided that they disguise the information so that the persons described are not identifiable to others and the discussions would not cause harm to persons who might identify themselves. The advantage of the APA approach is that it attempts to preserve confidentiality while also allowing professionals to share knowledge that could be important to both the theory and practice of psychology.

Were we to adopt such a standard, we would need to pay special attention to the opacity required for the disguise. The APA code requires that the person described not be recognizable to any other person. In many composition classes, this would be difficult to achieve because of the amount of information composition students come to possess about one another as a result of class discussion and peer review of drafts. Great care would be needed to ensure that no other class member who happened (as unlikely as this might be) upon the teacher/researcher's article could identify a student who is described without his or her permission. A commentary on the APA code suggests that psychologists might disguise cases by changing references to the sex, age, or ethnic background of the person, and that they might even meld features from various cases (Canter et al. 112). In some composition studies, however, such strategies would vitiate the worth of the description. Of course, following the APA model, a teacher/researcher could still present personal information about identifiable students, provided that the students have given written permission.

Although I hope that the preceding discussion of privacy and confidentiality might kindle a serious interest in these issues among composition researchers, I don't imagine that anything I've said might settle these matters. There are still other ways of thinking about this ethical question. Moreover, even if these two approaches discussed above are somehow woven together, they don't necessarily address all the important situations that could arise in our field. Consider, for instance, the status of a book like *Lives on the Boundary*, in which Mike Rose reports on his interactions over several decades with friends, teachers, and students in classes he's taken and classes he's taught. On the one hand, it would be difficult for him to contact some of these individuals for permission to portray them in the way that the first approach would require, and on the other hand it would be difficult for him to portray many of these individuals in the way that the APA principle requires. What sort of ethical principle could we devise that would address this sort of problem, or should future books like *Lives* be forbidden?

Ethics of Quoting Unpublished Writing—Copyright versus Consent

As a final example of issues in person-based research that we should address, I offer those intertwined with composition's long-standing tradition of quoting unpublished writing without permission. Most often, student texts are involved, sometimes being offered as evidence, sometimes as objects of analysis, sometimes as occasions for amusement. However, texts by faculty colleagues, university administrators, and other persons are also quoted without permission. Within the past five years, both NCTE and MLA have placed restrictions on the use of unpublished writing unless the researchers have obtained the writers' permission. However, these institutional actions have not completely settled the issue within our discipline. Other publishers of composition research have not adopted such policies and, indeed, both NCTE and MLA have received complaints from authors who believe they should not be required to obtain permission.[6] I want to discuss this issue briefly as a way of illustrating how the ethical framework of the federal regulation and of the *Belmont Report* can provide us with new ways of thinking about old issues in our field.

Published arguments concerning the practice of quoting unpublished writing without permission are rare. Over the years, however, I've heard many oral arguments on both sides. Regardless of their position, people usually justify their conclusion in legal terms, talking about copyright and property rights. Some argue that (morally if not also legally) students "own" their own writing and therefore must be asked for permission to quote it. Others maintain that when students submit their writing, they transfer ownership to their instructors. Some argue that the US copyright law permits use of unpublished work without permission provided that the amount reproduced falls within the act's definition of "fair use." Wishing to avoid restrictions on scholarship and taking the advice of its attorneys, NCTE adopted this position in 1994. That is, NCTE permits quotation without permission of brief excerpts from unpublished work by students and others, provided that publication of the material would not, in NCTE's judgment, violate the writer's privacy (Welshons). In deciding whether privacy might be violated, NCTE considers the nature of what the writer says in the quoted passage, not the nature of the student-teacher relationship. I've also heard composition researchers argue that the classroom is a public space so that what students write for a course is, in fact, "published" and therefore needs no special treatment that wouldn't be accorded a book or journal article. Among those opposing the application of a fair-use principle—at least with respect to student writing—is Joseph Harris, who contends that "we need to distinguish between citing the published work of a mature scholar and the semi-private writings of students, and for these reasons I believe student work should be quoted both anonymously and with permission" (440).

If we view the quotation of unpublished writing from the perspective of the *Belmont Report* and the federal regulation, we find that an alternative set of ethical principles could apply. These principles focus not on copyright but on consent. Consider the following situations. In the first, a composition instructor conducts a study in his or her own course after obtaining approval from the university IRB. Through the informed consent process, some students in the class have agreed to allow the instructor to use their writing as research data and to quote their writing in presentations and articles. Other students have decided not to participate, so the instructor is prohibited from including their work in the study in any way. The second situation involves the same students writing the same assignments in the same class, except that now the instructor has not made the course a subject of a formally planned study. Consequently, the instructor has obtained neither IRB approval nor the students' informed consent to use their writing in his or her research. However, the instructor keeps one paper for the purely pedagogical purpose of showing future students what a good response to a particular assignment looks like. After a few years, the instructor realizes that this paper provides a perfect illustration of a point the instructor wants to make in an article he or she is drafting. Despite diligent efforts, however, the instructor cannot locate the student author, who has graduated. Would it be ethical for the instructor to quote from the student's work without permission?

The federal policy does not apply to this situation because it pertains only to preplanned investigations. Nevertheless, its provisions can deepen our understanding of the ethical issues involved by suggesting two perspectives from which to consider the instructor's ethical obligations. The first perspective is that of the student whose work might be quoted. If the student would have declined to participate in a preplanned study, did he or she lose the right to decline to be involved in the instructor's research merely because the instructor hadn't planned to conduct a study during the semester the student took the class? Similarly, if the student would have consented to be a study participant, did the student lose the right to be asked for his or her consent? To put it another way, do the student's rights depend on what the instructor does or doesn't do?

The second perspective is that of the potential beneficiaries of the instructor's research project. Although the federal regulation would never allow the potential benefits of a study to justify enlisting someone as a research participant through coercion or the exercise of undue influence, it does instruct IRBs to take a cost-benefit approach when evaluating research proposals. Therefore, IRBs consider not only the perspectives of the potential participants but also of the potential beneficiaries of a proposed study. In the case of the writing instructor described above, these beneficiaries would be the future composition students who might enjoy better teaching because their teachers had read the instructor's article. Should these future students be deprived of this improved instruction simply because the instructor's insights weren't prompted in a class for which the instructor had planned a formal study? Is there some way for us to balance our ethical obligations to future students with our ethical obligations to students from the past? Could we distinguish circumstances under which it is ethical to quote unpublished writing from those in which it isn't?

To assure that they will be able to quote from student work that is submitted during courses that are not the subject of formally planned, IRB-approved research studies, some instructors ask students at the beginning of a course to sign forms allowing quotation from any work they produce during the term. From the "copyright" perspective, they may be doing nothing more questionable than what publishing houses do when they ask authors to sign a contract that gives the houses the copyright to as-yet unwritten work. However, the ethical framework of the *Belmont Report* and the federal regulation suggests that we should examine whether this practice involves an ethically doubtful situation in which the powerful teacher is making a request of less powerful students at a time when the students might be particularly eager to please. If so, would it be sufficient ethically for the instructor to use one or more of the strategies mentioned earlier, such as having someone other than the instructor request the permission, keeping the identities of those who granted permission confidential until the end of the term, and giving students a chance to confirm or withdraw their permission at the end of the term? Or does the instructor's systematic gathering of permissions mean that the researcher is actually engaged in a formally planned study requiring IRB approval?

As this brief discussion makes clear, thinking about quotation of student writing gathered outside a formally planned research project in terms of consent rather than copyright doesn't necessarily answer our ethical questions, but it does offer us new perspectives for considering them, ones that can enrich our understanding of the issues involved and increase the range of ethical principles from which we can build our own disciplinary position about it.

Where to Go from Here?

Composition theory and practice are built largely on knowledge created through various forms of person-based research. Our understanding of the writing process, collaboration, peer reviewing, student responses to our comments on their papers, and the impact of power and gender in the classroom—to name but a few of our many concerns—is richly informed by the results of quantitative and qualitative studies. Likewise, we have gained many insights about our students, our courses, and ourselves from articles and books in which the researchers report other people's attitudes, actions, and ideas that the researchers have learned about outside the context of formally planned research. And we have benefited from sharing with one another the unpublished writing and spoken words of other persons, particularly our students. We should recognize that we enter into ethically significant human relationships with these individuals not only when we involve them in some way in our own projects, but also when we read someone else's work to which they have contributed, wittingly and willingly or not.

Through this essay, I hope that I have persuaded you that, as a discipline, we ought to become much more reflective about the ethical dimensions of these relationships. However, I'm unsure what our next steps should be. The only point on which I'm certain is that we should take collective responsibility for increasing awareness of and compliance with federal and institutional policies designed to protect the participants in formally planned research. At the least, we should urge all graduate programs that prepare students to become contributing researchers in composition to educate about these policies. Also, the NCTE and MLA policies requiring researchers to obtain permission from research participants should be reframed so they are consistent with the federal policy, and other journals should consider formulating such policies as well.

However, many important ethical issues are not covered by the federal policy. The ones I've discussed in this essay are but a few representatives of a much larger group. How can we most effectively foster a discussion of these concerns? What role should our professional organizations play in leading it? What light can be shed on these issues by other discourses in our profession, such as the one on intellectual property rights? To what extent should we consult discussions of research ethics in other fields? I don't know the answers to these questions. Nor do I know what kind of outcome we should strive for, whether it's the creation of a code of research ethics for composition or simply a robust literature on the subject that individual researchers can draw on as they confront the ethical dilemmas involved with their particular studies.

I do, however, have one point to urge. In discussing research ethics, it's easy to become focused on principles and standards in a way that seems to ask, "What can we, in good conscience, take from other people?" We should remember, instead, that in person-based research we are the recipients of gifts. The volunteers in our formal studies hand us the gift of their time and cooperation. The persons whose unpublished words we quote have shared their experiences, ideas, and feelings with us. In comparison with the discomforts and dangers that participants in some biomedical research volunteer to endure, these are very simple gifts. But they are not trivial. No matter how we proceed in our discussion of research ethics, no matter what outcome we devise, let it be our goal to assure that both individually and as a discipline we treat these gifts—and their givers—justly, respectfully, and gratefully.

Appendix A: NCTE Form

Consent to Publication of Results of Research Study

_____ hereby states and agrees as follows:
                    (Name of Subject)

1. On or about _____ to _____
                              (Dates of research study)

I participated in a research study conducted by
_____ of _____
        (Name of Researcher)   (Name of Institution)

2. I understand that the results of this research study may be included in a manuscript which may be submitted for publication to the National Council of Teachers of English (hereinafter "NCTE") and that any such manuscript may also include all or some portion of my work, including writings and drawings, which I may have created or submitted as part of this research study.

3. I hereby consent to the publication by NCTE of any manuscript which describes or reports the results of this research study and I hereby grant and assign to NCTE all right, title, and interest, including copyright, which I may have in any such manuscript and in any of my works which may be included therein.

4. I understand and agree that I shall not be entitled to receive any royalty or any other compensation, from either the Researcher or NCTE, for my participation in the research study or for the use or publication of the manuscript or any of my works which may be included therein.

[CHOOSE ONE OF THE FOLLOWING:]

❏ 5. I was informed and understand that my identity will not be disclosed in any manuscript describing this research study or the results thereof and that a pseudonym may be used for me or to credit any of my work which may be included therein.

[OR]

❏ 5. I hereby consent to the use of my name in any manuscript describing this research study or the results thereof and to the use of my likeness in any photograph which may be included therein. I understand that I will receive credit by name for any of my work which may be included in any such manuscript. I further consent to the use of my name and likeness in any material used to promote the published work.

Signature: _____

Name: _____
                              (Please Print)

Address: _____

_____

Date Signed: _____

Appendix B: NCTE Form

Consent to Participate in Research Study and to Publication of Results

_____ hereby states and agrees as follows:
        (Name of subject)

1. I was informed and understand that _____
                                                    (Name of researcher)

of _____
                              (Name of institution)

is or will be conducting a research study briefly described as follows:

_____

_____

_____

_____

2. I have been asked to participate as a subject in this research study. I was informed and understand that my participation will consist of the following:

_____

_____

_____

_____

3. I was informed and understand that the results of this research study may be included in a manuscript which may be submitted for publication to the National Council of Teachers of English (hereinafter "NCTE") and that any such manuscript may also include all or some portion of my work, including writings and drawings, which I may have created or submitted as part of this research study.

4. I hereby irrevocably consent to participate in this research study. I further irrevocably consent to the publication by NCTE of any manuscript which describes or reports the results of this research study and I hereby grant and assign to NCTE all right, title, and interest, including copyright, which I may have in any such manuscript and in any of my works which may be included therein.

5. I understand and agree that I shall not be entitled to receive any royalty or any other compensation, from either the Researcher or NCTE, for my participation in the research study or for the use or publication of the manuscript or any of my works which may be included therein.

[CHOOSE ONE OF THE FOLLOWING:]

❑ 6. I was informed and understand that my identity will not be disclosed in any manuscript describing this research study or the results thereof and that a pseudonym may be used for me or to credit any of my work which may be included therein.

[OR]

❑ 6. I hereby consent to the use of my name in any manuscript describing this research study or the results thereof and to the use of my likeness in any photograph which may be included therein. I understand that I will receive credit by name for any of my work which may be included in any such manuscript. I further consent to the use of my name and likeness in any material used to promote the published work.

Signature: _____

Name: _____

(Please Print)

Address: _____

_____

_____

Date Signed: _____

[IF THE SUBJECT OF THE RESEARCH STUDY IS A MINOR,
ADD THE FOLLOWING:]

I am the parent or guardian of the above-named minor. I hereby irrevocably consent to the minor's participation in this research study and to the publication by NCTE of any manuscript which describes or reports the results of this research study upon all of the terms and conditions set forth herein.

Signature: _____

Name: _____

(Please Print)

Address: _____

_____

_____

Date Signed: _____

Appendix C: CCC Form

Permission Request

So that journals published by the National Council of Teachers of English can be protected by copyright against unauthorized use, it is necessary that consent to publish be obtained from persons who contribute to this work. This form gives such consent. Please sign and return this copy to the journal's editor. You may wish to keep a photocopy for your records.

I, _____ , consent to have my (writing/illustration) from

_____

used in an article entitled_____

by _____ to be

published by NCTE in their publication_____

I understand that I will receive no compensation. I hereby assign publishing rights for the contribution to NCTE, including all copyrights.

Name: _____

Address: _____

_____

_____

Phone: _____

Signature: _____
(if under 18, parent or guardian must sign)

Date Signed: _____

*Please find attached a copy of the material to be used.

Notes

1. Readers curious about the details of the tabulations reported throughout this article may obtain copies from me.

2. NCTE developed its current policy in the early 1990s when it reviewed and revised all its legal forms related to publishing in accordance with advice from legal counsel. MLA instituted this policy as it began publishing articles with this type of content. Details concerning the application of the NCTE and MLA policies are available from these organizations.

3. I learned which colleges and universities have IRBs or similar committees by using printouts of institutions that had Multiple Project Assurances or Single Projects Assurances on file with OPRR as of March 1, 1996 (all would have IRBs) and by calling the institutions not on the OPRR lists.

4. The Office for Protection from Research Risks' web site is http://www.nih.gov:80/grants/oprr/oprr.htm. The office also provides information by fax: (301) 594-0464.

5. Throughout this article, I am assuming that the potential research participants are adults. If they are minors, the federal regulation requires both parental permission and, if feasible, the child's assent to participation.

6. This information comes from telephone interviews with Phyllis Franklin, Executive Director of the MLA, Sandra Stotsky, editor of *RTE*, and Marlo Welshons, Managing Editor for Journals at NCTE.

Acknowledgments

I wish to thank two Miami colleagues who gently provided valuable advice as I was drafting this article: Susan Jarratt and Jean Lutz. I also thank *CCC* reviewers Davida Charney and Gregory Clark for their helpful suggestions. In addition, I am grateful to Marjorie McClellen, a member of Miami's history department who told me about the practices of oral historians.

Works Cited

American Anthropological Association. *Professional Ethics: Statements and Procedures of the American Anthropological Association.* Washington: AAA, 1973.

American Educational Research Association. "Ethical Standards of the American Educational Research Association." *Educational Researcher* 21.3 (1992): 23–26.

American Psychological Association. "Ethical Principles of Psychologists and Code of Conduct." *American Psychologist* 47 (1992): 1597–1611.

American Sociological Association. *Code of Ethics.* Washington: ASA, 1971.

Anderson, Paul V. "Ethics, Institutional Review Boards and the Use of Human Subjects in Composition Research." Kirsch and Mortenson 260–85.

Canter, Mathilda B., Bruce B. Bennett, Stanley E. Jones, and Thomas F. Nagy. *Ethics for Psychologists: A Commentary on the APA Ethics Code.* Washington: APA, 1994.

Ellis, Gary B. "Research Activities that May Be Reviewed Through Expedited Review." *OPRR Reports* 95-02. 5 May 1995.

"Federal Policy for the Protection of Human Subjects." *Federal Register* 56 (1991): 28003–32.

Fluehr-Lobban, Carolyn. "Informed Consent in Anthropological Research: We are Not Exempt." *Human Organization* 53 (1994): 1–10.

Franklin, Phyllis. Telephone interview. 3 July 1996 and 14 July 1997.

Harris, Joseph. "From the Editor: The Work of Others." *CCC* 45 (1994): 439–41.

Helmers, Marguerite H. *Writing Students: Composition Testimonials and Representations of Students.* Albany: State University of New York P, 1994.

Keim, Albert N. *The CPS Story.* Intercourse, PA: Good Books, 1990.

Kirsch, Gesa, and Peter Mortenson, eds. *Ethics and Representation in Qualitative Studies of Literacy.* Urbana: NCTE, 1996.

Kirsch, Gesa, and Patricia Sullivan. *Methods and Methodology in Composition Research.* Carbondale: Southern Illinois UP, 1992.

Lauer, Janice M. and J. William Asher. *Composition Research: Empirical Designs.* New York: Oxford UP, 1988.

Modern Language Association. "Statement of Professional Ethics." *Profession* (1992): 75–8.

National Commission for the Protection of Human Subjects of Biomedical and Behavioral Research. *The Belmont Report: Ethical Principles and Guidelines for the Protection of Human Subjects of Research.* Washington: US Department of Health and Human Services, 1979.

National Council of Teachers of English. "Consent to Participate in Research Study and To Publication of Results." Two-page form. Urbana: NCTE, no date.

———. "Consent to Publication of Results of Research Study." One-page form. Urbana: NCTE, no date.

National Public Radio. "Informed Consent and Nuremberg." Narr, Linda Werthheimer. *All Things Considered.* 9 December 1996.

Ohman, Richard. *English in America.* New York: Oxford, 1976.

Prior, Paul. "Tracing Authoritative and Internally Persuasive Discourses: A Case Study of Response, Revision, and Disciplinary Enculturation." *RTE* 29 (1995): 288–325.

Pritchard, Ruie Jane, and Jon C. Marshall. "Evaluation of a Tiered Model for Staff Development in Writing." *RTE* 28 (1994): 259–85.

Rose, Mike. *Lives on the Boundary.* New York: Free Press, 1989.

Shaughnessy, Mina P. *Errors and Expectations.* New York: Oxford UP, 1977.

Shor, Ira. *Critical Teaching and Everyday Life*. Chicago: U of Chicago P, 1980.

Social Sciences Research Council and Humanities Research Council of Canada. *Ethics: Guidelines for Research with Human Subjects*. Ottawa: SSHRCC, no date.

Stotsky, Sandra. "From the Editor." *RTE* 27 (1993): 132.

———. "Language Research Policies." *Encyclopedia of English Studies and Language Arts*. Ed. Alan Purves. Urbana: NCTE, 1994. 711–13.

———. Telephone interview. 21 March 1996.

United States Office for Protection from Research Risks. *Protecting Human Research Subjects: Institutional Review Board Guidebook*. Washington: GPO, 1993.

United States. *Trials of War Criminals before the Nuremberg Tribunals under Control Council Law No. 10*. Vol 2. Washington: GPO, 1949. 181–82.

Welshons, Marlo, Telephone interview. 28 July 1997.

7 The Ethics of Teaching Literature

Wayne C. Booth

Many teachers these days mistrust words like "ethical" and "literature,"
because they suggest a naïve return to old-fashioned questions and methods
that they consider by now utterly refuted. The mistrust is understandable
when we consider some of the extremer defenses of "traditional values,"
with their narrow definitions of literature: the many polarizing D'Souza-ist
and Himmelfarbian sermons attacking all postmodernist movements in the
name of traditional values and this or that canon.

Because of my persistent efforts, continuing here, to get all sides in current disputes to *listen* to the enemy, I have been accused by some of being
a Pomo, by others of being a Trad, and by some of being merely a cow-
ardly fence straddler. Easy labels fit hardly anyone. And what both defend-
ers and enemies of postmodernism too often ignore is a reassuring fact
underlying the vocabulary differences. Most of those now labeled "Pomos"
turn out, when you look at their work closely, to care as much about the
ethical or moral effects of literature and the teaching of literature as do the
"Trads." When we follow their lead in expanding the domain of literature
to include the whole world of "story," ranging from the ancient classics to
yesterday's soap opera, and when we then do a bit of deconstructing of
our other vocabulary differences, we find assertions about ethics and character, justice, responsibility, faith, hope and charity all over the Pomo
scene. In Jacques Derrida's recent work, for example, we find impressive
moral exhortation at almost every point: about justice, about responsibility,
about "Teaching and Learning to Give" (see his *The Gift of Death*).

Closer to home, a number of teachers of literature and composition at
colleges and universities have shown that they care intensely about ethical

Reprinted from *College English,* September 1998.

issues, although they express themselves in the language of postmodernism rather than that of traditional ethics. In last December's *College English,* for instance, there is Lee Ann Carroll's "Pomo Blues: Stories from First-Year Composition." The essay that will serve as my central example is by Elizabeth Anne Leonard, in the May 1997 issue of *CCC.* A PhD candidate, author, and teacher of writing, Leonard avoids traditional ethical language, even as she explores the ethical problem of how a responsible teacher can construct a self for herself that will in turn help students construct selves of the kind she hopes for:

> How can I teach [my students] to see themselves as constructed and yet not let the construction get in the way when the Muse knocks? How . . . can I encourage them to interrogate the academy and its power structures and simultaneously enjoy the experience of becoming a creator, a thinker? . . . *[I]f I'm changing students, how do I change them in ways that I feel are most useful to them? (222;* emphasis added)

Though some definitions of the word "useful" might raise problems here, is it not obvious that Leonard's project shares everything except vocabulary with many a Trad ethicist who wants teachers to build character? I might even call hers a moral project, if that word had not been corrupted to the point of suggesting some moral-*istic* project in the service of fixed rules.

The word "ethical" can perhaps shift us from judgments about specific commandments or codes toward joining Leonard's concern for the construction of a certain kind of person. Ethical thinking at its best has always pursued not literal "thou shalt nots" but a range of "virtues," characteristic habits of behavior considered admirable. Traditionally the virtues included every capacity or strength or competency or habit of mind and heart that the practicer, the self, the character (or his or her critic), could admire—or at least could bear to live with. A virtue was any excellence *(areté)* that could be praised, whether the successful navigation of a ship or throwing of a discus or raising of a family. (For the most influential work reviving the traditional sense of virtue as personal excellence, see Alasdair MacIntyre's *After Virtue;* the most challenging revival of ethical inquiry into the whole domain of "the self" is Charles Taylor's *Sources of the Self.*) Virtues in that broad sense obviously do include many of William Bennett's Sunday School list, but no list like his would ever include the striking virtue Leonard practices in constructing a challenging essay, or in thinking about how to create better "selves."

Throughout the history of thought about the virtues there has of course been controversy about whether this or that *virtù is* really a vice, or even—as in some Renaissance texts—merely an expression of taste. But what has not changed is that most ethical debaters, even among aggressive Pomos, have shared Leonard's implicit assumption that some people practicing one set of virtues are genuinely superior to some other people who may practice certain other virtues but lack some of the essentials. I cannot, for example, think of a single postmodernist who does not condemn, as ethically debased, all those who treat the "other" as enemy or as beneath contempt.

Through most of this history, debaters have recognized that no one Sunday School list of the essentials will work, when applied without relying on what came to be called casuistry—a much-maligned term for the necessity of weighing virtues against each other and making choices among them. (For a good introduction to casuistry, see Jonsen and Toulmin; for a deeper probing, with special reference to the Romantic period, see Chandler.) Ethical thought about truth-telling, for example, leads not to an absolute rule, "Thou shalt never under any circumstances lie, no matter how much harm the truth might produce" but rather "Try to become a kind of person, the kind who can think through why lying is generally bad but sometimes required in the service of other and often higher causes."

My first claim, then, is that the traditional ethical goal of building *character* can be harmonized with Leonard's effort to build *selves*—persons with a genuinely admirable, or "useful," ethical center. Although she avoids the words "ethics," "ethos," "morality," and "character," and although she never uses the word "literature," she obviously teaches literature, in my broad definition—the·world of story—and in doing so she hopes to produce results of the kind we all *ought* to hope for. Note that as an ethicist, I have a right to italicize that word "ought," one that is used by an astonishing number of writers who claim that there are no firm moral or ethical principles.

This claim obviously depends on a strong sub-claim, one that in itself is an ethical proclamation: the gaps and battles between pre-modern and modern and postmodern and post-postmodern are themselves the kinds of social constructs that can prove unethical, producing fake battles that we all *ought* to avoid.

Ethical Teaching and Its Opponents

What worries me far more than the ever-shifting misunderstandings over the terms for ethical criticism is the widespread neglect of the concern at the heart of Leonard's essay: how to *teach* ethical reading and writing—how "English," whatever we call it, can "change students in ways that are most useful to them." In the early decades of this century many books and articles, often influenced by John Dewey, talked openly about the goal of teaching as the building of character (see especially Dewey's *Democracy and Education*). But Dewey's complex case for ethical teaching quickly became caricatured with the slogan "teach the child, not the subject," as if working for the desired kind of child meant ignoring the value of learning skills and content. For reasons that I suspect nobody will ever fully explain, the words "moral" and "character" were banned from much of the academic scene in the fifties and sixties. Though of course they survived in religious writing, particularly of right-wingers, in "English" and other humanities departments they were pretty much abandoned. Only now do they seem to be coming back, and the return is still hotly contested by many. (See for example the "Symposium" on the teaching of morality in college courses, "Is Morality a Non-Aim of Education?" edited by Patrick White in *Philosophy and Literature,* in which seven of us "ethicists" try to persuade a professor of political science that all colleges should, and the better colleges actually do, teach ethics.)

As readers here will have long since inferred, my main hope is to strengthen that rebirth. It is not just that I'd like to see words like *ethical, character,* and *virtue* rescued from the dominance of the right-wingers who identify every Pomo movement with evil and decay. Much more important is the hope for a deeper kind of thinking about what any ethical teacher should work for in the classroom, regardless of whether the language is Trad or Pomo. We should seek selves for ourselves as teachers that, in Leonard's words, will change students in ways that we are sure are most useful to *them.*

(As I mentioned earlier, the word "useful" is itself deeply ambiguous. As a "pragmatic pluralist" who considers William James almost a saint, I do cringe when he succumbs to the phrase "cash value" to cover usefulness. When the useful is reduced to the free-market kind of utilitarianism, I go beyond cringing to passionate refutation. So did John Stuart Mill; throughout much of his later work he insisted that for Utilitarianism to work, it depended on the dominant presence of "men of noble character"—human beings judging the "useful" in genuinely ethical terms. See his chapter "Infirmities and Dangers" in *Utilitarianism.)*

I find it distressing that even the Pomos I admire join too many of the Trads in failing to talk about how to *teach* literature ethically. Recently I was invited to attend a conference in Wales on "Literature and Ethics"

(Aberystwyth, 4–7 July 1996; organized by Dominic Rainsford, with Andrew Hadfield and Tim Woods). I couldn't attend but I received abstracts of seventy-two papers. Many of them did address my first problem directly: they actually were working to harmonize the traditional language of ethics and the language of postmodernism, thus underlining my sense that ethical language is undergoing revival. But only one, only *one* paper out of seventy-two, even mentioned teaching or pedagogy or any of the problems connected with getting students to think about such matters.

Now I have no doubt that many of those three-score-and-eleven literary critics actually care a lot about teaching, and about the ethical effects of teaching this or that kind of story in this or that way. They just didn't bother to mention it, at least in their abstracts. . . .

As I labored to complete that paragraph, I suddenly wondered, "How often did I myself mention teaching in my own major ethical effort, *The Company We Keep?* So I checked, and found less than a page, out of 500 pages! While it's true that the whole book implies opinions about how we should teach, the least I could have done would have been to provide a full chapter explicitly developing the points I make on that one page.

That lone pedagogical anecdote went like this:

Our colleague on the University of Chicago College Humanities staff, Paul Moses, was an African American art historian. After being required, by staff decision, to teach *Huck Finn* year after year, he finally objected, as we worked together constructing the next year's list. His claim was that the book did harm to both his black and his white students. In other words, words that I'm sure he did not use: the book itself was bad ethical education. We fellow teachers on the staff thought that his objection violated everything we had been taught about the proper separation of genuine aesthetics—a concern for form and beauty and structure—and "didactic" matters:

> Our lengthy, heated, and confused debates with [him] never . . . honored his claim that teachers should concern themselves with what a novel might *do* to a student. . . . We had been trained to treat a "poem *as* poem and not another thing" and to believe that the value of a great work of fiction was something much subtler than any idea or proposition derived from it or used to paraphrase its "meaning." We knew that sophisticated critics never judge a fiction by any effect it might have on readers. And sophisticated teachers do not ask whether the works that they teach might harm students. "Poetry makes nothing happen" [Auden's famous line], we were fond of quoting to each other. . . . To have attended to Paul Moses's complaint would have been to commit—in the jargon of the time—the "affective fallacy."

> Paradoxically, none of this interfered with our shared conviction
> that *good literature in general* was somehow as vital to the lives of
> our students as it was to us. To turn them into "readers," and to get
> them to read the good stuff, was our mission. (4)

I would want to word that mission slightly differently now, stressing more
strongly—as in fact the book later does—better and worse ways of reading
and of teaching others to read. In any case, we were tacitly ethical critics,
while openly repudiating that role.

What I hope we *all* hope for is that more teachers will devote themselves
to the pursuit of some version of the ethical aims of education. Whether we
think of ourselves as Trads or Pomos, whatever our official specialty is called
(English, composition, writing, reading, speech, textual analysis, creativity,
linguistics, gender studies, racial issues, cultural critique, new historicism),
and whatever we think about the acceptability of a long sentence like this
one, let us join Leonard and *think* about the ethical aims of education: *what
kind of person pursuing what kind of ideas and practices and social
improvements do we hope to see emerging from our labors?* To paraphrase
Leonard's phrasing once more, what ethical improvements *in ourselves*
should we seek, in or out of the world of story, that will help our students
create selves most useful to them —useful not just in the utilitarian sense but
in the sense of yielding an ultimately rewarding life, working for an
ultimately rewarding and defensible society?

When we think of the aims of education in that broad sense, we're faced
with many opponents besides those I've already hinted at; some of them use
vocabulary that makes them sound as if they might be on our side.

Perhaps most prominent these days is what we might call the "Content
and Commandments Crowd": those who think that the way to improve
English education is to force teachers and students to work toward specific
pre-determined examination results on a statewide or national scale. When
President Clinton touts national standards, he talks as if he is the most
virtuous, most ethical pursuer of educational excellence in the world. Yet he
never really addresses the question of what kind of person or character or
self will be produced by the imposition of such rote standards.

Not long ago I heard a lively speech by the director of Chicago's school
reform/renovation/revival/resurrection project, Paul Vallas. It was absolutely
confined to how to raise scores on tests. In the question period a woman
asked him what kind of *person* his revolutionary efforts are designed to
produce; his answer was unhesitating: "The kind who can score higher on
those tests." *My* thought was: that means the kind who, the moment they

find out that I am a teacher of English, grimace and say, "Oh, I gotta watch my grammar!"

Now it's true that in Chicago, in this new program that puts low-scoring schools and teachers on probation, some scores have gone up a bit—but only in science and math. They've actually gone on falling in reading and writing and grammar and spelling. Is that surprising? Is it surprising that if teachers are driven to drill in vocabulary and grammar the scores in vocabulary and grammar continue to go down? What kind of student scores high in vocabulary? Obviously it's someone who has learned to love reading and writing and has thus learned hundreds of new words each week rather than reluctantly memorizing a short list imposed by a teacher obeying a principal who is obeying some external committee that is obeying the governor who is obeying President Clinton who is of course obeying God.

Who are the students who score high in grammar? Well, that depends on whether what you test is mere terminology for grammar, or actual usage. The ones who learn to use *effective* grammar are the ones who have learned to love reading and writing and speaking, at more and more complex levels. It's true that somewhere down the line, once students have become genuinely motivated, serious study of grammatical history and terminology can become not just interesting but fun. But if like me you were taught rote grammar mainly by teachers who were bored by it, you know just how deadly that can be. In my junior year in high school a fine first-year teacher who stressed engaged reading and writing left me determined to become an English teacher; I wanted to become someone like her. Then in my senior year I fell under a pious drillmaster in English-as-names-and-dates-and-grammatical-rules, and quickly changed my career to chemistry, where things could at least be interesting! Only in college, where my English teachers taught English as inquiry and my science teachers taught science as rote did I quickly change back.

Do the Content-and-Commandments Crowd really think that our dropout rate is caused by students not being taught this or that content? Students drop out mainly because they have learned that the classroom is not for them: boring, dull, empty of personal relevance, alien, "somebody else's idea of how to live, not mine."

What is especially troublesome about the over-emphasis on content or mechanical skills is that the "idea of how to live" that it conveys is utterly futuristic: "The point of learning today is to prepare for something tomorrow." Fourth graders must learn what they'll need in the fifth grade, whether they hate it or not; high school sophomores must memorize details about such-and-such a deadened classic, whether the teacher loves it or not, to prepare them for the junior year. The goal of the senior year is not to have a glorious, exciting year but to prepare for college admission, or to ensure that when some firm hires a graduate, she'll be a good speller, or will never say "between him and I," or will never, like Leonard in her title, use "which" when the rule books and grammar checks would require "that."

Obviously it's misleading to say that we want students who simply love us English teachers and our interpretations of a subject or text, though for many such emulation will be a useful first step. As Leonard's article implies, to seek emulation lands us in a paradox: We hope to produce a kind of person, and we don't want to be authoritarian about it, and yet we often realize, with some uneasiness about our arrogance, that the kind of person we want them to become is the same kind that we want to become—and want them to see us as already having achieved. Intentionally or not, every successful teacher is likely to impose an image of what an admirable person is, and that person then gets imitated. I remember how some of my fellow graduate students took up pipe-smoking after they'd fallen under the influence of Ronald Crane—holding their pipes with precisely his gestures. Far more of us took up his intellectual and pedagogical habits (virtues), many of them admirable but some now to me questionable.

That paradox and the controversies it generates are too often ignored by morally committed teachers. On the one side of the ethical crowd, too many moralists attempt to impose a mechanical code, like the ten commandments, or the twelve virtues of the Boy Scout oath I once chanted, or Stephen Covey's *Seven Habits of Highly Effective People.* (This simplistic book, translated into twenty-eight languages, has sold over ten million copies. For an excellent exposé of the dangers in such coding, see Wolfe.) It all comes down to "commands" like: our schools should produce students who don't cheat or steal or kill, students who honor their fathers and mothers, who stay off drugs and handle their sexual desires responsibly. Why? Too often the implied answer is: so they can succeed in the marketplace. Some virtue-touters never worry about whether students are motivated toward further learning: we should be training them to be "good citizens," which too often means those who will stay off welfare and passively accept low-paying jobs.

At the opposite extreme, a fair number of anti-conservatives, traveling under various names, put their commandments in equally routine unthought-through terms: liberation, creativity, empowerment, even rebellion. Always fight back, resist all institutional demands, wear a beard or hair-do or earring like mine. Some on the left implicitly lead students to drop out by spreading the notion that schools always and inevitably implant conventional or reactionary values that are not at all cool. So while the "content" buffs moan about ignorance of grammar or violation of codes, the conservative ethical crowd too often wastes time moaning about lack of courtesy or civility, or failure to implant work incentives. And meanwhile some of the self-and-social-construction crowd moan about our failure to produce revolutionaries.

It is not surprising that such differences produce the kind of controversy that might make us want to retreat into mere talk about verbal skills and vocabulary lists. Any one picture of ethical norms advocated aggressively by any one faction will seem offensive to other factions—a fact that leads some neutralists to extend the separation of church and state to separating moral and ethical talk from public schools. Do I want my child taught by someone who aggressively teaches that all abortion is wrong, or that no abortion is wrong? Do I want my child taught by someone who aggressively teaches that all ethical norms are merely socially constructed, and the goal of education is to show that they have no ultimate validity, or on the other hand that nobody who talks about our being socially constructed should be listened to? Of course I do not, so let's just keep all such stuff out of the classroom?

Why English Teachers, If They Teach Stories Ethically, Are More Important to Society than Even the Best Teachers of Latin or Calculus or History

Where does all this leave us, back in the classroom, suspicious of code-teaching, aware of ethical ambiguities, but committed to the ethical goal of producing students who are themselves committed to pursuing defensible values? Fortunately, there is one really effective answer to that tough question—an old answer, even a cliched answer, a *tired* answer but still the right answer: get them engaged with the world of story (including "literature" in the old sense) and teach them to deal critically with that engagement. Entice them not only into loving this or that book or fixed list but into loving *both* the seductions of story and the fun of criticizing those seductions.

To teach reading (or viewing or listening) that is both engaged and actively critical is central because it is in stories, in narratives large and small rather than in coded commandments, that students absorb lessons in how to confront ethical complexity. It is in dealing with narrative conflicts that they imbibe the skills required when our real values, values that are not *merely* social constructs, clash. To put the point again in jargon that I would never use with any but the most advanced students, literature teaches effective casuistry: the counterbalancing of "cases." It is in stories that we learn to think about the "virtual" cases that echo the cases we will meet when we return to the more disorderly, "actual" world.

Obviously no one story or list of stories will produce good ethical effects on every student. Many of our finest stories—Genesis, *Middlemarch, Absalom, Absalom!,* name your favorite—can have destructive effects when read uncritically; on the other hand, stories that the teacher detests, for whatever reason, can be taught in ways that hook students into the complex enterprise I'm probing here. The whole business boils down to teaching students how to read ethically—not just feeding them powerful narratives that have some chance of getting through to them at a given level but finding ways to teach them what might be called ethical or responsible reading (or listening).

That never totally successful process can be simplified as the quest for a kind of triple vision. First, students must learn how to engage fully and in a sense naïvely, practicing what Coleridge calls willing suspension of disbelief and what Peter Rabinowitz calls becoming the narrative audience: what might be called "genuine listening." They must learn the fun of being "taken into the narrative world"—often even in a sense *taken in,* experiencing the fun of total escape from the everyday world. Secondly, they must learn how to join simultaneously what Rabinowitz calls the authorial audience—the kind of critical audience that implied authors invite them to join as they distance themselves from the credulities of the story they are telling. The authorial audience knows, for example, that geese do not lay golden eggs, and it enjoys the fabulist's construction of a narrative audience who believe that they do. And yet it also joins the implied author in the metaphorical interpretation: when "geese" are laying "golden eggs," it's probably stupid to cut them open looking for more gold. Thirdly, students must learn how to become fully critical, skeptical readers and listeners, questioning both the "taking in" of the narrative "world" and the implied author's opinions about it: "Is it really, always wrong, when some situation (goose) is paying off, to reach for even greater pay-off by exploring the situation's (goose's) innards?" In short, students can learn the rich complex experience of combining full listening with critical analysis of what is "heard." They need to learn how to *think* about, and possibly reject, values of the story world they first "took in."

The irrefutable reason all this is important is that our most powerful ethical influences—except perhaps for parental modeling—are stories: it is in responding to, taking in, becoming transported by story that character is formed, for good or ill. Stories that listeners really listen to are powerful self-creators: they can create or reinforce bad ethos or good. They can transform us in self-destructive directions or they can turn us into would-be heroes.

Since no one story produces any one provable effect on every listener, it is probably impossible ever to obtain scientific proof of this claim. But it is obvious when we think about our own past experience that in entering the story world we get our strongest impressions of what are the most desirable ways to live. In Leonard's terms, we experience what we would most like our constructed selves to be—or what we would most like to avoid being.

We all know from both personal experience and observation of our students that when stories really work, when we are fully "taken in" by a story-world and feel ourselves loving and admiring or hating and detesting portrayed characters, our own aspirations and habits of thought are changed. The changes are inevitably less frequent and usually less dramatic for any highly trained teacher than they are for youngsters. But even for us, they are far more dramatic than is usually recognized. I have an elderly colleague who told me that reading Martin Amis's *The Information* recently changed his mind about assisted suicide: he's now seriously considering it. Another elderly friend reported recently that reading Kawabata's *Sound of the Mountain* had somehow inspired him, removing his depression over being so old.

When writing *The Company We Keep* I interviewed many people, from professors on up to kindergartners, asking them what stories had changed their lives. Almost everyone gave an immediate response. "When I read *Les Misérables* I swore I would always try to rescue lost souls like Jean Valjean, even if they steal my candlesticks." "Reading Sinclair Lewis's *Arrowsmith* was what persuaded me to become a scientist; idealized, pure inquiry, untainted by any motive but truth became my highest goal; only later did I realize how complicated that goal could become." "Reading *Pride and Prejudice* was what saved me from running off with the first boy I fell in love with: I recognized that he was really Wickham." "When I saw the movie *Philadelphia Story* I decided that it was time to give up being a teetotaler, and maybe even get drunk for the first time." "Reading *Tom Sawyer* led me for a while to be much more deceptive with my parents, imitating Tom's treatment of his aunt." "At fourteen I stumbled on *The Story of O* in my father's den, read it, and as I see it now it tainted my life for more than a decade." "In my teens I read Kerouac's *On the Road,* and I quit school and for a year went on the road, retracing the hero's journey. I regret that now, though of course I learned some good things from the experience." I was recently chatting with a twelve-year-old who had seen the movie *Liar Liar.* "How did it make you feel?" "Well," that pre-pubescent cool girl said, "it made me want to try not to lie as much as I've been doing." (All these quotations are from memory, not from tapes—therefore they should be read critically, "resistantly.") Every reader could add to my list.

The broad range of these experiences, from good to bad, further dramatizes the ambiguities of the word "ethical." The move toward the belief that lying to adults is cool or cruel is an ethical change, bad or good; the ethos has been either harmed or improved, depending on where it was before the change. An inferior or improved self has been constructed.

Practical Suggestions

I have six overlapping suggestions.

Suggestion One: Always include at least one work you consider extravagantly flawed, when viewed ethically, one that you suspect many students will themselves find repugnant: works like *The Postman Always Rings Twice,* or Mickey Spillane's *I, the Jury,* or the novel that intellectuals all over the world have overpraised, Celine's *Journey to the End of the Night* (the choice must always depend on your own best hunch about where the students already "are"). Too many of our lists are so biased toward values we ourselves embrace that students either get uncritically hooked or become bored and resistant.

Suggestion Two: Be sure to include some rival story that reveals that first story's dangers or stupidities. Provide at least one story that relies on values that contradict those relied on by the vile book. Seek out a story providing narrative proof of the risks involved in being "taken in" by the first choice. These two suggestions, when fused, will ensure that our reading lists, indeed our entire curricula, provide internal clashes among the values we worry about: stories celebrating *these* virtues that in themselves criticize stories celebrating *those* virtues, inculcating the right kinds of casuistry. What students really should "take in" is the excitement of dealing with value-conflict, of practicing "casuistry" in the good sense of the word.

Suggestion Three: Include some story in which the implied author, subtly calling for close reading, rejects the values espoused by appealing characters or especially sympathetic narrators: students must learn, to repeat, how to join the authorial, not just the narrative audience. I assume that most readers here have enjoyed witnessing students' delight in learning to join an author—Jane Austen, say—as she passes subtle judgment on a character who at first seems above it all—like Mr. Bennet. Even professional critics often show that they don't think enough about that kind of question. One reviewer of John Updike's recent novel, *The End of Time,* portrays it as a totally evil celebration of vicious moral flaws in the hero. She just didn't catch the perhaps too subtle ethical clues that Updike thought would be self-evident.

Suggestion Four: Teach the fun of locating within a given story signs of its implied author's unintentional incoherence or inadvertent revelation of flaws. Though some Pomos have carried this resistant quest so far as to kill all genuine listening, it is important for students to learn what too many teachers in my generation, emphasizing the quest for unity, failed to teach us: that many implied authors, even among the most perceptive, are ethically self-contradictory—just as we the readers are likely to be. Such internal conflicts can be, as Bakhtin stressed, evidence of wonderfully profound authorial probing, but they can also reveal sheer carelessness or commercial deceit.

I knew last summer that my grandson had loved the movie *Independence Day,* and after I'd later watched the massacre-packed thing on a plane flight, I e-mailed him a question about it. "Why is it that the only people who come out alive are the ones the makers have made us like most from the beginning?" He wrote back: "I hadn't thought of that trick. But it makes me wonder about the new Jurassic movie. How did they decide who gets hurt and who doesn't—and why does nobody get eaten?"

These first four suggestions dramatize the inherent conflict between any teacher's deepest critical interests and her sense of what conflicting narrative realities *these* students most need at *this* cultural moment. This conflict is dramatized in one of Lionel Trilling's most interesting essays, "On the Teaching of Modern Literature." He reports his experience at Columbia teaching a course in modern literature to freshmen. He chose the best modern works he could think of, judging them as a "literary critic." Since this was in the fifties, the works he chose as "best" all sharply criticized or undermined what he considered bourgeois clichés. His only *pedagogical* thought was that since the works were powerful they would wake his students up: an ethical goal. What he discovered was that his students were in effect already indoctrinated in anti-bourgeois convictions, and if they were to be challenged in their current values they needed some non-modern works. The list he constructed as best for students when he thought as a literary critic had to be changed when he asked himself, "What do *these* students most need?"

The point then is: never forget Trilling's confession about his error—his failure to think hard enough about pedagogy vs. lit. crit. Be sure to include at least one powerful story that challenges current hot clichés: Ishiguru's *Remains of the Day,* perhaps, or one of Austen's or George Eliot's works, or Gail Godwin's *The Good Husband,* or—well, why not?—the *Odyssey?*

We all know that none of these suggestions will work in all teaching situations. If you are faced with a class of non-readers who can't even handle works as complex as those I have mentioned, you'll have to translate all of my advice into more accessible works.

Suggestion Five: Turning from course lists to methods, we might fuse the four course-list suggestions by saying: make sure that you, along with the works you assign, are inculcating methods both of fully engaged reading—of understanding what the story itself is up to—and of critical oversight, of the *over*standing that results when we apply to a story values alien to it.

If you ask what is the best guide to combining understanding with overstanding the ethical effects of narrative, naturally I have a single absolute answer: my own book that I've already mentioned twice, violating my firm principle never to load my work with self-citations: *The Company We Keep.* Another work, one that is a bit more pertinent to the current scene, is *Authorizing Readers: Resistance and Respect,* by Peter Rabinowitz and Michael Smith. The book is precisely on this point: teaching students, high school or college, both how to respect the story's true intellectual and ethical demands and how to resist those demands responsibly.

Suggestion Six: Perhaps the most important methodological problem is how to build habits of genuine conversation, thoughtful talk by students who have learned to practice penetrating criticism of one another's readings—and of the teacher's own biases. The most important single product—to use that commercial term increasingly popular with administrators these days—is the kind of person who can criticize others not just negatively but productively, and that requires daily practice in genuine critical conversation. If I had time I would preach a bit about the difference between good and poor classroom discussion, dialogue and bullshitting, but instead I'll end with one institutional solution. Though it may appear too mechanical, it really works, regardless of what any teacher does in class. It is often hard to institute, especially in larger colleges, but I've experienced its blessings at three different colleges, small and large.

I suggest the installation of at least one campus-wide general-education requirement, one that instead of providing totally unrelated sections traveling under some general pious title will guarantee at least *some* shared reading experience by all students. We never arrive at really good judgments of a story by ourselves; we need the opinions, the company, of other readers, and not just of readers who have been indoctrinated in some one course. Every college should ensure shared encounters outside of class among readers of the same stories: the same novel, the same history, the same movie, the same autobiography.

No one reader's, no one teacher's, reading is ever complete, final, perfect. What we want to perfect is the kind of spontaneous conversation that both mitigates the harmful effects of bad stories or bad readings and strengthens the effects of good stories and good readings. If everyone on a given campus has wrestled with the same story, or even better the same list of stories, regardless of whether those stories are judged as ethically good or bad, spontaneous conversation will erupt, and shallow readings will be deepened, mistaken readings corrected, vicious stories exposed. Instead of deduction from fixed codes, or induction from some straw poll, a form of critical dialogue emerges that I like to call *coduction*.

How many institutions can boast, as Earlham College can, that every first-year student will share this year, in small humanities sections, a list like the following?

Demetria Martinez, *Mother Tongue*

Langston Hughes, *Montage of a Dream Deferred*

Euripides, *Medea* (a potentially dangerous work, by the way)

Aristophanes, *The Frogs*

Selections from Psalms, Proverbs, and the book of Job

Thoreau, "Civil Disobedience"

Thucydides, *The Peloponnesian War*

Impressive as that selection is, to me the precise choices don't matter a tenth as much as does the fact that every freshman at Earlham, when walking along the hall or planning to make love in a dormitory, will be likely to bump into somebody asking him or her "What the hell do you make of that Oresteeah, or however you say it? It turned my stomach when those Furies acted like that . . . And you know, my teacher doesn't like it either." And sometimes the reply will be, "Heh, man, you didn't get it right. What you gotta do is think of it this way—well, the way my teacher who loves it made the case was . . ."

None of this will ever prove to be easy. Teaching stories ethically is not only more important than any other teaching—a further proclamation from this overconfident retiree—it is more difficult than any other teaching. Teaching students how both to take in and not to be taken in by texts, how to unite ethical resistance and ethical respect, makes teaching the laws of thermodynamics look like child's play. This is not, however, a claim that only "English" is at the center. Stories dominate every field, even the hardest of sciences. Students can be harmfully "taken in," or genuinely liberated, by the explicit and implicit narratives that dominate every field: what could be more important than responding critically to the following story, "told" in many a textbook and popular account of science's triumphal march through history?

> Once upon a time ignorant people believed in gods of various kinds. Gradually, battle by battle, science, the only valid way of thinking, managed to knock down their superstitions. In this century we are at last moving toward complete mastery of the whole truth about the universe, as we pursue the final total theory just over our horizon.

I could cite here scores of books, published through the past two centuries, telling versions of this story. Some portray religion as totally annihilated in the war; some show it as fully and finally harmonized with science. My point is not to downgrade scientific storytellers but to invite them to recognize how often they enter into our "English" territory. Is it absurd to hope that, since we all live in the world of story, we English teachers can find ways of joining with teachers from all fields in pursuit of a common goal, ethical education? Whether we consider ourselves radical, liberal, or conservative, Trad or Pomo, scientists or humanists or anti-humanists, we surely must all aim to produce, using the world of story, not flunkeys who can only pass tests—though they can do that—but self-motivated learners. They should be living in their time with us in ways that make the path to further learning irresistible.

Regardless of our institutional base or theoretical differences, we all *ought* to share this loose-jointed but essential goal: to produce *this* kind of person, self, character, not *that* kind, even as we acknowledge that any one picture of "the best kind" always needs improving. It is in engaging with stories that "pictures" of life get improved.

The future of American education depends on teachers who vigorously pursue Elizabeth Leonard's question: "If I'm changing students, how do I change them in ways that I feel are most useful to them?"

Works Cited

Bakhtin, M. M. *The Dialogic Imagination: Four Essays.* Ed. Michael Holquist. Trans. Caryl Emerson and Michael Holquist. Austin: U of Texas P, 1981.

Bennett, William. *The Book of Virtues.* New York: Simon and Schuster, 1993.

Booth, Wayne. *The Company We Keep: An Ethics of Fiction.* Berkeley: U of California P, 1988.

Carroll, Lee Ann. "Pomo Blues: Stories from First-Year Composition" *College English* 59.8 (December 1997): 916–33.

Chandler, James. *England in 1819: The Politics of Literary Culture and the Case of Romantic Historicism.* Chicago: U of Chicago P, 1998.

Covey, Stephen R. *Seven Habits of Highly Effective People: Restoring the Character Ethic.* New York: Simon and Schuster, 1989.

Derrida, Jacques. *The Gift of Death.* Trans. David Wills. Chicago: U of Chicago P, 1995.

Dewey, John. *Democracy and Education: An Introduction to the Philosophy of Education.* 1916. New York: Free P, 1966.

Fox, Richard Wightman, and Robert B. Westbrook, eds. *In Face of the Facts: Moral Inquiry in American Scholarship.* New York: Cambridge UP, 1998.

Jonsen, Albert R., and Stephen Toulmin. *The Abuse of Casuistry: A History of Moral Reasoning.* Berkeley: U of California P, 1988.

Leonard, Alizabeth Anne. "Assignment #9—A Text Which Engages the Socially Constructed Identity of its Writer." *CCC* 48.2 (May 1997): 215–30.

MacIntyre, Alasdair. *After Virtue.* Notre Dame: U of Notre Dame P, 1984.

Rabinowitz, Peter. *Before Reading: Narrative Conventions and the Politics of Interpetation.* Ithaca: Cornell UP, 1987.

Rabinowitz, Peter, and Michael Smith. *Authorizing Readers: Resistance and Respect.* New York: Teachers College P/NCTE, 1997.

Taylor, Charles. *Sources of the Self: The Making of Modern Identity.* Cambridge: Harvard UP, 1989.

Trilling, Lionel. "On the Teaching of Modern Literature." *Beyond Culture: Essays on Literature and Learning.* New York: Viking P, 1965. 3–30.

White, Patrick, ed. "Symposium: Is Morality a Non-Aim of Education?" *Philosophy and Literature* 22.1 (April 1998): 136–99.

Wolfe, Alan. "White Magic in America: Capitalism, Mormonism, and the Doctrines of Stephen Covey." *New Republic* February 23, 1998: 26–34.

8 Going Public

Peter Mortensen

It isn't often that authors affiliated with composition studies reach an academic audience beyond their peers, much less a popular one outside of the academy. E. D. Hirsch managed to do so with *Cultural Literacy* in 1987, as did Mike Rose two years later with *Lives on the Boundary*.[1] Their commentaries on literacy drew the attention of academic and nonacademic readers alike. Yet surely Hirsch and Rose did not discuss literacy in all the depth and complexity both professional and general audiences might appreciate. More can be said. Indeed, more *must* be said, the stress here because an ethical imperative is at issue. In our journals and at our conferences, one finds repeated again and again the assertion that our work—our teaching, researching, and theorizing—can clarify and even improve the prospects of literacy in democratic culture. If we really believe this, we must then acknowledge our obligation to air that work in the most expansive, inclusive forums possible.

Of course, this is more easily said than done. As Joseph Harris argues, composition faces what Jürgen Habermas calls a legitimation crisis, it having to serve the often conflicting demands of professional academics and the general public (5). As it turns out, composition's struggle to build credibility within the academy has been a full time job. At the end of the day, little intellectual energy remains for the serious and difficult task of going public with what we do, with what we know.

Still, as I have said, we must go public. And we can. As I suggest in this essay, we are coming ever closer to publishing in ways that grant access to audiences outside the profession, beyond the academy. This is because certain modes of inquiry in composition studies now favor reports of

Reprinted from *College Composition and Communication,* December 1998.

research that are culturally and historically situated, enough so that nonspecialist and nonacademic readers can appreciate them. The impulse toward situated research reports, I argue, results from an evolving sense of ethical obligation to the individuals and groups whose literacies we study and to the publics we serve. But we are not alone in serving these publics. Journalists, essayists, polemicists, policy analysts, and others are writing about the same literacies we study. Indeed, sometimes they critique our teaching and research practices as part of their efforts to locate their observations and arguments in culturally and historically familiar territory. As I show, there is much to learn here, much to appreciate, and more to be wary of. And learn we should, for in failing to do so, we consign ourselves to mere spectatorship in national, regional—and, most importantly, local— struggles over what counts as literacy and who should have opportunities to attain it.

Ethics and Situated Reports

If we can say—as has been said before—that the appearance of Braddock, Lloyd-Jones, and Schoer's *Research in Written Composition* in 1963 catalyzed development of composition studies as a field of inquiry, then we may also say that concerns about the ethics of our inquiries have been with us from the start.[2] Midway through their report, Braddock et al. argue that "basic to a good design is the honest desire to discover or test some generalization about which the investigator does not believe he is fully informed, to discover or test some answer to a sincere question" (23). For them, honesty and sincerity are the hallmarks of good research design, of ethical asking and answering aimed at improving composition pedagogy. Left implicit is the chain of relationships that extends the authors' ethical concerns from pedagogy to student writing, and from student writing to the literate lives of writing students. Also unstated are the obligations of an honest and sincere researcher to those uncontrollable "writer variable[s]" whose immaterial presence forever complicates the analysis of student writing (6).

Spectral writer variables might still haunt composition researchers today were it not for Lynn, the twelfth-grade writer profiled by Janet Emig in her foundational NCTE research monograph some 25 years ago. That Emig had studied *writers*, not just *writing*, was—and continues to be—recognized as a turning point in composition studies (see Buxton v; North 197). The case study method Emig fashioned from interdisciplinary sources recast the role of student writers: no longer disembodied variables, their lives matter in the interpretation of writing (Nelms, "Reassessing" 121–22).

In keeping with case study method, Emig profiled Lynn's life in and out of school—her relationships with teachers, family, and community. Lynn, we learn finally, writes "often with great skill" despite being subjected to weak teaching. Emig leaves us with the "inescapable impression" that Lynn "is more sophisticated than her teachers, both as to the level of her stylistic concerns and to the accuracy and profundity of her analysis of herself as a writer" (73). End of chapter. No apologies.

And no apologies necessary. Lynn *is* a gifted writer whose talent is blunted by unimaginative teaching, by unimaginative teachers. This is *true*. The facts are evident in case study interviews and composing-aloud sessions conducted by "the investigator" (29). And clearly, if implicitly, what is true must be good, and therefore ethical. Besides, readers are warned in Earl Buxton's preface that they "will find the Emig report . . . at times disconcertingly outspoken" (v). So it is that Emig can render authoritative criticism of writing instruction and pedagogy that in her estimation is unethical—owing to its failure to tap the literate potential Lynn and students like her bring to the classroom.

Doubtless the most provoked and disconcerted of Emig's readers were Lynn's teachers. The *Composing Processes of Twelfth Graders* delivered them "bad news," broadcasting it across a wide network of teachers and researchers interested in high school and college writing instruction (see Newkirk). Few if any of us will ever know how the teachers took this news, for the teachers and Lynn's fellow students remain anonymous.[3] The value of anonymity goes unmentioned in Emig's study, perhaps because it is one of her method's first principles: the identity of subjects must be protected. Thus for Lynn's teachers, the reception of Emig's bad news was more or less a private affair. For everyone else, the bad news was not so bad at all, but rather the seemingly good news that the methods and ethics exemplified in Emig's study might well mean that "the learning and the teaching of composition may someday attain the status of science as well as art" (5).

If Emig agonized over her characterization of Lynn and her teachers, no trace of it appears in the pages of her research report. How could it have been otherwise? Such disclosure would surely have been perceived as gratuitous, since, in the universe of discourse on composition circa 1971, the truth-telling power of method rendered unnecessary any explicit attention to the ethics of representation. But time has reordered that universe. Across the span of 27 years, as qualitative approaches to research in composition have proliferated and evolved, *representation* has grown to be a—maybe *the*— problem of central significance. The truth Emig knew in 1971 no longer speaks for itself in 1998. It is instead embedded in constructs whose foundations are unstable, whose materials are unreliable. Contemporary theorists may disagree on exactly how representation is unstable and unreliable, but that it is so is generally agreed upon, not only in composition studies, but also in all disciplines invested in questioning "the *relationship* between the representational material and that which it represents" (Mitchell 14; see also Denzin and Lincoln 9–10).

Who may say what about whom, and how? This is a question of representation, one asked by more and more teacher-researchers who inquire into conditions of literacy and its teaching.[4] Emig answered the question silently, in keeping with the ethic of representation prevailing a quarter-century ago. Today, because our understanding of truth and language compels us to struggle openly with problems of representation, our ethics of representation must also be stated openly, whether for purposes of confirmation or contestation.

My own work in composition studies has given me the opportunity to study readers and writers—research subjects—and to reflect on how to conduct such inquiry. Yet most of what I know about research subjects comes not from this work, but from my experience *as* a subject. Some years ago, for the sake of curiosity and a few dollars, I became a subject— presumably a control subject—in an ongoing study of alcoholism among young men (see Schuckit and Smith). In 1988, on Fridays for a period of weeks, I reported at sunrise to a VA Medical Center near home. Electrodes were pasted to my scalp and taped to my chest. A physician administered intravenous doses of ethanol. Blood was drawn and urine taken. Then, intoxicated, I spent hours in a small, dark room performing tests of mental acuity and physical dexterity. I am assured that the results of my performance are kept under lock and key at the medical center, as are follow-up questionnaires I have completed over the past eight years detailing my use of (or abstinence from) drugs and alcohol. These data are linked to me only by an encrypted chain of reference, and so I am essentially unknown to the researchers. My contributions to their study have been aggregated with others so that, in print, I am merely one "healthy young man" among 300 or so, all of us protected by our anonymity, and by a code of ethics that specifies, above all, that our participation in this project must never jeopardize our physical, mental, or emotional well-being.

My experience illustrates precisely those ethical safeguards—concealment of identity and protection from harm—that, modeled on biomedical research, have long governed qualitative research on literacy and its teaching. Are these safeguards sufficient? Are they appropriate? Such are the ethical questions raised in our field, at once beset and enlivened by the crisis of representation. The tendency today is to answer the first question in the negative: promises of anonymity and care do not alone constitute an ethics of representation. Teacher-researchers thus must grapple with variations of the second question. What ethical considerations should—must—inform studies of writing and writing instruction?

One way to address this query is to identify what is troubling about the protections of anonymity and care. Simply put, the peril of anonymity is that it can lead to invisibility; at the same time, the institutional administration of care can slide easily into paternalism. In the worst case, then, the qualitative research subject is neither seen nor heard. Efforts to ameliorate the negative consequences of anonymity and care typically focus on giving voice and embodiment to subjects. With voice and embodiment, subjects may assume presence and agency in the text of research reports—presence and agency realized in recorded dialogue, in acknowledged collaboration, and in coauthorship. These efforts at inclusion—especially collaboration and coauthorship—demand that heretofore invisible and silent research subjects take an active role in interpreting the "data" recorded by a study's principal investigators. In effect, this interpretive charge makes researchers and subjects partners in a study's first audience. And if a study extends the charge to an even broader group, say a readership across the discipline, so much the better, especially from the perspective of an ethics of representation that abhors exclusion.

But gestures toward inclusivity have spelled considerable trouble for qualitative literacy researchers, both in the field and on the page. If it is true that *exclusion* is the chief ethical problem facing qualitative literacy researchers, it does not necessarily follow that *inclusion* is the sole and sufficient remedy. Inclusion multiplies the persons and communities who may make claims on the representation of research findings—an ethical good. But inclusion also opens the door to conflict in which, as Sandra Stotsky puts it, "ethical principles seem to collide, and the dilemmas (which cannot be easily or painlessly resolved) require much elucidation" (132). This process of elucidation has so far branched along several distinct paths, all of which illustrate the compromises we must abide if we mean to honor inclusion as an ethical good.

One path leads to the barrier that often separates composition researchers and theorists from teachers and students. That barrier can be removed, argues David Bleich, if we recognize in qualitative inquiry, specifically ethnography, the potential for "socially generous research": "Focusing attention on the classroom as an institution (a culture? a community?) can loosen the boundary between theorists and teachers, and between academic ethnographic work and the work of writing in classrooms" (176, 177). But this call for inclusivity is not so easily answered. The effort to tear down the barrier Bleich describes begins with an invitation. Like any invitation, this one, to erase long standing division, can be declined or ignored even as a researcher depends on its acceptance. Brenda Jo Brueggemann learned this in her dissertation study of deaf students' literacy at Gallaudet University. She initially fashioned a participant-observer role for herself that merged her research and teaching interests: she wanted to be the co-instructor of a composition class. But her offer of expertise was declined, and to remain at Gallaudet she had to position herself as a novice in the world of deaf college education. This refiguration, this repositioning, profoundly affected what she could see, know, and record. Rhetorically, repositioning meant that Brueggemann's first audience could not include those who knew most about teaching composition at Gallaudet.[5]

Brueggemann's case also illustrates another possible path toward a more inclusive audience, one that requires bridging the gap between teacher-researchers and students. Brueggemann invited two students featured in her study to comment on her ethnographic renderings of them. In one instance, that invitation was received and acknowledged, but never accepted in a way that could produce interpretive collaboration in Brueggemann's final write-up. In the other instance, the invitation was greeted, quite unexpectedly she says, with ambiguous silence. She concludes that we cannot make them participate if they only want to observe. We cannot require them to speak if they only want to remain anonymous or silent" (33).

Yet another path toward inclusivity finds teacher-researchers concentrating on ethical aspects of the rhetorical work that begins where fieldwork leaves off. As Bonnie Sunstein puts it, "When I write ethnography, I feel quiet guilt each time my informants speak and every time I enter their written words into my computer. . . . My processed version of them exists somewhere between *my* mind, *my* field notes, *my* computer, and eventually my reader" (177). Sunstein's observation underscores the point that even if everything goes well in the field—even if all one's invitations to be included are heartily accepted—the teacher-researcher as singular writer is left with the vexing (and often impossible) task of crafting sentences that fairly represent the outcome of that acceptance, that inclusion.[6]

Even the widest gesture of inclusion, collaboration at the point of inscription, in no way guarantees that teacher-researchers will surmount the difficulties to which Sunstein refers. Lucille McCarthy and Stephen Fishman found this to be so when they chose to co-author a report on McCarthy's naturalistic study of writing-across-the-curriculum in a college philosophy course taught by Fishman. Their work on "multivoiced" reports has led them to counsel collaborators on the following points: all parties—teachers, students, researchers—must enter a collaboration willing to change their thinking about composition and its teaching; collaborative relationships require continuing negotiation; accounts of such negotiations should appear in research reports; and the larger audience for the report should be carefully chosen to benefit all collaborators (172–73).

The path McCarthy and Fishman map in some detail, as well as those sketched more generally by Brueggemann and Sunstein, share a common endpoint: successful publication—made possible by the process of elucidation Stotsky urged, difficult and troubling though it may be. But does prizing elucidation in this way compromise the ethics of representation by assuring, falsely, that representation is *always* possible, that the ethical dilemmas faced by teacher-researchers are never insoluble, never paralyzing? Lester Faigley, writing of rhetorical problems similar to those under scrutiny here, reminds us that

> Bringing ethics into rhetoric is not a matter of collapsing spectacular diversity into universal truth. Neither is ethics only a matter of a radical questioning of what aspires to be regarded as truth. . . . It is a pausing to reflect on the limits of understanding. It is respect for diversity and unassimilated otherness. It is finding the spaces to listen. (239)

Apropos qualitative research, I take Faigley to mean, first, that we should not expect an ethics of representation to solve all of our problems by ratifying the truth of inclusive, multivoiced, even collaborative research reports. Nor should we expect the foregrounding of ethics to justify flight from stating what appears—given particular perspective and context—to be true. Instead, an ethics of representation should engender respect for that which heretofore has not been assimilated into representation. One unassimilated realm we should take more seriously than we do is that which exists beyond our discipline and outside the academy. In that realm are audiences that have for some time exhibited demand for what we know about literacy and language. But to date that demand has largely been met by commentators not affiliated with universities, writers often unaware of the specific ethical considerations I have just reviewed.

Crossing Boundaries

Yet just because "general" or "popular" audiences have shown interest in ideas we hold dear does not mean that we are conscious of how best to reach such readers. As I have argued up to this point, ethical developments in the study of literacy have compelled us to write research reports that are situated, that are contextualized in ways that nonacademic readers could potentially find inviting. But let's not be fooled. It is not easy writing for a "general" audience. That much we know from our own teaching: our students write better given an authentic purpose, and authentic purpose often depends on there being a knowable audience, even if that knowledge finally proves to be a fiction. Few in the composition community have been able to reach and engage nonacademic audiences with arguments that we, in the academy, deem important. (As previously mentioned, E. D. Hirsch and Mike Rose constitute the exceptions that prove the rule.) But there are writers from outside academe who have taken up these important issues, and it is to a book by one of them that I turn in this section: James Traub's *City on a Hill*, which examines, among other things, "remediation" in college composition.[7] Studying Traub's narrative enables us to glimpse the rhetorical moves necessary to reach a popular readership, allows us to discern what we already do well and what we must learn to do better.

Traub sets out to understand how City College of New York, once "one of America's great colleges," came to sponsor such a "vast remedial underworld" (9, 12). Assessing City's perceived decline, Traub asks, "Do the limits lie in the college or in the students?" (5). It emerges that Traub is concerned that students who pursue a course of remedial education at City College eventually graduate without the ability to think "critically" about intellectual problems. Far from being suspicious of a critical literacy—or at least a liberal version thereof—Traub is interested in a way to identify whether City College students are attaining critical literacy in the course of their college studies. If they are, as their predecessors reputedly did in City's heyday, then the open admissions "experiment" that has so changed the college might, after all, be deemed worthwhile.

Several chapters into *City on a Hill*, Traub's exploration carries him into the territory of composition studies, where he seeks to understand the "basic writing" program established by Mina Shaughnessy in the years following institution of open admissions at City College. Before moving ahead with his inquiry, he makes an interesting disclosure:

> I realized that if I wanted to get to the heart of the open admissions experiment I would have to become, in effect, a student, sitting in regularly on classes, seeing the same students day after day, and watching as the transformative process took hold—or didn't. (83)

Rather than fashioning a traditional journalist's "objective" stance, independent and free from bias, Traub strikes a deeply interested pose: he dons the mantle of the participant-observer.[8] But the participant-observer role was not familiar to some of Traub's reviewers, many of whom expected him to write with the "objectivity" of a journalist. He addresses this problem by engaging in dialogue—explicitly and implicitly—with another observer of the basic writing at City College, Marilyn Sternglass, head of the college's master's program in composition and a distinguished composition teacher-researcher.

In the midst of Traub's field research, Sternglass published an article in *Written Communication* reporting on her ongoing longitudinal study of City College student writers. The article took the form of a case study, which followed the writing development of "Linda" over her first three and a half years at the college. Sternglass characterizes Linda's achievements by observing her use of various "acts of discourse"—description, analysis, and interpretation among them—thought to "reveal the student's ability to use textual knowledge to move beyond recall and repetition of facts to . . . the creation of new knowledge" ("Writing Development" 244). Sternglass demonstrates that Linda made great strides toward sophistication in thinking and writing during her time at City; she also shows how Linda fell short of the institution's—and her own—goal of full fluency in composing academic discourse.[9]

Traub undertakes a similar study, mixing material from his interviews and observations with "data" Sternglass made available to him. What he brought to the table was a wealth of historical and political context—context Sternglass did not (and because of space constraints, probably could not) work into her report on Linda.[10] He asked to interview "Tammy," another of Sternglass's students, and to look at the writing she had done for the duration (about four years) of her participation in the longitudinal study.

In reporting the results of his inquiry, Traub glances sideways at the composition scholarship that stakes out the territory he attempts to map. His aim is to gather evidence to help answer whether Tammy's problems with literacy result from cognitive deficit or poor schooling. Traub observes that "composition theory since Shaughnessy has all but anathematized the imagery of deficit," having substituted for it the notion that college basic writers simply haven't had opportunities to acquire the conventions of academic discourse (117). In other words, the problems basic writers face are social and institutional in origin, not cognitive. But Traub is skeptical of this argument, and for support turns to composition scholars who embraced Jean Piaget's early theorizing about human development. Traub notes, rightly, that in this theorizing Piaget predicts the mastery of formal operations in early adolescence. If this is so, Traub reasons, college students unable to think in formal propositions must be cognitively deficient. Their supposed functional illiteracy, then, results from cognitive shortcomings, not lack of educational opportunity, so extending them additional learning opportunities is likely to do no good.[11]

Still, giving Sternglass's developmental taxonomy some credence, Traub is willing to grant that Tammy has made "remarkable" progress: "she had learned to write in the forms used by academics"; she knows how to insert a critical voice into academic commentary (132). But then Traub asserts that while this may be a kind of critical literacy, it is not the sort that most benefits individuals and culture—thereby touching on a controversy yet unresolved (and probably unresolvable) in composition studies.[12] He applies a standard of "intellectual discrimination" articulated by Theodore Gross, English chair and humanities dean at City College during the 1970s (132, 72).[13] Using Gross's measure, Traub is sure that Tammy falls short of being an "educated" person, one whose learning enables the unerring embrace of truth and morality (132). He concludes the chapter by voicing his suspicion that the well-meaning Sternglass is blind—as was Mina Shaughnessy before her—to the reality of Tammy's and Linda's modest achievements. But he concedes that this sort of "delude[d]" thinking may be an essential part of keeping the institution alive in the face of striking contradictions in its contemporary mission (133).[14]

The relationship Traub establishes with Sternglass is a fragile one. In his acknowledgments, he thanks her for being "especially generous in trying to persuade me of the wrongness of my views" (359). And he is careful to cite from the literature of composition studies (though he is less careful about citing current publications): the names of David Bartholomae, Patricia Bizzell, Min-Zhan Lu, Andrea Lunsford, Anthony Petrosky, and Mike Rose all appear as sources.[15] Yet Traub is finally unwilling to see Tammy and her fellow students as successes—and Sternglass as a successful teacher-researcher. He wants City College to be what he believes it once was: rather than "reproduc[ing] privilege" as Ivy League colleges did, "it gave poor, talented boys . . . the opportunity to make it into the middle class." City College thus was the "most meritocratic of institutions," and so it boasted "a moral status that no elite college could claim" (10). The erosion of standards, evidenced in Tammy's performance, has diminished that moral status, the very quality that once put a City College education on par with that available at Columbia, or Harvard, or Yale.

This is an engaging story. It gains its truth value, in part, by suggesting that Sternglass is too close to her students now to understand how they compare to those of the past. Traub claims to have the distance that Sternglass does not, yet he asserts that he is close enough to the scene of inquiry not to miss significant details. But composition scholars might well complain that, close or far, Traub never explicitly positions himself *vis-à-vis* the scene of inquiry, and thus must rely on institutional histories—S. Willis Rudy's centennial retrospective, for example—rather than experience to contextualize some of his claims. Traub avoids this positioning in part by limiting disclosures about his own background, about how his attitudes toward City College and its students have evolved over time.

Does it matter, for example, that Traub took his undergraduate degree at Harvard? That his father and brother did the same? That his mother attended Smith and his spouse holds a Yale PhD in art history? Does it matter that Traub grew up in New York's Westchester County, the son of Bloomingdale's former CEO, a man proud of transforming "a modest and slightly dowdy emporium . . . where Park Avenue maids shopped for their uniforms" into "one of the country's unique cultural institutions" (Traub and Teicholz xiii–iv)?[16] Were these details woven into Traub's account of City College, readers might themselves be better positioned to understand the perspective inhabited by the author and to judge the accuracy and reasonableness of his account.

Traub's difficulties with positionality notwithstanding, he has rendered what might be called an open text, one that invites (or at least allows) reinterpretation of his evidence and findings. That openness is partly visible in his dialogue with Marilyn Sternglass. It is still more visible in Jon Wiener's contentious review of the book for the *Nation*. Wiener, like Traub a Harvard alumnus, begins his review by criticizing Traub's attitude toward basic writing instruction at City College. Quoting a clumsy passage from the publisher's announcement of *City on a Hill*, Wiener argues that "if Traub had found his publicist's sentence in a City College student essay, he would have held it up as an example of the writer's hopeless inability to learn. The point is that poor writing is endemic in America today" (522). And later: "Traub obviously has never read the papers written by middle-class white college kids in freshman comp at the state colleges in California; their teachers get just as discouraged as their counterparts at City" (524). More intriguing are the conversations Wiener had with a number of the people Traub interviewed while on campus. Their collective portrait of Traub is unflattering: he was "uncomfortable," "incredibly condescending," "a tourist among the working class" (522, 524, 528). No doubt Traub was irked by these criticisms, and perhaps he was instructed by them. But the significant issue here is that Traub's text managed to provoke Wiener's complaints, and so has usefully extended ongoing discussions of literacy in higher education—discussions in which Traub cannot insist on having the final word.

If it is Wiener's contention that Traub was too distant from City College to get a good view of it, it is another prominent reviewer's opinion that just the opposite is true. A. M. Rosenthal, former executive editor of the *New York Times* and a City College graduate, fears that Traub has gone so far inside the college that he cannot

> make clear why his book is important to people outside New York who have no involvement in City College but are interested in the health of American higher education. The reason is that under one name or another remedial education is affecting a variety of colleges around the country. This is by no means just City's problem. (9)

This may or may not be so. Rosenthal's comment points to the irrepressible desire for inductive proof of universal truth, a desire that tends to efface particular differences, whether that difference is expressed in terms of ethnicity, class, gender, or in the more elusive terms of space and place. Traub takes pains to anchor his observations and analysis in a local history, one that need not necessarily approximate the history of other institutions elsewhere. Does that lessen the commercial value of *City on a Hill*? It does, probably. Traub's book earned a fraction of the national attention (and, presumably, the sales) enjoyed by Richard Bernstein's *Dictatorship of Virtue*, a best-seller that takes up in one chapter the controversy over a proposed first-year composition course at the University of Texas.[17] But if the notice *City on a Hill* received was largely from those who feel they have a direct stake in the future of City College, is there another sort of value at issue here?

Yes there is, and it is *ethical* value—measured in terms of a narrative's power to provoke local discussion and galvanize local action to address a local problem. Had Traub made a more general case about remedial writing in college, he would have passed silently into territory unknown to him, where the possibility of ethical representation would have been remote. Why remote? Why can't Traub's narrative of declining literacy standards serve as a keynote for understanding the "crisis" in "remedial" college writing instruction nationwide? The answer to these questions lies, in part, in the overreaching claims evident in Bernstein's account of composition at Texas. It is possible, as Bernstein unwittingly shows, to advance general conclusions about college composition that must bear considerably more weight than any local story can support. One way to avoid such generalization is to remain alert to the specific points of departure that eventually lead to particular conclusions. Attending to the historical pressures that shape these points tends to work against the kind of generalization Bernstein offers and Traub, for the most part, does not. Traub's book, then, is the more interesting of the two if we are looking for models of potentially ethical communication, even though Bernstein's book may model communication that is more successful (where success is figured commercially).

Traub grounds his story in the lively recollections of such City College alumni as Irving Kristol (from a brief memoir published in the *New York Times Magazine*) and Irving Howe (from the third chapter of his autobiography, *A Margin of Hope*). These and other luminaries speak of a time in the 1920s and 30s when a degree from City meant a chance, especially for young Jewish men, to rise out of impoverished circumstances into New York's burgeoning middle class. Could Traub tell the same story about literacy and hope for advancement in, say, Kentucky, where I now live? Could he strike the same stance? What attitudes prevailed—and prevail—where I live that might undermine the foundation Traub lays for his narrative of decline?

Quite simply, Traub's tale of an intellectual golden age gone by does not describe the Kentucky experience. More accurate would be an epic tale of suspicion, of the citizenry and its universities sharing little common ground and nothing like a common vocabulary. The problem here, recast in theoretical terms, revolves around the power undergirding Traub's authority. It once might have been acknowledged that, by virtue of its location and its history, City College represents *the* paradigmatic case illustrating the inability of remedial courses in composition to save higher education from the stain of functional illiteracy. But the postmodern analysis of institutional power rendered by Foucault and others suggests that no single institution can claim such paradigmatic status. Institutions of higher learning across the nation are empowered in peculiar and interesting ways, making it difficult to generalize about how such power shapes remediation in writing—and public discourse about it.

Reflecting on the local texture of that public discourse, I recall the remarks of former Kentucky Governor Wallace Wilkinson. While sitting as a university trustee several years ago, Wilkinson attacked professors for publishing esoteric research in "itty-bitty journals"—such as the British journal *Nature* (Lucke A1). Professors, Wilkinson argued, would be better off spending more hours in the classroom teaching and fewer hours writing. Around the same time, a similar idea was given voice by noted Kentucky author, UK alumnus, and former UK professor Wendell Berry, who asserted, sarcastically, that the "mark of a good teacher is that he or she spends most of his or her time doing research and writes many books and articles" (xiii).[18]

Readers might be tempted to label Wilkinson's comments anti-intellectual, as one writer did (Warth). For Berry we might reserve the term old-fashioned. But each makes a legitimate point (though one with which I must respectfully disagree). In their view of the university, professors should teach more and publish less. While the former governor likely envisions composition teachers simply instructing more students during a given week, Berry probably would allow for a kind of teaching that can be reconciled with the need, as I have been advocating, to speak publicly about academic literacies. But with conditions here and elsewhere even more complicated than I have described them, it is going to be difficult for any academic figure to cultivate *local* ground in order to address a *local* audience on a subject such as the literacy of college students.

Be that as it may, ethical representation demands that such local audiences be sought out by "public intellectuals" of local standing. How else, then, to predict whether the critical literacy taught in Kentucky college composition courses prepares students to fight against the social inequality and injustice that both Wilkinson and Berry would agree beset the commonwealth. And how else to explain why in Kentucky one kind of adult literacy training—college composition—has been relatively uncontroversial, while historically much controversy has surrounded adult literacy education outside the academy (see Mortensen, "Representations").

Henry Giroux underscores the importance of this mission:

> Public intellectuals . . . need to define higher education as a public resource vital to the moral life of the nation and open to working people and communities that are often viewed as marginal to such institutions and their diverse resources of knowledge and skills. (250)

But we need to be careful here. If composition teacher-researchers are to stand as public intellectuals, they may indeed wish to speak to the vitality of literacy for the "moral life of the nation," but they must also speak to the ethical concerns of the local—the community, the commonwealth, the region. Else they risk making generalizations that may be as attractive and forceful as they are baseless and misleading.

Should every composition teacher-researcher feel compelled to write as a public intellectual for popular audiences? Clearly not. Catharine Stimpson cautions that "not everyone can be a public intellectual" because "it demands a particular set of talents" that not all academics have ("Public Duties" 101). Still, Stimpson reminds us, "all academic professionals have public duties" (101). In composition, we can discharge these duties by writing for the communities we live in, communities likely much larger and more complex than the institutional ones in which we work. Few of us will write a book like Rose's *Lives on the Boundary*, but many of us are capable of sharing disciplinary knowledge with local audiences concerned about literacy. And, most of us are capable of reviewing a book like Rose's for local and regional publications. No less important, we might provide background information and testimony for lawmakers considering legislation relevant to our professional concerns. We might also write reports for school districts or state government agencies that are considering questions germane to our field (see Mortensen, *Remediation*). The list could go on. Unfortunately, there are few institutional rewards for writing in the public interest, although this may be changing.[19] And there are always dangers, chief among them making intellectually dishonest concessions to audiences not attuned to nuanced argumentation—what Michael Bérubé calls "selling out," or "abandoning one's principles and caving in to the demands of the market" (217).

Nor are there any guarantees (nor should there be) that interested publics will embrace whatever we share with them. Consider what two large organizations of literacy teachers and researchers recently learned. In March 1996, the NCTE and the IRA released their *Standards for the English Language Arts*. While the standards focus on K–12 literacy education, they are grounded in a tradition of theory, research, and practice shared with college teacher-researchers of literacy. NCTE and IRA were careful not to devise standards that could be interpreted as a national curriculum—lists of specific books to be read and skills to be mastered by all students in certain grade levels. Rather, the standards specify the conditions that research and teaching experience tell us must exist if students are to read and write in ways that will enable them to participate in democratic institutions and thrive in a post-industrial economy.

In the months following release of the standards, one complaint has been heard repeatedly: that they are vague. That criticism may have originated in official government comment on the standards offered by Michael Cohen, senior advisor to the US Secretary of Education (Sanchez). The *New York Times* sounded the same note in an editorial shortly after the standards appeared ("How Not"). Other newspaper editorialists and columnists soon advanced the same argument. In a Sunday editorial titled "English as Mush," the *Sacramento Bee* argued that the vagueness of the standards document was cover for a hidden political agenda. The *Bee* took particular issue with Standard 9, which envisions a world in which American "students develop an understanding of and respect for diversity in language use, patterns, and dialects across cultures, ethnic groups, geographic regions, and social roles" (3). That "sounds a lot more like an effort to shape political and social attitudes than a serious attempt to foster the teaching and learning of any real academic discipline," the *Bee* said. Of the twelve standards, Standard 9 points most emphatically to a plausible defense of the document's perceived vagueness. For the standards—for any research findings—to have a desirable and lasting effect, they must be fleshed out locally in conversations that can be responsive to interests that are likely to differ from place to place. But the *Bee* editorial is correct in one import respect (although for reasons unlike mine). The standards document *is* an effort to shape political and social attitudes, if by shaping we mean to imbue something heretofore undefined with form and substance. That, precisely, is what is ethical about the standards. They establish the grounds for consensus and difference on political and social issues, and provide the conceptual tools for translating that consensus and difference into local action—liberal or conservative, radical or reactionary.[20]

What vanity, though, to assume that our contributions are ever needed for such local action to move ahead. Others will do—or claim to do—what we can and should do better. Strong support for this contention can be drawn from the controversy that prefaced a 26 May 1998 decision by the CUNY Board of Trustees to eliminate "remedial" offerings throughout its system of senior colleges (see Healy and Schmidt for an overview). Individuals knowledgeable about the teaching of writing received scant attention during the course of the controversy. Aside from a letter to the *New York Times* by Marilyn Sternglass, little is to be found in the public record. That, ironically, left James Traub as one of the few commentators who entered the fray—in a

Times op-ed piece—with any demonstrable knowledge about college writing instruction ("Raising"). And yet how much could he contribute? As Patricia Donahue puts it in an incisive review of *City on a Hill*, it is "discouraging to note how *little* someone like Traub knows about what it is writing teachers actually do in the classroom, or, for that matter, what a critical pedagogical practice might look like" (121). What Traub lacks, according to Donahue, is an appreciation for writing students as the primary "subject" of representation in composition studies, with all the difficulty that entails (112). His aim to represent the "truth" of declining standards muddles the message about college students and "remediation," a message that could be presented in greater clarity and texture by composition teacher-researchers themselves.[21]

CUNY trustees approved a plan similar to Traub's proposal for a stratified CUNY: restricted enrollment for the senior colleges, but relatively open enrollment for the community colleges. Specifically, the trustees' resolution states that a student may obtain "remediation services at a CUNY community college, at a senior college only during its summer sessions, or elsewhere as may be made available" ("City University"). But can it be said that Traub's words influenced the trustees' resolution? No one has made that claim publicly, and the reason may lie in the resolution's details. For it is well known that New York Mayor Rudolph Giuliani would like "remedial services" to be offered "elsewhere" only, to be privatized (Healy and Schmidt A22).

Where, we might ask, did this idea come from? Apparently, according to the *New York Times*, from conservative journalist and social critic Heather Mac Donald (Arenson).[22] Like Traub, Mac Donald has spent time gleaning the field of composition. Her most recognizable harvest: an essay in the conservative policy journal *Public Interest* titled "Why Johnny Can't Write," in which she denigrates the usual suspects—Min-Zhan Lu, James Zebrowski [sic], John Trimbur, Marilyn Sternglass, and others—for "expending vast amounts of energy making excuses for their students" (11, 12). We might wish to dismiss Mac Donald's polemic as ill-informed and mean-spirited, but we should resist the temptation: the diffusion of her work across a broad network of influence demonstrates—structurally, if not ideologically—an approach that could be useful to composition teacher-researchers seeking to affect public policy on literacy issues. Mac Donald's *Public Interest* argument initially reached a modest audience in summer 1995, but its power was magnified shortly thereafter when George Will summarized it in his nationally syndicated newspaper column ("Teach"), and again two years later when John Leo made reference to it in his "On Society" column for *U.S. News and World Report* ("The Answer"). And Mac Donald recently returned to attacking composition teacher-researchers in a *City Journal* article outlining for Giuliani her agenda for reforming CUNY. She complains that "CUNY's remedial departments have been overrun by theory-besotted post-Marxists, who see in bad grammar a courageous blow against the racist patriarchy and a mark of freethinking individuality" ("CUNY" 67–68).[23]

Like it or not, Mac Donald has cultivated audiences whose attention translates into action with consequences for thousands of men and women whose literacy is our professional concern. Mac Donald makes the task look easy; her encounters with composition scholarship are glancing and facile—and arguably unethical. But it is her persistence that should command our attention. Her criticism of writing instruction for underprepared college students has been played out over a period of years in visible, credible forums (see Mac Donald "Downward"; Leo, "A University's"; Cook and Cooper; and Mac Donald "CUNY's" for an early sequence of commentary and response on remedial instruction).

Conclusion

This essay began as an argument that teacher-researchers should search for ways to accommodate their writing about college composition to broader, nonacademic audiences. To support this argument, I provided evidence of professional writers who have taken up the cause of speaking publicly, if not always ethically, about college composition. I then suggested that for such writing to be ethical, it may indeed be anchored in national concerns, but it must attend to the local because it is there that political and social issues of great consequence can be deliberated and acted upon.

The prospects of doing this work well are evident in Janet Emig's introduction to *Composing Processes*, in which she affirms her concern for the value of the persons and their ties to place represented in her study:

> The writer wishes to reiterate what she believes are the values of this study. . . . An experiment in capturing a process in process, the study provides certain kinds of data—humanistic data—that other kinds of inquiries into composition have not yet elicited. Perhaps its chief value is its steady assumption that persons, rather than mechanisms, compose. (5)

Two things are remarkable here. First is Emig's assertion—bold for the early 1970s—that composition should study *persons*, not *mechanisms*. And then there is the irony: Emig's self effacement, signaled here by reference to herself as "the writer," a tactic she adheres to throughout the book. A quarter-century later, introducing a collection on *Feminine Principles and Women's Experience in American Composition and Rhetoric*, Emig speaks in a voice that transforms "the writer" into "I" and "we," and in so doing lays the groundwork for thinking about composition scholarship as discharging a public duty.

Emig explains that she and her coeditor

> had been attracted into composition and rhetoric in part on ethical grounds, sensing and responding to its egalitarian and popular roots. We believe in common that all teaching possesses a moral dimension: teaching represents an ethical transaction with the learner, demanding responsibility, scrupulosity, and nurture. Now, perhaps, we would argue this as a feminist position; but we hold this commitment prior to our feminism, because it is made to all learners. Indeed, we each regard the learning and teaching of composition as democratic manifestations of a democratic society requiring serious, courteous, and equitable treatment of all persons across categories of age, gender, ethnicity, race, religion, class, sexual preference, and community status. (Emig with Phelps xv)

Good words to remember as we realize that the ideal of professionalism entails democratic values that encompass both academic and social realms—values shared, as Emig suggests, by colleagues and citizens alike. Teacher-researchers in composition should embrace this new professionalism, or else be willing to cede their authority to others whose aims and ethics in speaking about literacy may be inadequate to the task. To tolerate such inadequacy would mean turning our backs on the Lynns and the Tammys whose literacy it is at once our privilege and obligation to represent.

Acknowledgments

Many thanks to Janet Carey Eldred and Gesa E. Kirsch, always invaluable readers of my work.

Notes

1. Reception of *Cultural Literacy* among academics was mixed (see, for example, Smith, and Sledd and Sledd), as it was among nonacademic reviewers.

Rose's book, on the other hand, has been thoroughly embraced by readers on campus and off. Each has since shifted his focus toward matters of literacy in the schools, and the same pattern holds for reception of Hirsch's *The Schools We Need and Why We Don't Have Them* and Rose's *Possible Lives: The Promise of Public Education in America.*

2. North writes that "it would be no great exaggeration to call *Research in Written Composition* the charter of modern Composition" (17). Hillocks makes a similar point (xv–xvii). But it is worth remembering that the significance of such "Great Moments in Composition History" should always remain open to interpretation (Schilb 17).

3. But Lynn herself is no longer anonymous. Emig revealed Lynn's identity in an interview with Gerald Nelms. Nelms subsequently interviewed the real Lynn, Susan Gzesh, now an attorney practicing immigration law in Chicago and teaching at the University of Michigan ("An Oral History" 2–3).

4. I use the term *teacher-researcher* here in its widest sense. Most of us who study writing also teach writing, and the questions we ask as researchers cannot help but be influenced by what we do as teachers. Further, if the intent of publishing research findings is to inform and persuade, then researching always culminates in an act of teaching. Consider the following questions, more pointedly phrased. How best can student writing—and students writing—be characterized? To what extent can students of composition be involved as collaborators in research, rather than simply as subjects? What authority do students have in shaping, in advancing and suppressing, representation of their literate lives? A curious feature of these questions, one to be pursued in this essay, is that they tend to blur the line between writing "researcher" and "teacher" identities. Put another way, teachers and researchers of writing are both engaged in the work of representing what their students do when they write, as well as what *they* do when they observe that writing. So both entertain similar ethical questions relevant to representation. That is an enabling premise of my argument in this essay.

5. See also Helen Dale's account of her unmet desire to collaborate, even co-author, with a middle school English teacher in whose classroom she conducted a study of student writers' collaborations.

6. Elizabeth Chiseri-Strater notes that one way to salve the guilt Sunstein describes is to position oneself prominently in the text, so as to disclose one's point of view and, therefore, to acknowledge the distortions it might introduce. But there is risk associated with positioning for self-disclosure. In Chiseri-Strater's case, some readers of her ethnography, *Academic Literacies,* found her voice "self-indulgent and irritating," at least initially (127).

7. Traub's argument about the decline of college composition is but the most recent in a tradition that dates back at least to the attacks on composition at Harvard just before and after the turn of the century. For a selection of complaints, see Brereton, especially the essays published in popular journals of the day: an anonymous article in *Century Magazine* (238–41) and Thomas Raynesford Lounsbury's longer piece in *Harper's Monthly* (261–86). Cmiel lists additional magazine articles involved in the Harvard debate, among them contributions by Horace Scudder, E. L. Godkin, and W. W. Goodwin to periodicals such as *The Atlantic*

Monthly and *The Nation* (320, n. 10). See Connors for an interpretive history of such complaints.

8. Traub continues by observing that a social scientist might have found a less time-consuming way of reaching conclusions, gathering data rather than direct experience," a statement that indicates Traub's awareness that social inquiry is anything but a uniform science (83). He claims authority, just as would an ethnographer, by emphasizing that he "placed great value on sheer immersion, on the particular words and acts of particular people, and on the evidence of my own senses" (83).

9. Sternglass drew her analytical scheme from Richard Larson's FIPSE-funded work on writing portfolio assessment (circa 1986) at Lehman College, City University of New York. Larson's list of discourse acts is grounded in the speech act theories of J. L. Austin and John Searle (148). Interestingly, in more recent writing about Linda, Sternglass sets aside Larson's analytical scheme as a basis for making inferences about cognition from performance in writing (*Time* 204–22). Instead, she evaluates Linda's perspectives on knowing with regard to the epistemological categories posited by Belenky, Clinchy, Goldberger, and Tarule in *Women's Ways of Knowing*. More specifically, Sternglass works carefully with the notion of growth" in writing, with reference to Haswell's *Gaining Ground in College Writing*. One consequence of shifting from documenting discourse acts to assessing growth in thinking and writing is that Sternglass's argument becomes more accessible to nonspecialist and even nonacademic readers."

10. Sternglass's gesture to City College's history reads as follows: "Thus this study will not claim to make broad generalizations about the writing and learning processes of urban, high-risk college students in general, but it will attempt to account for the kind of progress that is possible for students of this background. The City College, justly famous for educating immigrant populations in the 1920s and 1930s in New York City, seems to be fulfilling that same role now for both minority and new immigrant groups in the city" ("Writing Development" 241). Let me stress that I consider Sternglass's *Written Communication* article to be an important contribution to knowledge in composition studies. Its importance is underscored by its recent inclusion in a new text for graduate students edited by Wiley, Gleason, and Phelps.

11. But Traub errs when he claims that "academics in the field have had to tie themselves into some serious knots to escape this conclusion" (129). He ignores Piaget's later research: research that places the acquisition of formal operations in late adolescence, the age of "traditional" first-year college students. Nor does Traub attend to a similar claim by Vygotsky that late adolescence is when young people can reliably engage in abstract, propositional thinking. Bergstrom and Villanueva represent just two of many sources in composition studies that explicitly address—and refute—the argument about cognitive development Traub appropriates. All of this is not to say that Shaughnessy's work should be exempt from criticism; see, for example, Harris' critique of her emphasis in *Errors and Expectations* on teaching grammar (76–90).

12. Traub had some insight into disagreements within composition studies over the usefulness of critical literacy as an analytical construct. For instance, he

"drew information and guidance" from James Williams' review essay of three books that, Williams argues, present a distorted vision of literacy because it is filtered through the lens of "neo-Marxist politics" (Traub 353; Williams 833). What he misses, though, is the discussion among those who accept critical literacy as a useful construct but disagree on how it ought to be defined and examined (see, for example, Lankshear and McLaren, published a year before *City on a Hill*).

13.   Traub reports that Gross's mild criticisms of open admissions led to his dismissal as humanities dean (72–74).

14.   Sternglass talks back to Traub at various points in the final report on her longitudinal study, *Time to Know Them*. She notes that Tammy (Sternglass calls her Joan) expressed disappointment in Traub's characterization of her (67–78). Sternglass's case study of Joan offers a fascinating counterpoint to Traub's (240–65).

15.   Careful to cite, yes, but not necessarily effectively (see Donahue 120). Still, Traub's treatment of composition literature is more even-tempered than his *New Republic* report on visiting the Fourth National Basic Writing Conference in 1992 ("Back"). In that report, Traub expressed amazement that critics of Mina Shaughnessy's theorizing about basic writing—Min-Zhan Lu in particular—would have any standing at such a meeting. Lu, Bruce Homer, Jerrie Cobb Scott, Pamela Gay, Tom Fox and Steve Parks were painted as "radicals," though radicals "uncomfortably, and even farcically, divided between their professional and ideological commitments." as if this divide were not a permanent condition of professional life (19).

16.   Biographical information on Traub, his parents, and his siblings can be found in the "Personal Afterword" of his father's memoir (Traub and Teicholz 397–403). Traub's spouse, Elizabeth W. Easton, completed her dissertation on the interiors of French painter Edouard Vuillard in 1989 and has subsequently curated several Vuillard exhibitions (Traub v, 360; Easton "Edouard Vuillard's Interiors" and *Intimate Interiors*). These details are offered to assist readers in identifying and situating Traub's authority as a researcher and writer (see Geertz for extensive use of such detail in locating the authority of well-known ethnographic writers).

17.   Most composition teacher-researchers are probably familiar with the controversy that grew from attempts to revise the first-year writing curriculum at the University of Texas early this decade. The conflict has been narrated by a number of the composition specialists close to the revision project, namely Linda Brodkey, Maxine Hairston, and John Ruszkiewicz. Brodkey—a central player in the controversy—has published most extensively, reaching readers by way of chapters in a number of high-profile edited collections (among them one from MLA ["Making a Federal Case"] and another from Routledge ["Writing Permitted"]). She has also republished and augmented her views in a new collection of her essays, *Writing Permitted in Designated Areas Only*. Hairston reached readers through an article in a prominent composition journal, and Ruszkiewicz aired his views at the profession's national conference. But aside from scattered newspaper coverage and a commentary by columnist George Will ("Radical"), the story of English 306 did not make an enduring impression outside the academy. That is, not until Richard Bernstein, former cultural correspondent for the *New York Times*, published *Dictatorship of Virtue*, a study of "how the battle over multi-

culturalism is reshaping our schools, our country, our lives," as the book's subtitle puts it. Among the book's favorable notices are those appearing in the *Wall Street Journal* (McGowan), *Commonweal* (Worth), and the *National Review* (Kramer). Negative reviews are forceful, but relatively few (for example, see Wilentz, and Stimpson, "Gunships").

18. It is worth noting that Berry spent the first two years of his academic career, 1962–64, directing the freshman English program at the University Heights campus of New York University, in the Bronx (Angyal 20–21). Berry left NYU and returned to Kentucky at a time when the university had embarked on a controversial program to transform itself into the elite urban institution it is today (see Baldridge 35–61).

19. The MLA Commission on Professional Service argues that such scholarship should be classified as "applied work," which "intersects with practical affairs and problem solving, making academic knowledge available in these areas. Beneficiaries of applied work might be government, industry, the law, the arts, and not-for-profit organizations" (164).

20. There is evidence that NCTE is willing to entertain serious oppositional critique of the standards within its own publications. In a recent issue of *Research in the Teaching of English*, two essayists question the claim that "students today read better and write better than at any other time in the history of the country" (*Standards for the English Language Arts* 5). Andrew Coulson claims that "this belief is not only wrongheaded, it is insidious, for it leads to the false impression that our educational system is fundamentally sound" (311). In a subtler voice, Lawrence Stedman asks. "Are these sweeping claims true?" and answers that they are, but need careful qualification (284).

21. See, for example, Ira Shor's call for an end to basic writing instruction in the CUNY system, and Karen Greenberg's forceful reply, both of which appeared in the *Journal of Basic Writing*.

22. With degrees in literature from Yale and Cambridge and a law degree from Stanford, Mac Donald spent part of the 1980s as an attorney with the US Environmental Protection Agency. After leaving the agency in 1987, Mac Donald moved to New York and took courses at New York University and the New School for Social Research. It was then that she became "a crusader against multiculturalism and other fashionable social theories" (Machan 64).

23. See also essays by Scott and Stelzer on the influence of *City Journal* and its publisher, the conservative Manhattan Institute.

Works Cited

Angyal, Andrew J. *Wendell Berry*. New York: Twayne, 1995.

Arenson, Karen W. "Some CUNY Officials Are Cautious about Mayor's Proposal, but Others See Disaster." *New York Times* 30 Jan. 1998: B7.

Baldridge, J. Victor. *Power and Conflict in the University: Research in the Sociology of Complex Organizations*. New York: Wiley, 1971.

Bergstrom, Robert F. "Discovery of Meaning: Development of Formal Thought in the Teaching of Literature." *College English* 45 (1983): 745–55

Bernstein, Richard. *Dictatorship of Virtue.* New York: Vintage, 1995.

Berry, Wendell. Preface. *Sex, Economy Freedom, and Community: Eight Essays.* New York: Pantheon, 1993. xi–xxii.

Bérubé, Michael. *The Employment of English: Theory, Jobs, and the Future of Literary Studies.* New York: New York UP, 1998.

Bleich, David. "Ethnography and the Study of Literacy: Prospects for Socially Generous Research." *Into the Field: Sites of Composition Studies.* Ed. Anne Ruggles Gere. New York: MLA, 1993. 176–92.

Braddock, Richard, Richard Lloyd-Jones, and Lowell Schoer. *Research in Written Composition.* Champaign: NCTE, 1963.

Brereton, John C. *The Origins of Composition Studies in the American College, 1875–1925.* Pittsburgh: U of Pittsburgh P, 1995.

Brodkey, Linda. "Making a Federal Case Out of Difference: The Politics of Pedagogy, Publicity, and Postponement." *Writing Theory and Critical Theory.* Ed. John Clifford and John Schilb. New York: MLA, 1994. 236–61.

———. *Writing Permitted in Designated Areas Only.* Minneapolis: U of Minnesota P, 1996.

———. "Writing Permitted in Designated Areas Only." *Higher Education Under Fire: Politics, Economics, and the Crisis of the Humanities.* Ed. Michael Bérubé and Cary Nelson. New York: Routledge, 1995. 214–37.

Brueggemann, Brenda Jo. "Still-Life: Representations and Silences in the Participant-Observer Role." Mortensen and Kirsch 17–39.

Buxton, Earl W. Foreword. *The Composing Processes of Twelfth Graders,* by Janet Emig. Urbana: NCTE, 1971. v–vi.

Chiseri-Strater, Elizabeth. "Turning In upon Ourselves: Positionality, Subjectivity, and Reflexivity in Case Study and Ethnographic Research." Mortensen and Kirsch 115–33.

"City University of New York Trustees Approve Resolution to End Remediation in Senior Colleges." Press release. 10 June 1998. 7 July 1998 <http://www.cuny.edu/events/press/june4_98.html>.

Cmiel, Kenneth. *Democratic Eloquence: The Fight over Popular Speech in Nineteenth-Century America.* Berkeley: U of California P, 1990.

Connors, Robert J. "Crisis and Panacea in Composition Studies: A History." *Composition in Context: Essays in Honor of Donald C. Stewart.* Ed. W. Ross Winterowd and Vincent Gillespie. Carbondale: Southern Illinois UP, 1994. 86–105.

Cook, Blanche Wiesen, and Sandi E. Cooper. "The Trashing of CUNY." Letter. *New York Times* 8 Sept. 1994: A25.

Coulson, Andrew J. "Schooling and Literacy over Time: The Rising Cost of Stagnation and Decline." *Research in the Teaching of English* 30 (1996): 311–27.

Dale, Helen. "Dilemmas of Fidelity: Qualitative Research in the Classroom." Mortensen and Kirsch 77–94.

Denzin, Norman K., and Yvonna S. Lincoln. Introduction. *Handbook of Qualitative Research*. Ed. Norman K. Denzin and Yvonna S. Lincoln. Thousand Oaks: Sage, 1994. 1–17.

Donahue, Patricia. "Talking to Students." Rev. of *Generation at the Crossroads*, by Paul Rogat Loeb; *Battling Bias*, by Ruth Sidel; and *City on a Hill*, by James Traub. *CCC* 47 (1996): 112–23.

Easton, Elizabeth Wynne. "Edouard Vuillard's Interiors of the 1890s." Diss. Yale U. 1989.

———. *The Intimate Interiors of Edouard Vuillard*. Washington, DC: Smithsonian Institution P, 1989.

Emig, Janet. *The Composing Processes of Twelfth Graders*. Urbana, IL: NCTE, 1971.

Emig, Janet, with Louise Wetherbee Phelps. Introduction. *Feminine Principles and Women's Experience in American Composition and Rhetoric*. Ed. Louise Wetherbee Phelps and Janet Emig. Pittsburgh: U of Pittsburgh P, 1995. xi–xviii.

"English as Mush." Editorial. *Sacramento Bee* 17 Mar. 1996, Forum: 4.

Faigley, Lester. *Fragments of Rationality: Postmodernity and the Subject of Composition*. Pittsburgh: U of Pittsburgh P, 1992.

Geertz, Clifford. *Works and Lives: The Anthropologist as Author*. Stanford: Stanford UP, 1988.

Giroux, Henry A. "Beyond the Ivory Tower: Public Intellectuals and the Crisis of Higher Education." *Higher Education Under Fire: Politics, Economics, and the Crisis of the Humanities*. Ed. Michael Bérubé and Cary Nelson. New York: Routledge, 1995. 238–58.

Greenberg, Karen L. "A Response to Ira Shor's 'Our Apartheid: Writing Instruction and Inequality.'" *Journal of Basic Writing* 16.2 (1997): 90–94.

Hairston, Maxine. "Diversity, Ideology, and Teaching Writing." *CCC* 43 (1992): 179–93.

Harris, Joseph. *A Teaching Subject: Composition since 1966*. Upper Saddle River: Prentice Hall, 1997.

Healy, Patrick, and Peter Schmidt. "In New York, a 'Standards Revolution' or the Gutting of Public Colleges?" *Chronicle of Higher Education* 10 July 1998: A21–A23.

Hillocks, George. *Research on Written Composition: New Directions for Teaching*. Urbana: NCRE and ERIC, 1986.

Hirsch, E. D., Jr. *Cultural Literacy: What Every American Needs to Know*. Boston: Houghton Mifflin, 1987.

———. *The Schools We Need and Why We Don't Have Them*. New York: Doubleday, 1996.

"How Not to Write English." Editorial. *New York Times* 14 Mar. 1996: A22.

Howe, Irving. *A Margin of Hope: An Intellectual Autobiography*. San Diego: Harcourt, 1982.

Kramer, Hilton. "How Democracy Perishes." Rev. of *Dictatorship of Virtue*, by Richard Bernstein. *National Review* 19 Dec. 1994: 53–54.

Kristol, Irving. "Memoirs of a Trotskyist." *New York Times* 23 Jan. 1977, sec. 6: 42+.

Lankshear, Colin, and Peter L. McLaren. Introduction. *Critical Literacy: Politics, Praxis, and the Postmodern.* Ed. Colin Lankshear and Peter L. McLaren. Albany: State U of New York P, 1993. 1–56.

Larson, Richard L. "Using Portfolios in the Assessment of Writing in the Academic Disciplines." *Portfolios: Process and Product.* Ed. Pat Belanoff and Marcia Dickson. Portsmouth: Boynton, 1991. 137–49.

Leo, John. "The Answer Is 45 Cents." *U.S. News and World Report* 21 Apr. 1997: 14.

———. "A University's Sad Decline." *U.S. News and World Report* 15 Aug. 1994: 20.

Lucke, Jamie. "Wilkinson Gets in Verbal Scuffle." *Lexington Herald-Leader* 22 Jan. 1992: A1, A9.

Machan, Dyan. "Free Lunch—No Dishes to Wash." *Forbes* 4 May 1988: 62+.

Mac Donald, Heather. "CUNY Could Be Great Again." *City Journal* 8.1 (1998): 65–70.

———. "CUNY's Open Admissions Fail Miserably." Letter. *New York Times* 15 Sept. 1994: A22.

———. "Downward Mobility: The Failure of Open Admissions at City University." *City Journal* 4.3 (1994): 10–20.

———. "Why Johnny Can't Write." *Public Interest* 120 (1995): 3–13.

McCarthy, Lucille Parkinson, and Stephen Fishman. "A Text for Many Voices: Representing Diversity in Reports of Naturalistic Research." Mortensen and Kirsch 155–76.

McGowan, William. "A Politically Incorrect Study of PC." Rev. of *Dictatorship of Virtue,* by Richard Bernstein. *Wall Street Journal* 4 Jan. 1995: A10.

Mitchell, W. J. T. "Representation." *Critical Terms for Literary Study.* 2nd ed. Ed. Frank Lentricchia and Thomas McLaughlin. Chicago: U of Chicago P, 1995. 11–22.

MLA Commission on Professional Service. "Making Faculty Work Visible: Reinterpreting Professional Service, Teaching, and Research in the Fields of Language and Literature." *Profession 96* (1996): 161–216.

Mortensen, Peter. "Analyzing Talk about Writing." *Methods and Methodology in Composition Research.* Ed. Gesa Kirsch and Patricia A. Sullivan. Carbondale: Southern Illinois UP, 1992. 105–29.

———. *Remediation in Writing.* Extended School Services Technical Report. Frankfort: Kentucky Dept. of Education, 1992.

———. "Representations of Literacy and Region: Narrating 'Another America.'" *Pedagogy in the Age of Politics: Reading and Writing (in) the Academy.* Ed. Patricia A. Sullivan and Donna J. Qualley. Urbana: NCTE, 1994. 100–20.

———. "Understanding Readers' Conceptions of Audience: Rhetorically Challenging Texts." *A Sense of Audience in Written Communication.* Ed. Gesa Kirsch and Duane Roen. Newbury Park: Sage, 1990. 267–79.

Mortensen, Peter, and Gesa E. Kirsch, eds. *Ethics and Representation in Qualitative Studies of Literacy.* Urbana: NCTE, 1996.

Nelms, Gerald. "An Oral History of Janet Emig's Case Study Subject 'Lynn.'" CCCC. Cincinnati, OH, 1992 (ERIC 345 277).

———. "Reassessing Janet Emig's *The Composing Processes of Twelfth Graders*: An Historical Perspective." *Rhetoric Review* 13 (1994): 108–30.

Newkirk, Thomas. "Seduction and Betrayal in Qualitative Research." Mortensen and Kirsch 3–16.

North, Stephen M. *The Making of Knowledge in Composition: Portrait of An Emerging Field.* Portsmouth: Boynton, 1987.

Rose, Mike. *Lives on the Boundary: The Struggles and Achievements of America's Underprepared.* New York: Free P, 1989.

———. *Possible Lives: The Promise of Public Education in America.* Boston: Houghton, 1995.

Rosenthal, A. M. "An American Promise." Rev. of *City on a Hill,* by James Traub. *New York Times Book Review* 2 Oct. 1994: 7, 9.

Rudy, S. Willis. *The College of the City of New York: A History. 1847–1947.* New York: City College P, 1949.

Ruszkiewicz, John. "'Reason Is But Choosing': Ideology in First Year English." CCCC, Boston, MA, 1991 (ERIC 331 058).

Sanchez, Rene. "Reading Standards Criticized." *Washington Post* 13 Mar. 1996: A3.

Schilb, John. *Between the Lines: Relating Composition Theory and Literary Theory.* Portsmouth: Boynton, 1996.

Schuckit, M. A., and T. L. Smith. "An 8-Year Follow up of 450 Sons of Alcoholic and Control Subjects." *Archives of General Psychiatry* 53 (1996): 202–10.

Scott, Janny. "Turning Intellect into Influence." *New York Times* 12 May 1997: B1+.

Shor, Ira. "Our Apartheid: Writing Instruction and Inequality." *Journal of Basic Writing* 16.1 (1997): 91–104.

Sledd, Andrew, and James Sledd. "Hirsch's Use of His Sources in *Cultural Literacy*: A Critique." *Profession 88* (1988): 33–39.

Smith, Jeff. "Cultural Literacy and the Academic 'Left.'" *Profession 88* (1988): 25–28.

Standards for the English Language Arts. Urbana and Newark: NCTE and IRA, 1996.

Stedman, Lawrence C. "An Assessment of Literacy Trends, Past and Present." *Research in the Teaching of English* 30 (1996): 283–302.

Stelzer, Irwin M. "Where Rudy Gets His Ideas." *New York Post Online Edition* 4 Feb. 1998. <http://www.nypostonline.com/commentary/3538.htm>.

Sternglass, Marilyn S. "At CUNY, Statistics Miss the Point." Letter. *New York Times* 11 Nov. 1997: A26.

———. *Time to Know Them: A Longitudinal Study of Writing and Learning at the College Level.* Mahwah: Erlbaum, 1997.

————. "Writing Development as Seen through Longitudinal Research: A Case Study Exemplar." *Written Communication* 10 (1993): 235–61.

Stimpson, Catharine. "Gunships on the Loose." Rev. of *Dictatorship of Virtue,* by Richard Bernstein. *Raritan* 15 (1995): 82–94.

————. "The Public Duties of Our Profession." *Profession* (1996): 100–2.

Stotsky, Sandra. "From the Editor." *Research in the Teaching of English* 27 (1993): 132.

Sunstein, Bonnie S. "Culture on the Page: Experience, Rhetoric, and Aesthetics in Ethnographic Writing." Mortensen and Kirsch 177–201.

Traub, James. "Back to Basic." *New Republic* 8 Feb. 1993: 18–19.

————. *City on a Hill: Testing the American Dream at City College.* Reading: Addison, 1994.

————. "Raising CUNY to a Higher Level." *New York Times* 14 Feb. 1998: A13.

Traub, Marvin, and Tom Teicholz. *Like No Other Store . . . : The Bloomingdale's Legend and the Revolution in American Marketing.* New York: Times Books, 1993.

Villanueva, Victor, Jr. Foreword. *Audience Expectations and Teacher Demands,* by Robert Brooke and John Hendricks. Carbondale: Southern Illinois UP, 1989. vii–xiii.

Warth, Robert D. "Interference Grows in the Fertile Soil of Ignorance Here." *Lexington Herald-Leader* 7 Mar. 1992: A13.

Wiener, Jon. "School Daze." Rev. of *City on a Hill,* by James Traub. *Nation* 7 Nov. 1994: 522–28.

Wilentz, Sean. "Sense and Sensitivity." Rev. of *Dictatorship of Virtue,* by Richard Bernstein. *New Republic* 31 Oct. 1994: 43–48.

Wiley, Mark, Barbara Gleason, and Louise Wetherbee Phelps, eds. *Composition in Four Keys: Inquiring into the Field.* Mountain View: Mayfield, 1996.

Will, George F. "Radical English." *Debating P.C.: The Controversy over Political Correctness on College Campuses.* Ed. Paul Berman. New York: Laurel, 1992. 258–61.

————. "Teach Johnny to Write." *Washington Post* 2 July 1995: C7.

Williams, James D. "Politicizing Literacy." Rev. of *Conversations on the Written Word,* by Jay Robinson; *Literacy and Empowerment,* by Patrick Courts; and *The Right to Literacy,* ed. Andrea Lunsford, Helene Moglen, and James Slevin. *College English* 54 (1992): 833–42.

Worth, Robert F. "E Pluribus, Plures." Rev. of *Dictatorship of Virtue,* by Richard Bernstein. *Commonweal* 4 Nov. 1994: 36–37.

III SERVICE LEARNING AND SOCIAL CHANGE

Service learning has become a major trend in American higher education, not only in English Studies but in many other disciplines as well. According to Schutz and Gere, "service learning . . . distinguishes itself from volunteerism by its emphasis on reflection as well as action [and] combines community work with classroom instruction." Service learning is significant because of its potential to enhance students' academic knowledge through critical reflection and experiential learning, its potential to connect colleges and universities with their surrounding community, and the potential to foster the educational goals of democracy and citizenship.

Aaron Schutz and Anne Ruggles Gere review the literature on service learning and trace its development in English Studies. They describe different ways in which service learning makes its way into English classes and explore its impact on students and on those being served. Among the critical questions they raise are, "To what extent and how does service learning meet curricular goals, enhance students' knowledge, benefit community members as well as students, and, finally, challenge stereotypes some students may hold of those who need help?"

In "Service Learning and First-Year Composition," Brock Haussamen takes a practical look at service learning. He explores how service learning can fit into a first-year composition classroom and examines both advantages and drawbacks of voluntary and required service learning course components. He concludes by making a case for the unique value of community service to a community college education.

Ellen Cushman explores the notion of "The Rhetorician as an Agent of Social Change" in an essay which won the Richard Braddock award for the best article of the year in *College Composition and Communication*. She argues for "seeing ourselves as both civic participants and as preparing students for greater civic participation," and illustrates her argument with an example of activist research she pursued in the community surrounding Rensselaer Polytechnic Institute. Her work sparked much animated discussion about the nature and purpose of "service" and increased teachers' and scholars' interest in service learning.

Finally, JoAnn Campbell takes a historical look at student writing and the "culture of service" at Mount Holyoke College. She examines how the college's mission and curriculum set out to prepare women for a life of service, encouraging them to pursue professions like teaching or missionary work. Campbell explores "the effects of gender on service, both as a concept and activity" and traces how a gendered notion of service continues to inform and influence contemporary discussions of service learning.

9 Service Learning and English Studies: Rethinking "Public" Service

Aaron Schutz and Anne Ruggles Gere

In recent years, service learning has begun to find a home in English departments, often by way of the writing program (Gere and Sinor; Herzberg; Minter, Gere, and Keller-Cohen; Watters and Ford). Unencumbered by a disciplinary identity, service learning has, for a number of years, moved freely within the academy, sometimes attaching itself to sociology or psychology, sometimes to education or social work, and, in the past few years, to English. Service learning, which distinguishes itself from volunteerism by its emphasis on reflection as well as action, combines community work with classroom instruction. Like other areas—film studies, say—that have nudged their way into the big tent of English studies, service learning owes its origins to students as well as faculty. On many campuses, the earliest forms of service learning emerged from student-developed community service programs, while university faculty or staff involvement came later. Fueled by renewed calls for volunteerism within the larger culture as well as increased interest in experiential learning, service learning has flourished on some campuses. At Stanford University, for example, student participation in service learning increased from 40 percent to 70 percent between 1984 and 1995 (Watters and Ford).

The growth in service learning has coincided with reconfigurations within English departments. Many English departments have begun to emphasize the social processes of consuming and producing texts rather than focusing entirely on "the best that has been thought and said" (Minter, Gere, and Keller-Cohen). Put another way, cultural studies has moved into English

Reprinted from *College English,* February 1998.

179

studies and taken up residence next to literary theory. Cultural studies brings with it questions about public policy and the relationship of the academy to the citizens who support it (Nelson; Smithson and Ruff). Consequently, it raises the decibel level of assertions that being political in the classroom cannot substitute for the kind of civic participation represented by service learning (Cushman). Both theoretically and practically, service learning fits particularly well in English departments that foreground the ways people read and write, attend to cultural studies, and entertain questions about public policy. Service learning has found an especially comfortable home in composition programs. As Anne Ruggles Gere and Jennifer Sinor show, the processes of contending with expectations, undertaking actions, and reflecting thoughtfully fit comfortably for both the writers and service learners who seek to locate themselves in a text or context. For instructors who teach classes that grapple with social issues related to literacy, or who wish to provide a venue for students to connect with the situated complexities of issues and communities outside the classroom, service learning provides a ready and practical solution—although, as this essay will try to show, truly effective and ethical service learning is not easy to initiate.

Before embracing either the theoretical or the practical attractions of service learning, English studies will do well to consider the nature and potential impact of this newcomer to the field. Certainly service learning has already met with its share of critics, ranging from those who explore the potentially oppressive impact of even well-intended efforts on those who are "served" (Maybach) to those who note that many projects seem to promote relatively simplistic and distorted "individualistic" visions of social problems among those who "serve" (Seigel and Rockwood; Herzberg). The popular press has also begun to question the usefulness of America's (and President Clinton's) new fascination with volunteerism as a solution for social ills, as seen for instance in a 1997 article in the *New York Times* (Cuomo).

One of the most persuasive critiques of service learning in the English department appears in Bruce Herzberg's "Community Service and Critical Teaching," where Herzberg discusses a two-semester service project he created with a colleague. In the first semester, students take an introductory sociology class where they "examine the ways that literacy is gained or not gained in the United States" (310), drawing on a range of critical readings on the social forces that surround literacy. At the same time, students take a short class to prepare them to be literacy tutors. In both semesters, students enroll in Herzberg's composition class, and in the second semester they serve as adult literacy tutors in a local homeless shelter.

While Herzberg notes that students generally "developed excellent tutoring relationships and all learned how to draw on their own resources both psychologically and pedagogically" (311), he is initially less than satisfied by the classes' other accomplishments. His complaints seem to fall into three general areas. First, he notes almost in passing that students "did not seem attentive . . . to the analysis offered by the shelter's assistant director, who explained that while the shelter provided critically needed services, it also undermined any sense of independence the residents might have." Second, he worries that his students "tended to see their learners, quite naturally, as individuals with personal problems" (311), finding it "extremely difficult to transcend their own deeply-ingrained belief in individualism and meritocracy in their analysis of the reasons for the illiteracy they see" (312); "very few of the students," he notes, "ever became indignant about what they saw." Finally, he reports that "they would like to know if there is a 'cure,' but they don't regard that as a realistic hope" (311); the students were not energized into social action by their experiences.

In the largest sense, Herzberg's concerns about the service learning experiences of his students derive from the fact that both the initial conception of and the response to the tutoring experience remained essentially "private." As Herzberg puts it, "If our students regard social problems as chiefly or only personal, then they will not search beyond the person for a systemic explanation" (309). They will fail to develop what Kurt Spellmeyer describes as "a social imagination, an awareness of the human 'world' as a common historical project, and not simply as a state of nature to which we must adjust ourselves" (cited in Herzberg, 317). Herzberg worries that service learning alone, without a critical classroom component, fails to enable students to become active participants in the public realm. However, he says that "time and work were on our side" in the different critically oriented academic classes that surrounded the tutoring experience, and that the students' research projects "show a sense of life as a communal project, an understanding of the way that social institutions affect our lives, and a sense that our responsibility for social justice includes but also carries beyond personal acts of charity" (315, 317). Interestingly, however, Herzberg reports that the tutoring project itself did not generally appear in the students' writings. He notes that this should not be surprising, since the academic portion of the class was not focused on the tutoring experience. Our own experience, however, leads us to consider another possible explanation for why the students did not write about or grapple fully with the social complexities inherent in their tutoring experience. Perhaps at least part of their reluctance arose from the limitations of tutoring *itself as* a tool for helping students "uncover" power relations and issues of social inequality in society. As we note below, while our example of a similar tutoring project, "Learning Communities," led to outcomes similar to those of Herzberg's effort, we nonetheless frame our results somewhat differently, interrogating the theoretical grounding of the terms "public" and "private" as they are applied to service learning.

It is important to point out that we will be using the words "public" and "private" in a manner that may be unfamiliar to many readers. These terms have been used over the years in a myriad of different ways for many different purposes. Part of our goal is to use the example of service learning to help us rethink the connections between and definitions of public and private as they are deployed in writing, literacy studies, and the field of English in general. Instead of treating, for example, the "private" as a *location* in which some people can be isolated, we examine both public and private as different *ways of interacting with other people,* modes of interaction that can occur in any space or location. In a simple sense, "private" (or, as we will explain, "caring") practices involve unique relations between pairs of individuals where one "cares" for another, while "public" relations involve collective relations between multiple individuals who join together in a common project. These conceptions of public and private, we argue, provide extremely powerful perspectives from which we might explore and critique different activities of service learning and their relation to the field of English studies.

"Caring" Tutoring

One of the most common forms of service learning is tutoring, and it is, we argue, no accident that Herzberg's critical comments about service learning involve a tutoring project. Tutoring is an activity that tends to enable certain kinds of discourse practices while discouraging others. At the same time, tutoring is inseparably intertwined with larger cultural understandings of what "tutoring" and "school" are supposed to entail. Students come to understand tutoring through their expectations of, participation in, and talk about the activity. Apprenticing students into a specific service learning context entails encouraging them to take on a specific kind of self and ideology, embodying relationships with those who are "served" and with communities beyond the context of the activity itself, that they can *then* discuss in class. This means that for community service learning to be successful in the manner Herzberg desires, the intellectual content of the academic class, the *talking about,* must map onto the *doing,* the activity of the service component. Otherwise, the academic material of the class will not clearly provide students with a useful structure within which to examine and evolve their assumptions about, for example, power and oppression in the service context.

In a manner very similar to that in the classes created by Herzberg and his colleagues, undergraduates in the "Learning Communities" project, developed by one of the authors, Gere, and her colleagues, participated both in after-school literacy tutoring programs (with elementary and middle school students who came to the program for a range of reasons) and in a weekly seminar that examined issues surrounding literacy learning. The class was designed to involve undergraduates in conscious reflection on their roles as students, tutors, and citizens, drawing on a range of reading and writing activities that evolved over the course of the different semesters of the class (see Nye and Young). Unlike Herzberg's project, a crucial and explicit goal of the "Learning Communities" academic seminar was to support the students in their tutoring contexts. It is important to note that the instructors of the different "Learning Communities" classes realized both that their students often entered seeing themselves as "liberal saviors," as instructor Morris Young put it, and that the structure of tutoring had the potential to enhance the students' vision of this "savior" role. Thus, the exercises, journals, and readings in the class were, in part, designed to grapple with these challenges. Because a number of the students met biweekly after their participation in the tutoring program, we could follow the development of their thinking through several semesters.

Like Herzberg's effort, the "Learning Communities" tutoring project draws implicitly on a model of service we want to call, after Nel Noddings, "caring." Noddings's work, especially her *Challenge to Care in Schools, is* cited often in the literature on service learning as a central theoretical model (Kahne and Westheimer; Wuthnow).

However, a close analysis of Noddings's theory of caring shows some important limitations. In Noddings's caring, the one-caring receives the cared-for in an attitude of "engrossment"; the cared-for "fills the firmament." At least initially, as ones-caring "we receive what-is-there as nearly as possible without evaluation or assessment" (*Caring* 34) from the cared-for. The first requirement of caring, then, is to "see" as completely as possible what the world "looks like" from someone else's point of view. As Noddings says, "although I can never accomplish it, entirely, I try to apprehend the reality of the other" (14). The "caring" associated with the close personal work of tutoring requires students to focus intensely on the individual being tutored.

Caring involves what Noddings calls "motivational displacement on the part of the one-caring," where "I receive what the other conveys, and I want to respond in the way that furthers the other's purpose or project" (*Challenge* 16*)* and "there is invariably this displacement of interest from my own reality to the reality of the other" (*Caring* 14). "My rational powers are not diminished but they are enrolled in the service of my engrossment in the other" (36). Caring represents less an attempt to cooperate on what we will call below a *"common* project" than an effort on the part of the one-caring to support and develop the *cared-for's* project.

The nature of tutoring and the caring for specific others inherent in it, its "motivational displacement," has the effect of limiting students' engagement with other, more "public" dimensions of their experiences. For example, Minter, Gere, and Keller-Cohen explore the many ways that tutors were led to negotiate multiple institutional and situational definitions and deployments of literacy. Yet, even though the "undergraduates could represent their negotiations of literacy's multiple meanings and discourses by juxtaposing scenes of reading and writing . . . undergraduates seemed unable (or unwilling) to move from these localized scenes to make larger, more explicit arguments about literacy." In fact, one student who "spent a large part of the semester on and devoted his final project to issues of race, racism, and education," wrote, nonetheless, that "tutoring did not have 'anything to do or too much [to do] with literacy'" (683). As with Herzberg's project, when it remained focused on "tutoring," "Learning Communities" did not enable students to move beyond the personal or "private" dimensions of their work to consider its larger, more "public" aspects as effectively as we would have liked.

We do not argue that tutoring is not a valuable practice to include in students' service learning experiences, but we do claim that its inherent emphasis upon caring and the "private" limits its capacity to support the goals of teaching students about more "public" issues such as social forms of oppression and normalization. First, no matter how caring a tutor might be, as Jaci Webb, Bruce L. Wilson, and H. Dickson Corbett have pointed out, without extensive knowledge of the context and communities in which a child lives, "caring" teachers tend to have a "limited view" of students' aspirations. (Merely "walking in the terrain of another's perceptions," as they recommend, however, may not be enough. Visiting an "alien" community without some common project to explore with those one meets there always risks becoming a form of voyeurism.) Therefore, the tutor generally remains the possessor of an expert knowledge of literacy that cannot be entirely transformed and contextualized through the tutor-tutee relationship.

Of course these limits are not absolute. In another paper about the "Learning Communities" project, for example, Caroline Clark explains how her student, Seth, shifted from an originally "giving" to a more "relational" or caring approach to tutoring. Clark notes that Seth began the project seeing himself as the giver of expert literacy knowledge to his tutee, David, "positioning" David as "needy or a victim, someone who needs help because Seth is there to 'help'" (14). David resists this positioning as helpless, and struggles to redefine what tutoring "is" with Seth. Slowly Seth seems to respond to David's resistance, and as their relationship develops, Clark notes that authority is increasingly negotiated between the two, and "clearly there is a marked change in the focus of service as 'help' to service as 'building relationships'" (20). Clark argues that the "opportunity to experience firsthand these pedagogical negotiations of authority enabled the college students, then, to begin to critique the preconstructing discourse of schooling and the power issues involved in teaching and learning" (21). Yet, while the relationship between Seth and David has become more caring, and while "Seth can now rely on David to share in that direction," as the tutor, Seth remains a representative of and a mode of access to an expert university discourse community. Although there are moments of promise, tutees like David never become equal participants in the relationship, as the child never possesses a store of knowledge or discursive skills that can be placed on the same level as that of any tutor—in a sense, this inequality is central to the very definition of "tutor." In response to similar issues, Carol Maybach worries that "if the representation of these groups in society primarily emphasizes their needs, the strengths of these same individuals become minimized" (228). Maybach ends her article by indicating that an evolved and adapted form of the practice of caring would suffice to move us beyond this marginalization, a conviction we do not share.

Further, in the absence of a connection to a tutee's larger community and of participation in a collective effort to transform social forces, the practice of caring encourages tutors to operate within a role that is as responsive as possible to the unique barriers that face the specific individual(s) they are working with. While an individual's barriers certainly include and are largely determined by larger social structures, these structures are invariably filtered through the perspective of an individual tutee. As tutors seek to meet the unique needs of their partners, these social forces can easily be constructed as individual problems and may even be located in some imagined "autonomous" self of the tutee (as deficiencies, as "bad" decisions) instead of in more complex relation to the society at large. An individual's problems can become "personal," "private" problems.

There were cases, as noted by instructors Emily Nye and Morris Young, for example, where students began to move beyond the limitations noted by Herzberg. One student, Arnelle, interviewed her tutee "in order to learn about his family, and to determine Lawrence's attitude about learning. Her project broadened as she and Lawrence distributed a survey to fourteen eighth graders 'to see what they thought teachers could do in order to improve students' learning abilities'" (13). Through this project, Nye and Young argue, Arnelle "learned more about herself as a learner." Beyond this learning, however, we wonder if Arnelle's project may represent the beginnings of a shift beyond the "caring" nature of tutoring toward something that looks more like a "public" project where both Arnelle and Lawrence might collaborate with increased equality on a common project. Hannah Arendt argued that even a group as small as two could form a "public" space if they engaged together in a common project ("Philosophy"). Supported by the instructors, some students moved creatively beyond what we argue is the initially "caring" structure of tutoring.

The strength of tutoring as a mode of service is its ability to promote close individual relations between tutors and tutees. Yet, without a deep connection to a tutee's communities, the effort to create such a relation may be seriously constrained. Thus, it is not surprising that tutoring often fails to change college students' visions of their tutees as lacking a free-floating "expert" knowledge that they can provide. At the same time, as a practice largely focused on the development of caring relationships with specific "others," tutoring has limited capacity to dislodge what Herzberg sees as upper- and middle-class college students' individualistic and meritocratic visions of success and failure in our society. This limitation can be traced, we argue, to the essentially "private" nature of the tutoring relationship, where arenas of "public" discourse have little place, even when tutors are encouraged to reflect on more "public" issues in the class that accompanies the tutoring activity. What we have noted is a *tendency* of the tutoring context, not an absolute limitation-different students, of course, respond differently, as the other papers published on the "Learning Communities" project attest. Below, we examine a different approach to service learning that may begin to overcome some of the limitations both we and Herzberg have seen in the practice of tutoring.

"Public" Action in a Writing Course

In an advanced argumentative writing class taught by author Aaron Schutz, college students were asked to choose a problem that bothered them in the world and that had an actual audience they could speak to. Schutz provided some initial ideas, focusing on university-related issues that also had implications for the community outside the university, and students brainstormed about topics, finally arranging themselves in groups around five selections: gender equity in athletics at the university, the relatively new night entry policy at the student union, the problem of limited parking at the university, whether university athletes should be paid, and the lack of student participation in student government. The students' task was to write a paper together about the topic arguing for a specific change and addressing the audience they had chosen; they were encouraged to actually present these papers to their audience. In essence, the students were asked to define their problem and present a well-argued proposal for change. Students moved toward the final paper via periodic reports on what they had accomplished. They collected a range of data for their projects, the bulk of which consisted of interviews, but also including university and student documents as well as other more traditional published material. Although this writing project looks very different from the more traditional tutoring effort described above, we will argue that it does, in fact, constitute a foundation for "service learning" projects where students can respond to what they see as a community need, with implications for other, more extensive efforts. The classroom itself constituted what we are calling a "public space" in which students could begin to articulate and address these community issues.

The gender equity group was made up of two women and two men. Two of the participants, both women, were students in the university's Kinesiology program, and thus sports were a focus of their academic careers. Later, Schutz discovered in conversation that their topic arose because one of the men had a friend on the men's gymnastics team that was, at that time, threatened with extinction in the name of gender equity. An early note from one of the women indicates that she, too, was concerned about and questioning this decision. After doing some interviews and research on this topic, however, the group shifted its focus to the question of women's basketball, a sport with little visibility (and little success) at our institution. As they shifted to the women's basketball topic, the entire group showed an increasingly personal commitment to the issue. In their final presentation to the class, both of the women referred to their experience as athletes and noted that this experience informed the evolution of their paper. The men were clearly significant contributors to the paper as well, however, doing a significant amount of the research and writing. From a topic that struggled with the "fairness" of gender equity, their paper evolved into an effort that explored complex issues about their own community and its complicity in attitudes toward women's athletics. The project became an effort to intervene in the social construction of women's identities, an effort at "cultural work" in Gere's terms. This paper was eventually published as a multi-page spread in the student newspaper, an emergence into a social space beyond the classroom.

After extensive discussion, the group decided that a central problem with making women's athletics equal to men's had to do with fan interest and participation. After interviewing representatives from the successful University of Iowa women's basketball program, the students decided that the "target" audience for their paper was the promotional department of the athletics department, and that the most efficient avenue for change would be a fundamentally different approach to marketing our school's women's basketball team. The traditional approach of focusing on students and alumni as fans, they argued, was not the most effective. "Students tend to be apathetic and closed-minded to women's athletics," they wrote; "often at times they have trouble overlooking the way women's sports were in the past." Instead, drawing on the Iowa experience, the students wrote that the school should seek out a fundamentally different audience, older women and youth in the community.

First, after speaking with a number of older women in the community, and with the Iowa marketing department, they argued that older women would be more appreciative of women's achievements instead of focusing on the differences between men's and women's athletics as "deficits." Second, the group recommended that the school reach out in a systematic way to a much younger audience as both a long- and a short-term strategy. The students noted that

> by appealing to the youth, Iowa can hope to espouse tolerant atti-
> tudes towards women's athletics before persisting stereotypes influ-
> ence these kids negatively. The objective of appealing to the youth
> is to make women's sports more socially acceptable in years to come.
> If schools can successfully market [to] grade school boys and girls,
> they may be able to generate an interest in women's basketball that
> persists into adulthood. Instead of being ashamed of their athletic
> ability, young girls will begin to feel good about their participation
> in sports.

In the end, the students admitted that "our promotions are only temporary." They noted that society tends to feel that something is wrong with women who "compete," placing them in the untenable position of not being women, but not quite being men either, and remembered women they knew who had resisted wearing their own varsity jackets, fearing they would not be seen as "feminine" enough. "Permanent success" they concluded, "is primarily dependent on society's change in attitudes toward women and athletics. . . . Women's basketball games need to be appreciated as women's basketball games rather than the game that men have been playing for years. As attitude changes in women's sports occur slowly, the next generation needs to be encouraged, supported and looked at in a positive way." This group's excursions into new areas of the social world helped them begin to understand and address communal needs.

The group that examined the night entry policy at the student union was made up of two women who identified themselves as African American, and two men who identified as Jewish: Elizabeth, Mary, Alex, and Sam. The new night entry policy required those who wished to attend weekend parties at the union to have student IDs or be guests of students. In their initial prospectus, the students wrote that they had questions both about exactly why the entry policy was initiated and about which groups were affected by the policy. Initial conversations with the students indicated that they generally agreed that the policy disproportionately affected African American student groups, although all agreed they did not know enough about the policy.

As with the gender equity paper, the students' research consisted mainly of interviews. The students reported that they explicitly took advantage of their different social positioning in the university community to do research. In the section of the paper written primarily by Alex, he noted that

> group work is often difficult because members may have different backgrounds and opinions on controversial issues. However, this was the strength of our search to answer the question of why the Union policy must be revised. Elizabeth and Mary are both African American students who use the Union as their social environment. . . . On the other hand, Sam and I (Alex) are both white students who use the Greek system as our social environment. These racial and social differences helped us greatly because we were able to look at all perspectives and keep open minds. Had we all been from the same homogenous background, it is quite possible that we would have missed the other side of the issue.

In their presentation, the group indicated their agreement with this statement. Sam wrote later about a discussion the group had comparing the experience of Jewish and African American students, noting that "Mary, Alex, Elizabeth and I learned a great deal about ourselves through this project. . . . I feel extremely lucky to have taken part in this project with them." In written evaluations Schutz did not see until after grades were passed in, Elizabeth wrote that the group project "was a good experience and gave students the opportunity to exchange ideas and work together." Mary wrote that she thought it would "be time consuming, but it turned out pretty well. It's a cool idea." While it is doubtful that the group operated in as bias-free a manner as Alex and Sam seemed to think, it was clear from their writings and their presentations that all four felt that their perspectives were valued and made important contributions to the paper as a whole. Thus Alex goes on to write in his section of the paper that

> our heterogeneity also helped us in terms of our research. Because of the different social crowds that we associate ourselves with, Sam and I were able to obtain interviews from white fraternity and soror- ity members, while Elizabeth and Mary gathered their research from members of the Black community. This is not to say that we are all racist and refuse to befriend members of different racial backgrounds. Rather, we realized that our social differences were our strengths and that by using these distinctions we could acquire a vast amount of information.

The group's paper represented a complex understanding of the differences of opinion and social positioning of those involved in the night entry policy dispute. In the end they did not propose a specific solution, but explored the points of view on both sides, focusing on the issues of the "black community and how the new union night-entry policy has harmed it." The paper explores both the opinions of the union's administrators (who refused to discuss whether the policy had racial implications) and how the policy was received by and affected the African American community, which generally did not have its own venues for parties and thus was most affected by it. It traces the history of the implementation of the policy, which occurred without any public comment either from African American groups using the union or from a range of other groups, including the owners of restaurants located inside the union, the union's security personnel, and even the union's manager.

The paper did not end up accusing the university administration of overt racism, although it indicated clearly that fear of African American violence in particular was a direct cause of the policy. In their final report the students noted that they did not focus on the issue of racism because of its complexity and "difficult ambiguity." They found that within the Black Greek Association there were "mixed emotions as to whether the new policy is directed towards African American students," and that "every member felt that a new policy was needed, but not this particular one." At the same time, however, Mary noted that the policy "may be racist even if it was not planned to be," and Alex pointed out that while Elizabeth and Mary had both been carded at the union numerous times, he and Sam had never been asked for their IDs. In their presentation to the class they noted that the African American groups had many questions about the consistency with which the policy was applied to different groups. The group focused on the fact that, because of the historical situation of the African American community, "the major problem is that it is affecting African American students and other students of color because they are the main groups to use Union facilities." The context created by the group's presentations to the class and the dialogues that ensued around them constituted a local public space, if a small one, in which the different perspectives and backgrounds students brought with them were brought to bear on a common issue.

The paper appeals not for a specific solution but for a more open dialogue among all the users of the union that might lead to a more equitable solution, noting that despite the statements of the administration, other unions they had contacted around the country with similar problems had arrived at different and yet workable solutions. Elizabeth and Mary noted in the section they wrote together that their group

> debated whether or not we wanted to create an alternative Union night entrance policy in our conclusion. Then we realized that this would defeat the entire purpose of this project. We are here to say that a policy can not be constructed with only the input of a select group. . . . We believe that the policy should be altered, but the process of creating a final policy should be changed too.

The group then recommended further research involving all users of the union, restaurant owners in the union, and other affected parties, among other outreach efforts.

Despite the fact that this argumentative writing class, unlike the tutoring projects described above, did not include extensive readings on normalization or social oppression, the practice entailed in these students' projects clearly uncovered for them many of the complexities of the operations of power in their own community and in the larger society. The analysis entailed in the paper writing and the need to conceptualize a specific audience led both groups to complex and multi-faceted conclusions. This was not automatic, however, and the class clearly could have been much improved by more talk about the activities involved in writing the paper. The other three groups, which we have not discussed in detail, were far less successful. Even in the case of parking, however, their project provided the potential experiential "stuff" that might have made such analyses possible in ways the practice of tutoring clearly did not. Still, the limitations of projects focused mainly on students' self-interests, like parking, as well as the often homogeneous nature of university classes, indicate the need to move beyond the preliminary approach presented here toward efforts that help students construct "public" projects in conjunction with other communities—generally beyond the university—with different needs and visions of the world.

We would argue, however, that both of these projects are examples of "service learning." Although they did not involve caring for specific others outside the university community, they encouraged students to enter their own community, take responsibility for an issue that had relevance in and beyond their own community, and reflect on it. Each of the two cases we have examined represents an attempt by students from different backgrounds to collectively articulate and promote specific changes in aspects of their own multiple communities. In one case, the students' project resulted in an actual intervention in the larger community through its publication in the school newspaper. Their "service" represented an effort to alter the position of women athletes in the university and in society at large. While the night entry group did not take this last step, their formation of a "public space" in class nonetheless represents a form of action.

"Public" Service

The practice aimed for in these groups represents more what Arendt and Maxine Greene call "public" action than it does Noddings's caring, even when it is conducted in the small space of the classroom. According to Arendt and Greene, public spaces are created when multiple individuals come together around a common project. In fact, given that Hannah Arendt and others have argued that these kinds of vibrant "publics" must be *local* (Arendt discusses the danger that large numbers can present for the creation of public spaces [*Human Condition* 43]), classrooms themselves might productively be reconceptualized as potential "publics" in their own right. In this kind of local public space, "being seen and being heard by others derive their significance from the fact that everybody sees and hears from a different position" (Arendt 53) on this common project. In a public space, therefore, people can take distinctive yet communicable stances on common issues. They can act *with* others by bringing their unique potentials to bear upon a common project. And unlike Jürgen Habermas's view of the public, the relation in Arendt's public is not one aimed at consensus, at some imagined "collective consciousness"; the goal is not to erase the distance between us, "but to be able to speak, listen, and act together across it" (Bickford 171).

Thus, while caring encourages individuals to give their motivation and interests over to the projects of specific others, the "public" in Arendt's terms requires that individuals retain their points of view as they work together on common projects. Unlike Noddings's vision of caring, while people must listen carefully to others' points of view and must be prepared to change in response to what they hear, participants in public actions do not perform "motivational displacement"; they do not give up their own projects in the service of others. Instead, they attempt to fit their own projects with those of others.

Individuals participating in "public" practices are focused not on the unique perspectives of specific "others," but on the common effort located between multiple individuals. In caring, one cares for the "other," whereas the public is more focused on what Arendt sometimes calls "the love of the world"; it is focused on the elaboration of the common project and the maintenance of a space in which individuals might "appear" in some relative equality, taking coherent positions around such a project. Clearly, service learning informed by "public" practices offers an alternative *to* the "private" personal growth perspective; *it* moves away from what Harry Boyte sees as a disavowal of policy questions, of "seeing service as an *alternative* to politics" (766).

At this point, we might be expected to claim that as service learning finds a place in English studies we need to connect it with more explicitly "public" projects if our goals for it include guiding students toward better citizenship. Certainly we do believe that more self-consciousness about the relationship between the "ideology" of a given service experience and the academic learning of the classroom will enhance service learning in English departments. We also believe that the essentially "private" nature of tutoring poses problems for a pedagogy that seeks more "public" ends. But we resist an easy conclusion based on a dichotomy between "private" and "public." Rather, we seek to complicate the ways we think about both terms, presuming that service learning's role in English studies will be more productive if we proceed with a fuller understanding of its complexities. Arendt was quite clear that "action" always took place in situated contexts, and that no theoretical framework could ever tell us beforehand what would be appropriate for a specific situation. Arendt's and Greene's description of the public, like Noddings's vision of caring, is only a general theoretical guideline for conceptualizing the creation of public spaces. Each public space, to be successful, as is clearly shown in the above examples, must draw on and be responsive to the local histories, social realities, and individual personalities involved in any particular issue. Public spaces are concretized not by the achievement of some abstract ideal, but by the appropriation of the idea of collective action into a local, messy, and complex context.

Much of the dichotomous thinking about "public" and "private" derives from academic feminism's attention to separate spheres, the divisions between the (masculinized) public and (feminized) private spaces occupied by women and men in the nineteenth century. Despite the fact that individual scholars portrayed their work as speculative and historically contingent, the separate spheres concept has become, as Nancy Hewitt laments, "the most widely used framework for interpreting women's past in the United States" (301). The vocabulary of separate spheres was also appropriated by political historians, most notably Habermas and Geoff Eley, to argue for the emergence of a public sphere of politics that contrasted with the previously closed and private world of Westminster and the royal court. These two uses of private—one to designate the domestic world occupied by women and another to designate a male-dominated center of power— illustrate the difficulty and danger of treating "private" as a monolithic concept. Similarly, the term "public" carries multiple and often conflicted meanings. As Nancy Fraser explains, it can refer to three analytically distinct things: the state, the economy of paid employment, and arenas of public discourse. Furthermore, she argues, this concept depends upon masculinist gender constructs and brackets social inequities. And the boundaries between public and private are always arbitrary and determined by power relations.

Here, we are exploring conceptions of the public and the private as different, local, discursive practices, as varying approaches to relations among individuals. And, as Fraser points out, we cannot escape the ways in which these different practices reflect the workings of power in society. Joan C. Tronto and Julia T. Wood, among others, point out, for example, that caring tends to be a practice engaged in more consistently by those who are in more subordinate positions in society: women, people of color, people of a lower social class, among others. Thus, even though our public/private distinction does not include a "location" in which some people (women, for example) can be isolated from the public, neither is it a neutral concept that somehow escapes inscription into larger cultural forces of inequality.

Fraser's demonstration of the problems inherent in framing "public" and "private" in dichotomous terms has implications for our thinking about service learning. Seeing these two concepts as entirely separate would make it impossible to see, and value, the ways in which Schutz's students' "private" personal interests intersected with the "public" ones they addressed in their papers. Similarly, a dichotomous perspective makes it difficult for us to recognize and affirm the extent to which students in the tutoring program did, in fact, begin to see many of the complexities of the operations of power in their own community and in the larger society, as Minter, Gere, and Keller-Cohen, Nye and Young, and Clark, among others, have pointed out.

It would thus be inaccurate for us to say that tutoring and the project in the argumentative writing class represented, somehow, "pure" forms of the private and the public. As we noted above, tutoring itself is not a defined "practice" so much as it is an activity, inseparably interrelated to cultural visions of what it ought to entail. Efforts like Herzberg's and that of "Learning Communities" have attempted to enhance the more emancipatory and socially responsive aspects of tutoring, and they have had some success. Much the same could be said about the argumentative writing class. Clearly in the groups in the writing class caring remained an important aspect of the relationships among the students.

It is important to note, therefore, that both Noddings and Arendt recognize the interconnectedness and mutually supportive aspects of public and private practices. As Noddings says, "when people have loving regard for one another, they can engage in constructive conflict—although it is by no means easy, even then" ("Conversation" 115). Private—in our terms, caring—relations provide the foundations for more critical public spaces; they provide environments within which unique individuals are encouraged to advance their own specific projects, and where they are nurtured as they explore their own situated visions of the world. Arendt also clearly understands this interdependence of the public and private (see Skoller 111; Benhabib 211). A focus on the creation of a local "public" does not mean that caring relations are somehow excluded, nor does a focus on caring relations exclude interactions with larger social issues.

The public, in the sense that we mean it here, is constituted by local, largely face-to-face, activity. Thus, each of the papers presented by the groups in the classroom represents a strategic emergence into the larger "social" realm, as Arendt called it, in which some of the multivoiced quality of the group seems to be collapsed in favor of a more unified statement. The groups operated rather like the women's writing clubs studied by Gere, which enabled their members to regulate "the information about them and their activities that circulated to nonmembers. Clubs, in other words, provided spaces where women could exert some control over the terms of their representations" (44). The "intimate practices" of these clubs included *both* "public" *and* "private" (caring) practices (see 46–47). As with the groups in the argumentative writing class, the practices of reading and writing positioned clubwomen to make strategic emergences into the larger social realm (see also Scott). In the writing class, there appeared to be multiple levels of "emergence" into larger publics which, in the case of the newspaper article published by the women's athletics group, led eventually into the social sphere outside the classroom. Smaller "publics" within the writing groups (e.g., the Jewish men and the African American women in the night entry group) came together into a larger local public, the entire writing group. This group then reported back to the local group of the classroom to receive feedback both from the instructor and from the rest of the class. And finally, most groups at least attempted to aim their paper at an audience outside the classroom. Each shift represented a movement into a different level of risk, interpersonal relationship, and institutional structure, and the different levels may have allowed the development of multiple, often very small, public and private spaces, each of which allowed different modes of presentation of the self and the group. What this shows is that there were multiple levels of "service learning" going on in these projects.

We assert that a "public" model of service learning begins to respond to the limits of a "caring" approach to service. In "public" service, we must create structures that allow those who are "served" to become more active members of a public space where the differences participants bring with them become productive and crucial contributions to the development of the common project, "fueled with a new vision of service through cooperation rather than domination" (Maybach 235). In fact, service efforts like the one we have described that focus on the needs of the students' campus community may make it more difficult for students to treat the "others" they meet there—often their own peers—as less than equal participants, countering students' tendency to assume an attitude of *noblesse oblige. As* one of our reviewers pointed out, moreover, "there is a need for and a real interest in on-campus service projects."

The approach we have discussed does not represent an unrealistic attempt to eliminate all inequality, but instead seeks to create practices that might both foreground inequality and take advantage of "difference." This may mean promoting multiple public spaces within larger ones, as both Iris Young and Nancy Fraser point out. Thus, the fact that in the union night entry group the two subgroups wrote different sections of their paper can be seen as a productive outcome. Although the paper fit together quite well, the Jewish men and the African American women maintained, nonetheless, their own spaces within which to speak. Thus it is probably more representative of a common public space *because* these separate voices were maintained.

The creation of "public" efforts that explicitly reach out to new communities, as Herzberg's project and "Learning Communities" did—even if the students remain on campus—is crucial to ensure the development of public practices that do not become exclusionary. Throughout history we have examples of "public" spaces that excluded those who were "other," including, of course, the Greek *polis,* which defined only propertied men as truly human (Arendt, *Human Condition);* even the white, Protestant, middle-class clubs formed by women at the turn of the century, despite their many positive aspects, often excluded and stereotyped working-class women and women of color (Gere). Outreach efforts that attempt to include those from different communities as relative equals (even if they can never entirely succeed) may serve to destabilize any group identities that would otherwise be supported through the monolithic "othering" of outside groups (see Connolly).

Instead of assuming that what they offer is automatically of use, students need to discover how they might contribute to a local context with a history and set of complex issues all its own. "Public" service requires a different approach to the literacy skills students take with them into a service context from that encouraged in the practice of tutoring. Students need to begin not as teachers but as learners in a community setting, where the goals and purposes of a "service" effort are not established beforehand. Perhaps students would see the contexts or agencies in which they were offered entrée as places where they would be given "assignments" in the way that Linda Adler-Kassner describes as working for her "at-risk" students. To be successful, service learning projects need to create spaces where college students are given opportunities to be "cared-for" by those they wish to serve, moments where they require initiation into the practices of a

community they do not understand, moments where *they* are the learners
instead of the experts, as all participating negotiate common projects
together. We are talking "contexts," here, because "public" service would
require students to enter relationships with *communities* and not with easily
isolated individuals. In this approach, the activity of service learning itself
may provide an opportunity for students to rethink the nature of literacies
and discourses as they operate in different communities.

English and Service Learning

In his recent book, *The Employment of English: Theory, Jobs, and the Future
of Literary Studies,* Michael Bérubé explores what he describes as "the
profession's competing . . . fiscal and intellectual imperatives," arguing that
two current crises, the lack of decent jobs for most new PhDs and the
struggle between literary and cultural studies, should not be considered in
isolation from each other. Bérubé issues a call for cultural studies that
"articulates the theoretical and critical work of the so-called public
intellectual to the movements of public policy" (322), an articulation that
would lead the profession of English toward greater involvement with public
politics and policy. Yet, even as he makes this recommendation, Bérubé
expresses a healthy skepticism about the value of inserting policy into
cultural studies. As he says, we might "underestimate—or, worse, ignore—
the difference between theoretical work on such subjects [debates over race,
ethnicity, clothing, cuisine, music, science, and technology] and the
practical political effects such work can have for the people we're talking
about if not necessarily to" (337).

   Bérubé's hesitation hinges on differences he perceives between two
"publics," the literary public sphere and the public policy sphere and the fact
"that most cultural studies intellectuals, myself most assuredly included,
have not yet begun to think seriously about how best to negotiate that
difference" (340). As our discussion of the various dimensions of "public"
service learning indicate, we share Bérubé's concerns about the various
meanings assigned to "public" and the implications of these for the field of
English studies. Yet, we, like Bérubé, do not see the solution in backing away
from the term. As he writes, "while we've been making the case against
imposing or presuming a common American culture, the New Right has
worked assiduously to destroy the material foundations of what can at least
potentially sustain us as a common society. That's why their attacks on the

realm of the public are so important, and why it is so important that we reclaim and rejuvenate 'the public' in the name of the people" (342).

In our view, service learning can act as one entry point for English studies to begin this reclamation process because multiple public and private spaces, operating at multiple levels, allow myriad kinds of difference to emerge into dialogue. Fluid and fragmented spaces like these allow the complex and multifaceted nature of discourse, as well as its imbeddedness in large social structures, to be more effectively explored and contested. Service learning provides a way for those in positions of privilege and power in the university to place themselves in the positions of "learners," as they request and negotiate entrée into communities, often disenfranchised communities, within and beyond their own and attempt to discover, in conjunction with those in these new communities, what they can offer to those they wish to "serve." "Public" service focuses not on "helping" others but on joining them as relative equals in a common project of social change. Service learning projects can encourage us to engage in dialogue about (talk "to" and not just "about") the implications of a *specific* literate activity for a *specific* context and to the *specific* goals we intend to pursue. This allows us to see the work of English studies, in all its different configurations, as always precariously poised between myriad locations, activities, and discourses—each with its possibilities and limitations.

Done effectively, service learning fits well into an English Studies that is reconsidering its own boundaries and internal relationships because it brings into classrooms discourses and activities in the world outside the academy, mediating the relationships between the discourses and needs of the academy and those of actual community contexts. As many have long pointed out, the idea of a classroom as separated from the larger community in which it is situated cannot be disconnected from the issues of power, oppression, and exclusion this disconnection involves. Service learning provides a means for faculty and students to complicate this idea of the "classroom" and the approaches to discourses, writing, and literacy that it constructs. But we must think carefully about how we take advantage of this opportunity. Despite our best intentions, if we are not careful we may end up reinforcing ideologies and assumptions that we had hoped to critique. *How* we step outside the classroom, how we enter into service learning relationships with communities beyond our own, will be crucial in determining our success.

Works Cited

Adler-Kassner, Linda. "Digging a Groundwork for Writing: Underprepared Students and Community Service Courses." *College Composition and Communication* 46.4 (1995): 552–55.

Arendt, Hannah. *The Human Condition.* Chicago: U of Chicago P, 1958.

———. "Philosophy and Politics." *Social Research* 57.1 (1990): 73–103.

Benhabib, Seyla. *The Reluctant Modernism of Hannah Arendt.* Thousand Oaks: Sage, 1996.

Bérubé, Michael. *The Employment of English: Theory, Jobs, and the Future of Literary Studies.* New York: New York UP, 1998.

Bickford, Susan. *The Dissonance of Democracy: Listening, Conflict, and Citizenship.* Ithaca: Cornell UP, 1996.

Boyte, Harry. "Community Service and Civic Education." *Phi Delta Kappan* June 1991: 765–67.

Calhoun, Craig, ed. *Habermas and the Public Sphere.* Cambridge: MIT P, 1992.

Clark, Caroline. "Literacy Learning, Outside In: Beyond Service as Violence." Paper presented at the 1997 Conference on College Composition and Communication, Phoenix.

Connolly, William E. *Identity/Difference: Democratic Negotiations of Political Paradox.* Ithaca: Cornell UP, 1991.

Cuomo, Mario. "Two Cheers for Government Charity: No Amount of Volunteerism Can Let Government Off the Hook." *New York Times* 27 April 1997: E15.

Cushman, Ellen. "The Rhetorician as an Agent of Social Change." *College Composition and Communication* 47.1 (1996): 7–28.

Eley, Geoff. "Nations, Publics and Political Cultures: Placing Habermas in the Nineteenth Century." Calhoun 289–339.

Fraser, Nancy. "Rethinking the Public Sphere: A Contribution to the Critique of Actually Existing Democracy." Calhoun 109–42.

Gere, Anne Ruggles. *Intimate Practices: Literacy and Cultural Work in U.S. Women's Clubs, 1880–1920.* Urbana: U of Illinois P, 1997.

Gere, Anne Ruggles, and Jennifer Sinor. "Composing Service Learning." *The Writing Instructor* (in press).

Greene, Maxine. *The Dialectic of Freedom.* New York: Teachers College P, 1988.

Habermas, Jürgen. "The Public Sphere." *New German Critique* 3 (1974): 45–55.

Herzberg, Bruce. "Community Service and Critical Teaching." *College Composition and Communication* 43.3 (1994): 307–19.

Hewitt, Nancy. "Beyond the Search for Sisterhood: American Women's History in the 1980s." *Social History* 10 (1985): 299–321.

Kahne, Joseph, and Joel Westheimer. "In the Service of What? The Politics of Service Learning." *Phi Delta Kappan* May 1996: 593–99.

Maybach, Carol Weichman. "Investigating Urban Community Needs: Service Learning From a Social Justice Perspective." *Education and Urban Society* 28.2 (1996): 224–36.

Minter, Deborah Williams, Anne Ruggles Gere, and Deborah Keller-Cohen. "Learning Literacies." *College English* 57.6 (1995): 669–87.

Nelson, Cary. *Disciplinarity and Dissent in Cultural Studies.* New York: Routledge, 1995.

Noddings, Nel. *Caring: A Feminine Approach to Ethics and Moral Education.* Berkeley: U of California P, 1984.

———. *The Challenge to Care in Schools: An Alternative Approach to Education.* New York: Teachers College P, 1992.

———. "Conversation as Moral Education." *Journal of Moral Education* 23.2 (1994): 107–18.

Nye, Emily, and Morris Young. "Service Learning and the Literacy Connection." *The Literacy Connection.* Ed. Alice Horning and Ron Sudol. (Forthcoming).

Scott, James C. *Domination and the Arts of Resistance: Hidden Transcripts.* New Haven: Yale UP, 1990.

Seigel, Susan, and Virginia Rockwood. "Democratic Education, Student Empowerment, and Community Service: Theory and Practice." *Equity and Excellence in Education* 26.2 (1993): 65–70.

Skoller, Eleanor Honig. *The In-Between of Writing.* Ann Arbor: U of Michigan P, 1993.

Smithson, Isaiah, and Nancy Ruff, eds. *English Studies/Culture Studies: Institutionalizing Dissent.* Urbana: U of Illinois P, 1994.

Tronto, Joan C. "Beyond Gender Difference to a Theory of Care." *Signs* 12.4 (1987): 644–63.

Watters, Ann, and Marjorie Ford. *A Guide for Change: Resources for Implementing Community Service Writing.* New York: McGraw Hill, 1995.

Webb, Jaci, Bruce L. Wilson, and H. Dickson Corbett. "Understanding Caring in Context: Negotiating Borders and Barriers." *The Urban Review* 25.1 (1993): 25–45.

Wood, Julia T. *Who Cares? Women, Care, and Culture.* Carbondale: Southern Illinois UP, 1994.

Wuthnow, Robert. *Learning to Care: Elementary Kindness in an Age of Indifference.* New York: Oxford UP, 1995.

Young, Iris Marion. *Justice and the Politics of Difference.* Princeton: Princeton UP, 1990.

10 Service Learning and First-Year Composition

Brock Haussamen

Introduction

"Service learning" refers to the use of voluntary community service as an integral part of an academic course. In a cycle of experience and reflection, students apply their skills and knowledge to help people, and in the classroom, they reflect on the people, social agencies, and communities they have encountered and on the nature of service. Service learning is not primarily social assistance; it is a pedagogy, one that addresses not only the issue of how best to learn but also the question of the best purposes of learning. The words of the Rutgers University service learning motto express the good will, "Serving to Learn. Learning to Serve."

As one of Raritan Valley Community College's trio of service learning coordinators, as well as an English professor, I encourage colleagues to try service learning, and I help find appropriate agencies for their students. The applications of service learning extend all across the curriculum. Accounting students help agencies keep their financial records. Students in physical education courses conduct exercises with children or the elderly. Students in sociology and psychology courses observe social and individual behavior while they help at adolescent drop-in agencies, community mental health centers, and group homes for the developmentally disabled. Students in the sciences, math, communications, education, computer science, and marketing have all volunteered for service that has augmented their academic training, their career preparedness, and their community awareness.

Reprinted from *Teaching English in the Two-Year College,* October 1997.

Service learning is a new branch of experiential education. It differs from the two older branches of internships and cooperative education in that service learning is unpaid, requires fewer hours—at Raritan Valley, usually 30 hours a semester or less, depending on the faculty member's specifications—and is only one of the components within a course instead of being a course or program unto itself. Service learning has taken root at all levels of education since the 1980s as many educators have acknowledged that while graduates may go forth successfully trained as aspiring private professionals, many are also unprepared and unwilling to accept roles in the public community. Racism on campuses, the national cynicism about politics and government, and the decline of volunteerism have forced a recognition that in a democracy citizenship education cannot remain merely an extracurricular activity.

In the field of English, literature often lends itself to community experiences. The literature of women, of law, of AIDS, of African American and Eastern cultures can all lead to service learning projects. However, here, I describe service learning in first-term composition, where it has rich potential to affect many college students.

Optional Service Learning in English I

Service learning can be organized in two basic ways in any course. It can be an optional project, or it can be required or strongly recommended for all students. In English I at Raritan Valley, service learning fits well as an optional alternative for the research paper assignment that is the culminating course project. Different instructors approach the research assignment in different ways, but the community can be a resource for most of them. Over the years, I have usually assigned a biographical essay about a member of the student's family, a paper drawing on both interviews and library sources. Now, with the service learning option, an alternative assignment is for the student to spend at least fifteen hours in a nursing home in conversation with a senior citizen and to write the researched biography about that person instead of a family member. To prepare for this project, I telephone the volunteer coordinators at several nursing homes, ask whether they can arrange suitable pairings if students contact them, and then give the students the list of nursing homes, contact persons, and phone numbers to select from on their own. Generally, about half the students in a class express initial interest in this assignment, and half of those complete it.

One problem with service learning as an option is the compensation for the additional hours it requires. In actuality, most students completing service learning do not look back on the time spent as onerous at all, and many put in additional hours. But at the start of the semester, for community college students holding jobs, thirty hours, even fifteen hours, sounds like a lot. So an incentive helps. The carrot I offer is that the students completing the nursing home project will be excused from the final exam. The omission of the exam does not compromise the course for those diligent enough to finish the required paper, and it does not, for that matter, save students much time, but it is an attractive incentive. In other courses across the college, and at other colleges, faculty often adjust the writing requirements of those students choosing a service learning project or give them extra credit in some form. This element of service learning management, however, is unsettled and controversial, for on the one hand, the student's time commitment should be acknowledged, and yet faculty should seek to adhere to the principle of giving academic credit only for the evaluated academic results of service, not for the time alone.

The students at Raritan Valley who volunteer for the nursing home project spend an hour or two at a time during the middle portion of the semester befriending an elderly man or woman. Each week I ask a couple of these students to talk in class about what the resident is like, what the home itself is like, how they feel about being there, how they think they are perceived, and what sources they are finding in the library that amplify the life stories they are hearing. Such reflection is indispensable to service learning as a pedagogy, for students, although they usually feel good about their community work, are not particularly inclined to contemplate it after they leave it behind each week. Reflection—through discussions, journals, and research—prompts the student to unpack a host of impressions and to reach for an understanding of them. Service by itself is not learning; the learning occurs in the examination and analysis of the service.

Listen to student Marie Hocker, who juxtaposed historians' accounts of the Battle of Guadalcanal with the reminiscences of World War II veteran, Stan, now 80 years old,

> mostly deaf, single-legged, nearly blind without bottle-thick glasses.
> . . . He speaks his mind bluntly. "Anybody don't want to hear, don't
> have to listen." I have listened to Stan for the past two months, and
> have learned more than I had imagined I would.

In hearing and telling the story of Stan's life and of Guadalcanal, Marie saw the issues of human need that permeate both the past and the present. She concluded:

> One of these days you'll come to see me and I won't be here, he tells me. "Where're you going, Stan?" I ask. "I don't know. Somewhere where the food is good and people treat you decent." I think back on his time on Guadalcanal. He was fighting then for "somewhere where the food was good and the people treat you decent. . . ." I want to believe that the odds are not as overwhelming now and that the spirit of those who fought at Guadalcanal lives on in those who take care of the Guadalcanal survivors. I want to believe that Stan's American Dream will still come true. Stan, may the food be good and the people treat you decent, always.

English I with Required Service Learning

The optional mode of service learning of the sort I have described has advantages and disadvantages. It gives the faculty member who is trying the method for the first time an opportunity to get the feel of it, to see how it fits with the course objectives, and to see how the students respond. On the other hand, when only a few students in a class are carrying out such involved projects, those students require extra time and attention, and their experience of the course may become significantly different from that of the other students. For these reasons, many faculty who have tried the optional model have gone on to teach sections in which service learning is a standard requirement of the course. Raritan Valley now offers as many as a dozen such classes across the disciplines each semester.

One of these has been a section of composition subtitled "Writing and Learning in the Community." The service requirement is indicated in the published course schedule so that students are aware of it when they select that section. The course draws students who have volunteered in the past or have wanted to do so—and predictably others as well who arrive at the first class claiming that they had no idea what that service thing meant but the section fit in their schedules. A few of the disenchanted ones drop the course, but more often those who grudgingly start the service go on to become fully engaged. While one might expect that altruism or at least a sharp sense of responsibility would be a criterion for successful service learning, in fact a student does not need either in order to find service learning eventually gratifying.

The partnership between a composition class and the community can be of different kinds. One relationship has come not from service learning at all but from the study over the last couple of decades of the role of community in the nature of discourse and the writing process. Writers, it has been emphasized, write not just as individuals but as members of communities. (Joseph Harris has surveyed this topic in a fine essay.) The awareness of discourse communities has inspired service courses organized around writing that is needed in and by community services and groups—newsletters, pamphlets, flyers, histories. The anthology *Writing for Change*, edited by Ann Watters and Marjorie Ford, includes examples of such projects.

Another connection between the writing class and the community is through tutoring. Composition students explore the theme of literacy and, with some basic training in tutoring, help high school students or other community members to improve their writing skills. Bruce Herzberg has written about a fully developed version of this approach at Bentley College in Massachusetts.

But my design has been simpler, because I wanted a model that other English faculty could easily adopt and, if they did so, for which community placements could be found in large numbers. I invite students to pursue any kind of community service they are interested in, as long as it is unpaid (so a current job in a care center doesn't qualify), is helpful in nature, and is likely to be something the student would learn from (I allowed one student in his third year with a volunteer fire company to use that as his service, but it never became a new experience for him in any way; I should have established more particular goals with him at the start). The minimum time required for students is thirty hours over the semester; students hand in a time sheet, initialed by a supervisor, at midterm and at the end.

Often their service interests turn out to be career-related; they check out what it is like to work in hospitals or day care centers or county government or art therapy. Sometimes they follow up a community involvement that they are already familiar with—a nursing home around the corner from their house, a service program at the family church. I describe a variety of agencies on the first day of class and evaluate the students' own suggestions for placements, and I press them all to make phone calls for interviews quickly because getting started can easily consume three weeks. (At colleges without a service learning or other volunteer office, faculty can obtain listings of volunteer opportunities from local governments, from comprehensive agencies such as United Way, and sometimes from local newspapers.)

The writing assignments for the course parallel those given in other composition sections; final papers emerge from the same process of drafts and peer discussion, and they are held to the same standards. The difference is that all of the papers are about community and service. They include narratives and essays on such topics as an incident in the past when the student did or did not help someone, definitions of community, a description of the volunteer site and its clients, and arguments on whether service should be required or not. The students also keep a journal. I give them a list of questions to consider such as, "What did someone say to you that surprised you?" "If you were in charge, what changes would you make at the agency?" "What conflicts did you experience or observe at the agency? What caused them?"

The research assignment is a problem-solution paper. Students select some element of the social problem that their agency is dealing with. They research the sources of the problem, the conflicting points-of-view involved, and the possible solutions. Grasping such complexity does not come easily to most of them, and I emphasize the multiple nature of causes and options. They interview the director of their agency, and they include their experiences at the agency in their discussion. Their writing process often includes coming to grips with contrasts between the written sources and their firsthand impressions. They are expected to draw conclusions and make recommendations.

Here are some examples of their topics: One student at a day care center with children from distressed families did her research on problem children in a preschool setting, on how to humanely control and discipline children who may have become accustomed to neglect and harsh punishment at home. A student coaching a Pop Warner football team studied the dilemma of competitive, high-pressure parents on the children's playing field. Another student helping at a community theater compared the complaints from local arts and theater groups about lack of government funding with demands from individuals about their entitlements to welfare.

For readings in the course, I sometimes use *Writing for Change*, at other times my own assortment of essays and stories. (The old chestnut "The Lottery" by Shirley Jackson takes on new life in discussions about community involvement!) Many teachable essays about social problems appear on newspaper op-ed pages. *Education for Democracy*, edited by Benjamin Barber and Richard Battistoni, is a large, exemplary collection that includes readings about service learning itself. (See the appendix for organizations that provide extensive information about service learning, including sample course syllabi.)

Service Learning, English, and Democracy

As the semester progresses, students ask pointed questions about why
community service is part of their English course. I tell them that the purpose
is not to solve community problems but to improve their education. I tell
them that I believe their education ought to promote not only their
professional and personal development but their development as
community members as well. That is accomplished by using their
communication skills to reflect on their community experience. And indeed,
students not only have plenty of material to write about, but as any teacher
of service learning quickly discovers, students need to do a great deal of
talking about their first encounters with hyperactive children, or frail elderly,
or the poor. Students have much to say about the agencies themselves, the
confusions of getting started there, their verdicts about whether people are
being helped effectively or not. But as they talk in class, write about their
experiences, give each other advice and support, and read related narratives,
their frequent comment is that the course acquires a reality for them that
other courses have not had. They, like service learning students in general,
report increased confidence in themselves both as learners and as someone
"who can make a difference." All this is their way of expressing the
fulfillment of the primary goal of service learning: to bring the academic
world and the democratic community into a closer relationship.

Benjamin Barber of Rutgers University is an eloquent advocate of
citizenship education in a democracy, and among what he considers to be
the political benefits of service learning, two are also curriculum goals of
English. First, service learning students listen. They must pay careful attention
to the unfamiliar words they hear from the unfamiliar people they work with.
And listening, Barber points out, is an essential but endangered skill in our
talkative, media-dominated democracy; it is through listening that people
understand each other and find the possibilities for political compromise.
The other skill is imagination. Successful service learning students must
stretch their vision in their study of people from different backgrounds, and
such imagining, the capacity for informed social empathy, is a critical art in a
democracy ("The Democratic Imperative").

Occasionally, of course, listening and understanding go awry, and service
learning does not work well for a student. Some students do not become
engaged at their agency. They report that they stand around a lot or are bored
or that no one is telling them what to do. Asking them to explain in detail
what the situation is—who the people are and exactly what they are doing—

is a helpful preliminary step in encouraging participation. Only once have I encountered the opposite sort of difficulty: a girl was so involved in listening to the overwhelming problems of young teenagers at an after-school center that she herself began to feel overwhelmed. She willingly wrote in her journal about what she was hearing (and asked me not to read certain pages), and I encouraged her to talk in class, where she felt supported by the other students. She gradually found her bearings at the agency and has since become a peer counselor in a high school.

In such cases, and whenever I think it might be worthwhile, I telephone the volunteer's supervisor around mid-semester to share information and suggestions. These calls sometimes uncover another problem that can arise, which is that the agency is not using or supervising volunteers effectively. This may occur in a large organization such as some hospitals, or in any agency that is not prepared to provide volunteers with some structure. For a while, I steer volunteers elsewhere.

Let me conclude by pointing out that while many four-year institutions have service learning programs, service learning has a special impact at community colleges, where students come from the local community and, to a large extent, will remain in it. Community service is integral to the notion of the community college. Many service learning students say they want to continue working at their agencies after the semester ends; some of them do for a while, and a few go on to take regular positions there. But for all of them, service learning deepens their relationship to their home community and increases the chance they will participate in that community again in the future.

Appendix

Several major organizations provide information about service learning:

Corporation for National Service/1201 New York Avenue, NW/Washington, DC 20525/202-606-5000, Ext. 136. http://www.cns.gov/learn.html. The federal agency that directs Americorps also provides grants for collegiate service learning through its program Learn and Serve America: Higher Education.

Campus Compact Center for Community Colleges/1833 West Southern Avenue/Mesa, AZ 85202/602-461-7392. http://www.mc.maricopa.edu/academic/compact

American Association of Community Colleges/One Dupont Circle, NW, Suite 410/Washington, DC 20036-1176/202-728-0200, ext. 254. http://aacc.nche.edu/speproj/service/resource.html. A center for information about both selected model service learning programs as well as service learning in community colleges nationwide.

National Society for Experiential Education/3509 Haworth Drive, Suite 207/Raleigh, NC 27609/ 919-787-3263. http://www.tripod.com//nsee. An organization that predates the service learning movement, NSEE publishes excellent materials on teaching through service learning.

National Service Learning Cooperative (K–12) Clearinghouse/University of Minnesota/1954 Buford Avenue, Room R290/St. Paul, MN 55108/800-808-7378. http://www.nicsl.coled.umn.edu A clearinghouse for a wide range of information about organizations, materials, and specialists.

Works Cited

Barber, Benjamin R. "The Democratic Imperative for Civic Education." Address: Princeton University. 16 Nov. 1995.

Barber, Benjamin R., and Richard M. Battistoni. *Education for Democracy: Citizenship, Community, Service: A Sourcebook for Students and Teachers.* Dubuque: Kendall, 1993.

Harris, Joseph. "The Idea of Community in the Study of Writing." *College Composition and Communication* 40 (1989): 11–22.

Herzberg, Bruce. "Community Service and Critical Teaching." *College Composition and Communication* 45 (1994): 307–19.

Watters, Ann, and Marjorie Ford. *Writing for Change: A Community Reader.* New York: McGraw, 1995.

11 The Rhetorician as an Agent of Social Change

Ellen Cushman

In his "Afterthoughts on Rhetoric and Public Discourse," S. Michael Halloran finds that "the efforts of citizens to shape the fate of their community . . . would surely have been of interest to American neoclassical rhetoricians of the late eighteenth and early nineteenth centuries" (2). Unfortunately, he sees an "apparent lack of interest in such 'Public Discourse' among new rhetoricians of late twentieth-century English departments" (2). One way to increase our participation in public discourse is to bridge the university and community through activism. Given the role rhetoricians have historically played in the politics of their communities, I believe modern rhetoric and composition scholars can be agents of social change outside the university.

Some critical theorists believe that the primary means of affecting social change is to translate activism into liberatory classroom pedagogies. This paper seeks to address other ways in which we can affect social change, something more along the lines of civic participation. As Edward Schiappa suggests, "pedagogy that enacts cultural critique is important but it is not enough. . . . We should not allow ourselves the easy out of believing that being 'political' in the classroom is a substitute for our direct civic participation" (22). I agree. I hope here to suggest ways we can empower people in our communities, establish networks of reciprocity with them, and create solidarity with them. Using a self-reflexive rhetoric, I'll describe the limitations of my own role as a participant observer in a predominately Black (their term) neighborhood in a city in upstate New York. I hope to reveal a tentative model of civic participation in our neighborhoods which I

Reprinted from *College Composition and Communication,* February 1996.

believe illuminates some paradoxes in postmodern approaches to composition.*

Approaching the Community

One of the most pressing reasons why composition scholars may not work in the community has to do with deeply rooted sociological distances between the two. Many universities sit in isolated relation to the communities in which they're located—isolated socially and sometimes physically as well. Rensselaer, for example, where I'm a fourth year aPhiD candidate[#], is isolated socially and physically from the community.

The Hudson borders Troy on the East, rolling hills on the West. Most of downtown developed along the river valley, while RPI expanded up one of these hills. People in the city generally call those associated with RPI "higher ups." Rensselaer students often call people in Troy "Troylets," "trash," or "low lifes." RPI was originally built closer to the city, beginning at the West edge of

---

* This paper is a multivoiced, self-reflexive look at our roles as rhetoricians. As such, I hope to turn our work as scholars inside out, upside down, back in upon itself. I've included many voices in this paper because this was the only way I seemed able to capture the range of reactions I've had to the theories and practices of critical pedagogues and cultural studies theorists—from initial enthusiasm to disillusionment to frustration and anger. And so I've organized this paper as a hall of mirrors. The central image is the argument that rhetoricians can be agents of social change outside the university and a brief explanation of how this plays out in research. To create this image, I use a narrative voice to tell a story of possibility. The footnotes with various markers are the next set of mirrors and reveal more background for my argument. In these footnotes, I use a self-critical voice hoping that we will pause for a brief moment to examine our discourse. The numbered endnotes include the theorists I find most useful in reflecting my argument. Here I use an academic voice in a conscious effort to work within the system. Finally, we have the appendices. In these I don't want to cite specific authors because the onus to consider the ramifications of using critical discourse remains on all of our shoulders. Yours and mine. With these asides, I want to point to trends in the discourse I've heard at conferences and read in the work of many composition scholars. I've appended these, first, because they reflect the main argument by revealing my initial frustration and, many times, anger, which prompt this paper; and, second, because they're written from this anger, I risk being dismissed as inflammatory, a risk I hope to reduce by making them an aside; third, these asides have significant personal value to me. They're the best translation of my street-tough face-breaking, fight-picking voice that I can manage for an academic audience. Given this activist research, my white trash history, and being only one pay check away from returning to the streets, I'm very far from that voice, that way of being, no matter how many books, computers, students, and teachers I sit in front of.

[#] An aphid is a type of louse. So an aPHiD brings the "lo" together with "use." The plural of louse is lice. When I graduate, I'll have a License to create knowledge from the people I study. Do da. Do da.

the valley, but for reasons too complicated to go into here, RPI expanded up the hill. The relationship between Rensselaer and Troy is best symbolized by the Approach, what used to be a monument of granite stairs, pillars, and decorative lights, but is now barely recognizable as a walkway.[1]

The city gave the Approach to Rensselaer in 1907 as a sign of the mutually rewarding relationship between the two. Once an access way to the university on the hill, literally and figuratively, the stairway was pictured on many of the notebooks of students in the Troy City school district. Walk into any diner in the city and folks can remember the Approach pictured on their notebooks when they were growing up. Even in the late 1950s, students and city officials worked together to maintain this connection as part of a "civic betterment project."

Unfortunately, the Approach fell into disrepair during the early 1970s as a result of disagreements between the city and university about who should have responsibility for maintenance. Now angry graffiti, missing stairs, and overgrowth symbolize the tattered relationship between the city and RPI. Young fraternity boys are rumored to use the Approach for initiation during rush week, and certain ski club members have skied down the Approach as a testament to their ability and courage. While Troy natives look at the Approach in fury and disgust, the city and RPI continue to negotiate over its upkeep and hopeful repair.

I spend time describing this symbol of the relationship between the university and the city because I don't think this relationship is an isolated example of the sociological distance between the university and the community. It's precisely this distance that seems to be a primary factor in prohibiting scholars from Approaching people outside the university. Everyday, we reproduce this distance so long as a select few gain entrance to universities, so long as we differentiate between experts and novices, and so long as we value certain types of knowledge we can capitalize on through specialization.[2] This history of professionalization might be one reason academics have so easily turned away from the democratic project that education serves to ensure—civic participation by well-rounded individuals.[3]

Malea Powell, an Eastern Miami and Shawnee Indian, suggests that the theorizing of academics necessitates a distance from the daily living of people outside academe, particularly those people we study. Although she's found "a location for healing in theory," she also knows these theories are used to "civilize unruly topics," with a similar assumption of manifest destiny that colonists use(d) to civilize unruly Native Americans. "Central to telling the 'American' story is the settlers' vision of the frontier, a frontier that is 'wilderness,' empty of all 'civilized' life." In order to colonize, the settlers denied the very existence of Turtle Island's original people. Powell sees that

> this denial this un-seeing . . . characterizes our "American" tale. For the colonizers it was a necessary un-seeing; material Indian "bodies" were simply not seen . . . the mutilations, rapes, and murders that made up 'the discovery' and 'manifest destiny' were also simply not seen. Un-seeing Indians gave (and still gives) Euroamericans a critical distance from materiality and responsibility, a displacement that is culturally valued and marked as "objectivity."

Scholars reproduce this colonizing ideology when we maintain a distance from people. In search of an area of interest we look to stake our claim over a topic, or in Powell's words, "define a piece of 'unoccupied' scholarly territory . . . which will become our own scholarly homestead." If the scholarly territory happens to be occupied by other scholarly endeavors, our job demands that we show how these original scholars fail to use their territory well, thereby giving us manifest justification for removing their theories from the territory through expansion, co-option, or complete dismissal. In some fundamental ways we shirk our civil responsibility and always already enact violence under the guise of objective distance, and the thin veil of 'creating' knowledge.

Powell (and I) "don't mean to disable scholarly work here." But I believe that in doing our scholarly work we should take social responsibility for the people from and with whom we come to understand a topic. I'm echoing Freire who shows that when we theorize about the oppressed we must do "authentic thinking, thinking that is concerned about *reality*, does not take place in ivory tower isolation, but only in communication" (64). Once we leave the classroom, we're again in ivory tower isolation, unless we actively seek our students in other contexts—particularly the community context.

Activism begins with a commitment to breaking down the sociological barriers between universities and communities. And if we see ourselves as both civic participants and as preparing students for greater civic participation, then activism becomes a means to a well-defined end for Approaching the community. Recent work by Bruce Herzberg reveals one model for how rhetoricians can enter into the community. His thoughtful article on "Community Service and Critical Teaching" shows how he manages to link his writing courses with community agencies.

> The effort to reach into the composition class with a curriculum aimed at democracy and social justice is an attempt to make schools

> function . . . as radically democratic institutions, with the goal not
> only of making individual students more successful, but also of mak-
> ing better citizens, citizens in the strongest sense of those who take
> responsibility for communal welfare. (317)

I'm not asking for composition teachers to march into the homes, churches,
community centers, and schools of their community. I'm not asking for us to
become social workers either. I am asking for a deeper consideration of the
civic purpose of our *positions* in the academy, of what we do with our
knowledge, for whom, and by what means. I am asking for a shift in our
critical focus away from our own navels, Madonna, and cereal boxes to the
ways in which we can begin to locate ourselves within the democratic
process of everyday teaching and learning in our neighborhoods. For the
remainder of this paper, let me offer some brief considerations of what such
activism might ideally entail, as well as some practical limitations of trying to
live up to this ideal. For these considerations, I draw upon my own activist
research in a primarily African-American inner city.

Short Changed

Most current accounts of activism in cultural studies don't do justice to social
change taking place in day-to-day interactions. I think activism can lead to
social change, but not when it's solely measured on the scale of collective
action, or sweeping social upheavals. (See the appendix on "Slippery
Discourse.") Rather, we need to take into our accounts of social change the
ways in which people use language and literacy to challenge and alter the
circumstances of daily life. In these particulars of daily living, people can
throw off the burdens placed upon them by someone else's onerous
behavior. In other words, social change can take place in daily interactions
when the regular flow of events is objectified, reflected upon, and altered.
Daily interactions follow regular patterns of behavior, what sociologist
Anthony Giddens terms "routinization." These interactions result from every
individual re-enacting the social structures that underpin behaviors.
Giddens' notion of the "duality of structure" captures the ways in which
individuals' behaviors manifest overarching social structures. When the
routine flow of events is impeded or upset, we have an example of
deroutinization—of what can be the first steps to social change on
microlevels of interaction. I've found that people disrupt the status quo of
their lives with language and literacy and that the researcher, when invited to
do so, can contribute resources to this end.

For instance, Raejone, a 24-year-old mother of two, applied to a local university. As she composed her application essay, I offered some tutoring and access to Rensselaer computers. This was the first time she had applied to college. In another example, Lucy Cadens moved to a safer, suburban apartment complex. With my (and others') letters of recommendation, she obtained decent housing that accepts her Section 8. To facilitate the process of transferring her social services from one county to another, she asked me to complete a letter of certification which stated how many children she has in her new apartment. This is the first time Lucy has lived outside of the inner city. These precedents mark the very places where people deroutinize the status quo of wider society, together, during activist research.[4] Over the course of two and a half years of research, these people and I have worked together during numerous literacy events to create possibilities, the promising, if minute, differences in opportunity: together we've written resumes, job applications, college applications, and dialogic journals; when asked to do so, I've written recommendations to landlords, courts, potential employers, admissions counselors, and DSS representatives; one teen and I codirected a literacy program that allowed six children to read and write about issues important to them and that united resources from Rensselaer, Russell Sage College, the public library, and two philanthropic organizations. Since together we unite resources and grease the mechanisms of wider society institutions, all of these literacy acts carve possibilities from the routine ways these institutions, agencies, courts, and universities have historically worked in constraining ways.

I need to emphasize the difference between missionary activism, which introduces certain literacies to promote an ideology, and scholarly activism, which facilitates the literate activities that *already* take place in the community. For example, the Cadens' household had become too crowded with extended family. Lucy's daughter, Raejone, and her two children decided to seek housing from the philanthropic organization that rented to Raejone's mother. This agency had many units available and a short waiting list, but as the months passed, Raejone realized that her name never moved up the list. Her sisters also applied for housing but encountered similar foot dragging. Raejone found housing through a private landlord and then wrote a letter to this housing agency. In it she protested the inadequate treatment she received. Raejone and the directors of this housing program met to discuss the letter, and since then, Raejone's sisters have been offered housing by this agency. Raejone's letter caused the people who were simply reproducing their typical behavior to pause and consider the impact of their actions. In effect, the people in this housing program have altered the ways in which they treat Raejone and her family. Raejone, without any of my assistance, potently enacts her agency in order to challenge the routine foot dragging she faced.

Often this type of social change would be overlooked or underestimated with the emancipatory theories we currently use. Those who choose to say resistance only counts when it takes the form of overt and collective political action might describe us as using nothing more than coping devices with this literacy. Choosing to see this interaction in isolation, they may be correct; however, Scott reminds us that thousands of such "'petty' acts of resistance have dramatic economical and political effects." (*Domination* 192). These daily verbal and literate interactions mark the very places where composition teachers can begin to look for the impact of our critical pedagogy and activism, both in the classroom and when we approach the community.[5]

Red Robin Hoods

If we view social change at a micro level of interaction, we can begin to see where activism fits into the particulars of daily living. Activism means accepting a civic duty to empower people with our positions, a type of leftist stealing from the rich to give to the poor. To empower, as I use it, means: (a) to enable someone to achieve a goal by providing resources for them; (b) to facilitate actions—particularly those associated with language and literacy; (c) to lend our power or status to forward people's achievement. Often we are in a position to provide the luxuries of literacy for people. Since we're surrounded with the tools for literacy all day long, we often take for granted the luxury of the time and space needed for our literacy events. We schedule our work days around papers we read and write; our research is often carried out in libraries—clean, well lit, with cubicles and desks to use as we silently mine books for information;* and we return to our homes or offices to trace out an idea with pen and paper or at the keyboard. Our time is devoted to reading and writing with spaces and institutional resources often provided for us. But when we approach the community, often we will be forced "to recall the material conditions of writing," to remember that "we do confront such complex material questions as how to provide equality of access to computers for word processing." (Gere 87).

---

* We mine data in our scholarly homeplots looking for a gem of an idea others will value.

The reading and writing used for individual development in many communities is a valued, scarce, and difficult endeavor. We may say to ourselves that reading and writing is more important than some daily worries, such as cleaning, taking care of children and grandparents, and cooking, but often one of the primary ways people build a good name for themselves outside of work is to be solid parents, providers, doers. Mike Rose reminds us in *Lives on the Boundary* as he describes Lucia, a returning student and single mother, and notes "how many pieces had to fall in place each day for her to be a student. . . . Only if those pieces dropped in smooth alignment could her full attention shift to" the challenges of literacy for her own development (185). In *All Our Kin*, Carol Stack also describes similar domestic demands which must take priority over time for oneself in order for people to maintain their social networks of reciprocity. In other words, before people can devote their time to reading and writing to improve themselves, their social and family duties must be in place. Many women in the neighborhood in which I am immersed say they "wish there were more than 24 hours in a day," or they qualify their literate goals with, "if I had time, I could study that driver's manual." Yet, for a researcher, seeing the need for time is only half of the equation; the other half is doing something about those needs.

Empowering people in part enables them to achieve a goal by providing resources for them. Since it's difficult for many of these women to clear time alone while they're at home, we often schedule one or two hours to be together during the week when they know they won't be missed. We've spent time in places where we have many literate resources at our disposal including bookstores, libraries, my apartment (not far from this neighborhood), as well as the Rensselaer computer labs and Writing Center. During these times we've cleared together, we've studied driver's manuals, discussed books, gone through the college application process, as well as worked on papers, resumes and letters they wanted to write. Because we have worked together, these people who want time away from the neighborhood have achieved their literate goals.

Empowerment also happens when we facilitate people's oral and literate language use as well as lend our status for their achievement. The people in this neighborhood recognize the prestige of the language resources and social status I bring from Rensselaer and ask for assistance in a number of their language use activities.[+] One woman had just received an eviction

---

[+] In addition to language resources, I make available many of my material resources: clothes, small amounts of money, food, and rides to the doctor, stores, and DSS offices.

notice and asked me to "help [her] get a new place." She asked if we could practice mock conversations she might have with landlords over the phone. She thought this practice would "help [her] sound respectable, you know, white." As we practiced in her dining room, she wrote what we said on the back of a Chinese take-out menu for future reference. Once she set appointments to see an apartment, she contacted me so we could view the apartments together because "having you with me will make me seem respectable, you being from RPI and all." She differentiates between the social languages we speak and she wants to practice these languages with me.[6] She also identifies one way she can use my position for her own ends. She eventually got an apartment and thanked me for what she saw as my contribution. (See the appendix on "False Consciousness.") I've found that the luxury of literacy can easily be transferred from the university to our neighborhoods when we expand the scope of our scholarly activities to include activism. While empowerment may seem one sided, as though the scholar has a long arm of emancipating power, the people in communities can empower us through reciprocity.

Much Obliged

The terms governing the give-and-take (reciprocity) of involvement in the community need to be openly and consciously negotiated by everyone participating in activist research. As Bourdieu terms it, reciprocity describes a gift-giving and receiving behavior which can produce a mode of domination if the gift is not returned. "A gift that is not returned can become a debt, a lasting obligation" (126). Depending on the terms of the exchange, this obligation can either be in the form of a monetary debt, which imposes "overtly economic obligations by the usurer," or, in the form of an ethical debt, which produces "moral obligations and emotional attachments created and maintained by the generous gift, in short, overt violence or symbolic violence" (126). Reciprocity in exchange networks quickly produces power relations where the likelihood of oppression depends upon the terms of the giving and receiving.

While Bourdieu depicts reciprocity networks by studying the bonds maintained in relations between kin-people and tribal chiefs, this notion of reciprocity applies to the ways in which we enter into the community. With an idea of how exchanges create and maintain oppressive structures, activists can pay conscious attention to the power structures produced and maintained during their interactions with others outside of the university.

Reciprocity includes an open and conscious negotiation of the power structures reproduced during the give-and-take interactions of the people involved on both sides of the relationship. A theory of reciprocity, then, frames this activist agenda with a self-critical, conscious navigation of this intervention.

Herzberg's work exemplifies reciprocity well when interpreted in terms of the give-and-take relationship between the researcher and community. Through a "service-learning program," students at Bentley became adult literacy tutors at a shelter in Boston and wrote about their experiences in Herzberg's composition classroom. At the outset, the rules were established for what types of information could be exchanged between the tutor and learners. The students "were not allowed (by the wise rules of the shelter and good sense) to quiz their learners on their personal lives and histories" (315). Before these tutorial sessions began, the boundaries for exchange of information were set. Students tutored, wrote, and received college credit; Herzberg gave his time and energy, which eventually earned him a spot in this journal; and although this article does not make clear what the people in the shelter received and gave from this involvement, he indicates "the tutoring, as best [as they] could determine, appeared to be productive for the learners at the shelter" (316). From his work, we begin to see how bridging the university and community establishes give-and-take relationships that must be openly and carefully navigated.

It may seem that the activist research I described in the previous section is one-sided, that I may sound like a self-aggrandizing liberator of oppressed masses. But this just isn't the case, since these people empower me in many ways. Referring back to my original definition of empowerment, they've enabled me to achieve a primary goal in my life: getting my PhD. They've let me photocopy their letters, personal journals, essays, and applications. They've granted me interviews and allowed me to listen to their interactions with social workers, admissions counselors, and DSS representatives. They've told me stories and given me the history of this area through their eyes. They've fed me, included me in their family gatherings for birthdays and holidays, and have invited me to their parties and cook outs. They've read my papers and made suggestions; they listened to my theories and challenged them when I was off mark. (See the appendix on "In Ivory Towers, We Overlook.") As I write my dissertation, they add, clarify and question. In some very important ways, we collaborate in this research. In fact, the two women whose writing I refer to most frequently in this article, signed a release form so that you may read about them today. To quote from the CCC "consent-to-reprint" forms, Raejone and Lucy understood that they "will receive no compensation" for their work and that they "assign publishing rights for the contribution to NCTE, including all copyrights." They have given me the right to represent them to you and have facilitated my work in doing so. They've also lent me their status. They've legitimized my presence in their neighborhood, in masque, and in some institutions simply by associating with me. Through reciprocity, they've enabled me to come closer to achieving my goal everyday; they've facilitated my actions; and they've lent me their status.

The Access in Praxis

Often we don't have to look far to find access routes to people outside of the university. Any kind of identification we may have with people in our communities, to some extent, acts as a point of commonality where our perspectives overlap, despite our different positions. These points of convergence, I think, come closest to Freire's notion of solidarity. Solidarity manifests itself when there are common threads of identity between the student and teacher. To achieve empowerment through critical consciousness, the teacher "must be a partner of the students in his relations with them" (62). A partnership connotes people working together toward common goals. Freire finds "one must seek to live with others in solidarity . . . [and] solidarity requires true communication" (63). I believe that access to people with whom we identify is the initial building block for the solidarity and communication needed in activism.

Many access routes into the community have been established by philanthropic organizations, churches, community centers, and businesses. Before an access route is chosen, though, significant research needs to be done to see how the community developed, what types of contributions are needed, and whether or not there's precedent for the work proposed. After I spoke with representatives in many philanthropic and social service agencies, I volunteered in a bridge program between Rensselaer and a community center. Once there, I proposed a summer literacy program, but when this was over, I soon realized that I needed to reposition myself in the community. When I stopped volunteering, the women in this community found it easier to identify with me as a person and not as an organizational member.

Although I'm white, the women in this neighborhood and I identify with each other in many ways: we're no strangers to welfare offices, cockroaches, and empty refrigerators. We've held our chins out and heads up when we haven't had enough food stamps at the check out line. We've made poor (and good) choices in men and have purple and pink scars to prove it. We know enough to take out our earrings before we fight. We know abuses and disorders and the anonymous places people turn to for them. Since many of these people came from the Carolinas, and since my great-great-grand parents were in the Trail of Tears, we know why, on a crisp January day, a cardinal in a pine tree gives us hope.

Once we locate an access route into the community, we can begin the long process of self disclosure and listening from which we can begin to identify with each other. For Freire, communication is the main way to achieve this identification: "Through dialogue, the teacher-of-the-students and the students-of-the-teacher cease to exist and a new term emerges: teacher-student with students-teachers. The teacher is no longer the-one-who-teaches, but one who himself is taught in dialogue with the students, who in turn while being taught also teach" (67). Through communication, the exchange of questioning and asserting, we come to identify with each other and challenge the bases for our differences.

While this type of dialogue can take place in the classroom, the very power structure of the university makes it difficult to establish and maintain dialogue and solidarity. There's only so much we can get to know about our students within the sociological confines of the academic composition classroom. (See the appendix on "Freired Not.") Yet when we approach the community, we maneuver around the sociological obstacles that hinder us in the classroom from communicating with our students in ways that show our identification with them. Said another way, activism starts with some kind of identification with people outside of the university, an identification that often can flourish in a context where both the scholar and people together assess and redraw lines of power structures between them.

No Mother Teresas Here

With the initial components of activism roughed out this way, I need to provide some important caveats. Let me show a few of the limitations of this kind of praxis with reference to shortcomings and mishaps in my own ethnographic fieldwork. My first concern in folding open activism this way is that these principles will be read as altruistic, when in my experience activism establishes an interdependency. Activism can't be altruistic because we have to be in a position to participate in our communities. The very same position as scholar which distances us from the community also invests us with resources we can make available to others. And we need these luxuries in order to be stable enough to give our time, knowledge, and resources. This means we must work very hard in the academy with the support of our community in order to garner the status and resources that we then return to the community.

I don't mean to simplify the process of gaining luxury here because I recognize that becoming an agent of social change in our neighborhoods requires time and energy. As a funded graduate student, I'm particularly fortunate to have the time and money to do this activist research. My teaching assistantship requires an average of twenty hours of work per week, and since I'm through with course work, I'm only on campus when I'm teaching, writing on the computers, or researching in the library. While I know my professors have 3/2 and 3/3 course loads, I've heard of other professors who have 5/5 course loads and hundreds of students every semester.[7] Yet, at the risk of sounding pollyannic, we've already seen precedents for the type of scholarly civic participation I suggest. Perhaps through the reciprocity of activism, we might fold together our scholarly and civic duties.

Since the relationship established in activism centers upon reciprocity, an interdependency emerges. One of the ways in which we've maintained a mutually empowering relationship is through open and careful navigation of the reciprocity we've established. While this reciprocity may sound easy to maintain, many times requests have to be turned down. I've asked to record certain people and have been refused: I've also asked for examples of certain types of writing people didn't feel comfortable giving me, so I went without. Likewise, one person asked me to co-sign on a car loan (which I couldn't); and another person asked me to sign over any royalties I receive from a possible book to the families on the block (which I'm still considering). Everyone in this research realizes what we stand to gain from the work, and reciprocity helps prevent the work from becoming altruistic.

If we ignore the give-and-take established in activist research and instead choose to paint ourselves in the bright colors of benevolent liberators, we risk becoming what Macedo so delicately terms "literacy and poverty pimps" (xv). When we adopt a fashionable theory of emancipatory pedagogy and activism without considering the structural constraints imposed by reciprocity, we capitalize on other's daily living without giving any of these benefits in return. But here's the paradox—we need to make activism part of our research and teaching, so that we can make a living in the university. How else will we be able to give in equal amount to what we take?

Accessive Force

The degree to which we gain entrance into the daily lives of people outside the university in some measure depends upon who we are. The boundaries of our access must be negotiated with the people. Often, leftist posing assumes a here-I-am-to-save-the-day air, takes for granted immediate and complete entrance into a community, presumes an undeniably forceful presence. In my own work, I've overstepped the boundaries of my access working under similar assumptions. Six months into this research on a summer afternoon, I joined a large group of teens and adults playing cards, sipping beer, and talking on a front stoop. I was dealt into a game of 21 and listened to gossip and news. Lucy Cadens had a boyfriend (Anthony) who was seated in one of the folding chairs at the end of the stoop. Lucy had been gone for a few minutes, and he and I chatted until it was my turn to deal.

Later that day, Lucy called me away from the stoop and asked, "You want to tell me about Anthony?" I thought she was referring to a complaint a parent made to the center staff about him, and told her I wasn't at liberty to talk about it. She looked confused and asked me if I was talking to him that day. I told her of what I thought was an innocent conversation about gambling in Atlantic City. "They told me he was fishing with you," she said with her hands on her hips. I was shocked; what I thought was a simple conversation was actually him flirting with me. I told Lucy that I would keep a much safer distance from him and asked if she thought I should make that a unilateral decision about interacting with men in the neighborhood. She said I should be careful about who I talked to and about what, but that I could be polite to them. Since then, I've negotiated this boundary much more carefully and have gathered the majority of my notes from the children and women of the neighborhood. In this way, the access I presumed I had was fundamentally limited along gender lines. The lines of access must be charted, recharted, and respected in activist research. I had overstepped a boundary, albeit unintentionally, and realized my liberal presumption of unlimited access was pompous and shortsighted.

The Best Laid Approaches

Civic participation requires careful understandings of how our position will work, or not, within the given organizations of people. As mentioned earlier, I originally gained access to this neighborhood as a literacy volunteer and researcher through a bridge program between Rensselaer and the neighborhood center located in the heart of this community. As a volunteer, the social workers expected that I follow the same rules of conduct that they were institutionally bound to follow. However, I soon realized that the roles of researcher and volunteer contradict each other in important ways.

As a volunteer, a team player, I was expected to tell the social workers any details I might be privy to which concerned the private lives of the people in this neighborhood. I often visited the homes and sat on the stoops with people when the social workers were bound to stay in the center—their liability insurance did not cover them if something happened to them outside the center. As a researcher, though, I needed to walk between both worlds, the home and community center, but I was bound to the ethics of participant observation which dictate I can not reveal information about my informants. Unfortunately, the center staff felt threatened by my peculiar position and worried that I would jeopardize their standing within the community with the information I had about the workings of their institution. As a result, they asked me to discontinue my volunteer work with them.

When we first consider bridging with communities, especially if we hope to do research at the same time, we must chart the internal workings of the institutions in order to see the ways we might, or might not, fit in. I initially believed I could simply volunteer and do research—"surely people will welcome the time and resources I offer." Here I was guilty of leftist posing disguised as philanthropy. Because I assumed this, I didn't negotiate my role within this organization well at all.

Even with these limitations, we can begin to participate in our communities despite (to spite) the sociological distances we must cross. Cultural studies models of empowerment and critical pedagogues are derelict in their civic duties by not including an expanded version of activism. Through activism, we've taken the first, tentative steps toward social change outside of the social confines of the university classroom. Finally, we not only fill a civic responsibility with activism, but also inform our teaching and theories with the perspectives of people outside the university. We begin to see just how deficient our estimations of our students are when we immerse ourselves and contribute to their everyday literacy and hidden belief systems.

The roads into the communities aren't paved with yellow bricks and sometimes may seem unapproachable, but access can generally be gained with observation and informal interviews to see who is already in the neighborhood and how they got there. Along the way relationships need to be navigated openly and consciously with close attention paid to boundaries and limitations in our access and intervention. Of course, I'm ignoring one potential means of access into the community—our students. But then, this assumes that we have solid enough relations with them to be able to follow them beyond the moat surrounding the ivory tower.

Appendices

Slippery Discourse

Many researchers believe that they can promote *social change* and *empower* students through critical literacy and emancipatory pedagogy. Yet we often hear the terms *social change* and *empowerment* used as though the nature of their outcomes is clearly established and reflected upon. This slippery discourse leads us to believe that we're all after the same ends: "enfranchising outsiders," having "social impact," creating a more "just society," offering a "liberating ideology," honing students' "awareness and critical consciousness," challenging "the oppressive system," "encouraging resistance," and of course, "interrogating dominate hegemony."[†] Just how these end products of critical pedagogy lead to *social change* and *empowerment* isn't clear to me from these discussions. In fact, some scholars make no distinctions between *social change* and *empowerment,* as though to empower is to liberate, and to liberate is to produce social change.[8] Underpinning this slippery discourse is an equally slick assumption—*social change* and *empowerment* lead to some kind of collective action or resistance involving the masses of people we teach.[9] When we view the impact of critical pedagogy from these grand levels, though, we miss the particular ways in which our teaching and research might contribute to students' abilities to take up their civic responsibilities once they leave our classrooms. We need a theory of social change and empowerment that captures the complex ways power is negotiated at micro levels of interaction between people, which would allow us to better characterize the impact of our work. With such a theory, we're less likely to paint ourselves as great "liberators of oppressed masses."

[†] These trends in discourse I culled from many of the collected essays in *Composition and Resistance.* Since these discourses often make one think of saviors, the footnote marker seems particularly apt.

False Consciousness

Many critical theorists portray themselves as brokers of emancipatory power, a stance that garners them status at the expense of students. One way to make a position for themselves in the academy is to diagnose their students as having "false consciousness." Once labeled as having "false consciousness," students can be easily dismissed and diminished by critical theory.[10] Yet, the many scholars who do immerse themselves into the daily living of people find, predictably, hidden ideologies—belief systems that contain numerous, clever ways to identify and criticize onerous behavior.[11] In some fundamental sense, the discursive posturing we so frequently hear would not be able to legitimize itself, if it didn't diminish others in its wake. The label of false consciousness, then, reveals more about the speaker's limited access to students and communities, than it reveals about the level of people's critical abilities. If cultural studies theorists were to visit the homes and streets of the people attending their classes, they would likely hear critiques of the dominating sociological forces.[12] Therein we see the fundamental problem in building our models of cultural studies: we're sociologically distanced from the cultures we study.

In Ivory Towers, We Overlook

When we fail to consider the perspectives of people outside of the academy, we overlook valuable contributions to our theory building. Without a praxis that moves between community and university, we risk not only underestimating our students' pre-existing critical consciousness, but we also risk reproducing the hegemonic barriers separating the university from the community. That is, we become guilty of applying our theories from the sociological "top-down," instead of informing our theories from the "bottom-up." In fact, it appears many value the idea more than the people, a value that bolsters the sociological distance of the university from the community. I've even read arguments *supporting* the social isolation of theorists in the academy from people in communities. In other words, we exclude many of the people we're trying to empower for the sake of positing (what we sure as hell hope will be) liberating ideas. The flaw in this logic seems so obvious: How can we study ideologies, hegemonies, power structures, and the effects of discursive practices when we overlook community discursive dispositions—the place where these language practices are first inculcated, generated and consequently reproduced in the social habitus?[13] Thus, many postmodern theorists remain tucked within their libraries and don't engage the very people they hope to help. They will send their theories down to the people and engage each other in postmodern conversations (over pomo tea perhaps) in their postmodern universities.

Freired Not

When we begin to turn cultural studies in on itself in a self-reflexive manner, we see its limiting assumptions and paradoxical stances as it's applied to composition studies. And this is indeed a shame, because the political and sociological theories it employs are very useful in expanding our roles as rhetoricians to include more perspectives from the margins. In the opening of *Pedagogy of the Oppressed*, Freire evaluates the oppressors in society: "To affirm that men are persons and persons should be free, and yet, to do nothing tangible to make this affirmation a reality, is a farce" (35). What he means by tangible is left up to interpretation; I suggest he means activism.[14] If we let *tangible* be synonymous with activism, then to what extent is promoting critical consciousness in our classrooms "activist?" My sense is that we're not doing enough because we're acting within the role of the teacher that has been perpetuated by the institution, and thus keeps us from breaking down the barriers between the university and community. In fact, many critical pedagogues have betrayed their activist agenda in their classrooms by characterizing their students as "dull," "numb," "dumbly silent," "unreflective," "yearning" and/or "resentful."[∞] They place themselves in the oppressive position by relegating students to the category of the "unfortunates." Pedagogues are only two letters shy of becoming demagogues. About these characterizations, Freire might say: "No pedagogy that is truly liberating can remain distant from the oppressed by treating them as unfortunates" (39). What these researchers fail to remember is that the students they teach are in a prime position for critical reflection precisely because they are disenfranchised: "Who are better prepared," Freire asks, "than the oppressed to understand the terrible significance of an oppressive society?" (29).

[∞] As found in the popular collection of essays, *Contending with Words*.

Notes

1. While this idea of the physical surroundings having significance isn't novel, it is often overlooked as a tool to critique our own context, the university setting. Bakhtin, for example, finds that "everything ideological possesses semiotic value" (929). In other words, "any physical body may be perceived as an image. . . . Any such artistic-symbol image to which a particular physical object gives rise is already an ideological product. The physical object is converted into a sign" (928). This allows us to critique how even the construction and setting of the Approach can take on significance. Thus, "a sign does not simply exist as a part of a reality— it reflects and refracts another reality" (929). The stairway is a sign of the connection between the city and university, a connection that needs maintenance.

2. Cheryl Geisler offers a cogent summary of these ideas in the second chapter of her recent book on expertise in the academy. Further, Bowles and Gintis present a Marxist analysis of the ways in which schooling serves to perpetuate the class hierarchies necessary for modern capitalism to flourish.

3. Mike Rose's latest work reveals the rich and complicated ways in which primary and secondary school teachers still move toward this democratic principal. His book challenges the country's impoverished discourse used to describe education, and takes steps toward envisioning a discourse of possibility centered on a fundamental belief in the strong ties between education and democracy.

4. Activist research expands upon notions of *praxis*. Originally developed by Aristotle, praxis resembles "phronesis, action adhering to certain ideal standards of good (ethical) or effective (political) behavior" (Warry 157). Marx embellished this political agenda for participation in his "Eleventh Thesis," and some applied anthropologists have since adopted praxis as a term describing, loosely, ethical action in the research paradigm geared toward social change. For example, Johannsen brings postmodern critiques to ethnography and finds that research as praxis demands that we actively participate in the community under study. While expanding the participant side of social science research is necessary in order to achieve praxis, examinations of praxis in social sciences are for the most part "wholly theoretical and with only occasional reference to methodological or pragmatic concerns associated with planned change, intervention, or action research" (Warry 156). Even though applied anthropology, a subfield of anthropology, provides theoretical models for how praxis enters into the research paradigm (see Lather), many scholars still need to do the work of intervention at the community level.

5. Some may question the potency of such activism and the extent to which these literacy events really did challenge the status quo. In his classic social scientific study entitled *Black Families in White America*, Andrew Billingsley depicts some of the historically rooted everyday struggles of African-Americans in achieving social and geographic mobility. Education "is a most reliable index and a potent means of gaining social mobility and family stability in our society. The absence of systematic training and education during slavery and reconstruction depressed the social structure of the Negro people most, just as the presence of education in small and scattered doses proved such a powerful source of

achievement" (79). Raejone's application essay for college suggests one way we worked against this historically rooted absence of education that Billingsley mentions in an effort to create the presence of higher education in her family. Similarly, the literacy which contributed to Lucy's relocation to a suburban area loosens "the tight white noose around the central cities [that] has kept Negro families from being able to penetrate suburbia in any appreciable numbers" (74).

6. Different types of discourses constitute different contexts, an idea Bakhtin described well as the difference between "everyday genre" ("what ordinary people live, and their means for communicating with each other") (*Dialogic* 428) and "social languages" ("the discourse peculiar to a specific system of society [professional, age group, etc.]) (430). Thus, "heteroglossia" allows us to understand how "language is stratified, not only into linguistic dialects . . . but also—and for us this is the essential point—into languages that are socio-ideological: languages of social groups" (272).

7. I found Pauline Uchmanowicz' recent article particularly disturbing. She describes her "dog years" as a part-time college writing instructor at two institutions where she teaches "between twelve and sixteen scheduled classes per week" and is paid "a little over half the salary of a full-time teacher for teaching double the course load" (427). Add to this burden her commute of five hundred miles every week and lack of job security, and I begin to worry that the luxury needed for activism is out of reach for many composition teachers.

8. Jennifer Core insightfully critiques "some shortcomings in the construction of 'empowerment' by critical and feminist educational discourses which create problems internal to their discourses" (54). For example, she identifies how the agency of empowerment stems from the teacher, while the subject of empowerment is usually the student. As the center of activity in these discourses, the teacher is more important than the students—a practice that contradicts the theoretical emphasis on the student.

9. I think many of us work so closely from Freire's model of pedagogy we believe the impact his literacy projects have will be in equal kind and type to the impact our classes may have. However, Freire cautions "it is impossible to export pedagogical practices without re-inventing them. Please, tell your fellow American educators not to import me. Ask them to recreate and rewrite my ideas" (Macedo xiv).

10. James Scott, a political scientist, makes a convincing argument against the label of "false consciousness." His ethnographic fieldwork in Malaysia depicts not only the social forces which daily influence Malay peasants, but also reveals their unseen defiance and hidden ideology used to challenge these forces. He differentiates between those public and private behaviors that relate to power struggles. The peasants appear to cordially accept the authority of landlords in their public encounters with them: however, they actually fought this oppressive ideology in private spheres. This resistance Scott terms as the difference between "public and hidden transcripts," and reveals how these peasants have devised a number of ways to challenge their subordination. These forms of often "low profile, undisclosed resistance" create the infrapolitics of larger society (198), but also suggest the limitation of the notion of false consciousness. Since most researchers

and teachers aren't privy to the hidden ideologies of their informants/students, we miss the ways in which resistance and critical consciousness are constructed in subtle, often unnoticed ways.

11. For example, Keith Basso found that Western Apaches have clever, elaborate systems of mocking "the Whiteman." Luis Moll immersed himself in a Mexican-American community in Tucson, Arizona, and characterized complex systems of knowledge and strategies shared by households in order to "enhance survival within harsh social conditions" (225). Carol Stack in *All Our Kin* found African-Americans devised many strategies to undermine the welfare institution's influence in their fund allocation, including withholding information, foot dragging, and misrepresenting census data. Perhaps with more access to their students' communities, critical scholars would not be so quick in their dismissal of their students' critical abilities.

12. Fundamental to activism, I believe, is not only a basic trust in the potential and abilities of people, but also a basic mistrust of assessments that diminish and dismiss others. Brian Fay, a philosopher of social science, describes the ontological values of critical social science this way: "An active creature . . . is intelligent, curious, reflective, and willful" (50). All people have these qualities regardless of their socio-cultural circumstances. Activism has roots in a genuine care and respect for all people. Anything short of this and our work quickly takes on a paternalistic, patronizing, and ingenuine flavor.

13. Pierre Bourdieu's sociological model of the *habitus* describes dispositions as patterns of behavior, such as language behaviors, which then combine to make the "acquired system of generative schemes, the habitus" (54).

14. As Giroux points out, "though Freire provides the broad theoretical framework needed to help bridge the gaps that plague radical education in North America, his analysis in key places warrants further substantiation and depth" (136). For the sake of this argument, I believe that in North America, teaching is different from activism. Teaching is institutionalized because a certain social status is constructed around the knowledge used in this role (see Berger and Luckmann). Yet, activism in the politics of the community is not institutionalized, per se, rather, it's a civic duty that all people can potentially fulfill without needing specialized knowledge related to schooling (Geisler: Bowles and Gintis). So activism is more closely related to civic duty and teaching related to an institution. I see these two activities on the same continuum of the democratic process, as potentially mutually informative, but not interchangeable projects of democracy.

Works Cited

Bakhtin, Mikhail. *The Dialogic Imagination.* Ed. Michael Holquist. Austin: U of Texas P, 1981.

———. "Marxism and the Philosophy of Language." *The Rhetorical Tradition.* Ed. Patricia Bizzell and Bruce Herzberg. Boston: St. Martin's, 1990. 924–63.

Basso, Keith. *Portraits of "The Whiteman."* Cambridge: Cambridge UP, 1979.

Beach, Richard, et al., eds. *Multidisciplinary Perspectives on Literacy Research.* Urbana: NCTE, 1992.

Berger, Peter, and Thomas Luckmann. *The Social Construction of Reality.* New York: Anchor, 1966.

Billingsley, Andrew. *Black Families in White America.* New York: Simon, 1968.

Bourdieu, Pierre. *The Logic of Practice.* Stanford: Stanford UP, 1990.

Bowles, S., and H. Gintis. *Schooling in Capitalist America.* New York: Basic, 1976.

Fay, Brian. *Critical Social Science.* Ithaca: Cornell UP, 1987.

Freire, Paulo. *Pedagogy of the Oppressed.* New York: Herder, 1971.

Geisler, Cheryl. *Academic Literacy and the Nature of Expertise.* Hillsdale: Erlbaum, 1994.

Gere, Anne Ruggles. "The Extracurriculum of Composition." *CCC* 45 (1994): 75–92.

Giddens, Anthony. *The Constitution of Society.* Berkeley: U of California P, 1981.

Giroux, Henry. *Ideology, Culture, and the Process of Schooling.* Philadelphia: Temple UP, 1981.

Gore, Jennifer. "What We Can Do for You! What *Can* 'We' do for 'You?'" *Feminisms and Critical Pedagogy.* Ed. Jennifer Gore and Carmen Luke. London: Routledge, 1992. 54–73.

Halloran, S. Michael. "Afterthoughts on Rhetoric and Public Discourse." *Pre/Text: The First Decade.* Ed. Victor Vitanza. Pittsburgh: U of Pittsburgh P, 1993. 52–68.

Herzberg, Bruce. "Community Service and Critical Teaching." *CCC* 45 (1994): 307–19.

Johannsen, Agneta. "Applied Anthropology and Post-Modernist Ethnography." *Human Organization* 51 (1992): 71–81.

Lather, Patti, "Research as Praxis." *Harvard Educational Review* 56 (1986): 257–77.

Macedo, Donald. Preface. *Politics of Liberation.* Ed. Peter McLaren and Colin Lankshear. Routledge: London, 1994. xiii–xix.

Moll, L. "Literacy Research in Community and Classrooms: A Sociocultural Approach." Beach et al. 211–44.

Moll, L. and Stephen Diaz. "Change as the Goal of Educational Research." *Anthropology and Education Quarterly* 18 (1987): 300–11.

Powell, Malea. "Custer's Very Last Stand: Rhetoric, the Academy, and the Un-Seeing of the American Indian." Unpublished essay. 1995.

Rose, Mike. *Lives on the Boundary.* Boston: Penguin, 1989.

———. *Possible Lives: The Promise of Public Education in America.* New York: Houghton, 1995.

Schiappa, Edward. "Intellectuals and the Place of Cultural Critique." *Rhetoric, Cultural Studies, and Literacy.* Ed. Frederick Reynolds. Hillsdale: Erlbaum. 1995. 26–32.

Scott, James C. *Domination and the Arts of Resistance.* New Haven: Yale UP, 1990.

———. *Weapons of the Weak.* New Haven: Yale UP, 1985.

Stack, Carol. *All Our Kin: Strategies for Survival in a Black Community.* New York: Harper, 1974.

Uchmanowicz, Pauline. "The $5,000–$25,000 Exchange." *College English* 57 (1995): 426–47.

Warry, Wayne. "The Eleventh Thesis: Applied Anthropology as Praxis." *Human Organization* 51 (1992): 155–63.

12 "A Real Vexation": Student Writing In Mount Holyoke's Culture of Service, 1837–1865

JoAnn Campbell

Speaking at the third anniversary of the Mount Holyoke Female Seminary, on July 30, 1840, Williams College president Mark Hopkins described the ideal Mount Holyoke student:

> Let us suppose her beautiful in person, and, I will not say accomplished, for there clings to that word something of ostentation which I do not like, not accomplished, but possessed of accomplishments, and simple and elegant in manners. Let us suppose her intellectual faculties so exercised and balanced, that she has extensive information and good judgment, in connection with the lighter graces of imagination and fancy; and then that she so combines simple piety and the severer virtues with practical goodness as to awaken mingled respect and affection, and we have a combination, certainly possible, of solid and brilliant qualities such as might well remind a person of no extraordinary enthusiasm of that expression in the Revelations, 'And I saw an Angel standing in the sun.' (17)

Hopkins's comparisons of women and angels, and later women and vines around the sturdy male oak tree, were standard nineteenth-century rhetorical devices. Such imagery explains his preference for the phrase "possessed of accomplishments" rather than "accomplished." Angels work quietly, serving for the sake of service and not for attention or accolades. So too women in nineteenth-century institutions of higher education studied for knowledge that would help them be of service to their communities rather than for self-glorification or edification. Subjects that were considered accomplishments

---

Reprinted from *College English*, November 1997.

were feminine, less serious, and taught in finishing schools. Ada Snell, a teacher at Mount Holyoke College, noted that verbal ability, in particular "spoken English," was downplayed at Mount Holyoke: "This fact may be owing to the position of women at the time and also possibly that Elocution or Reading seemed to Mary Lyon to be an accomplishment and not a study. That the subject was suspect—merely an ornamental branch of learning—is evident from the fact that it was classified with painting and music in the list of extras" (20). A rhetoric of service, on the other hand, was the chief argument used to raise money for serious women's colleges, for as Susan Conrad observes, "intellect severed from virtue and duty was unthinkable" (22).

My examination of hundreds of themes from Mount Holyoke, Vassar, Smith, Wellesley, Radcliffe, Harvard, and Amherst indicates that the first generation of women to attend US colleges negotiated two worlds with competing demands: a social world that expected women to be of service to family and community, and an academic world that valued individual intellectual performance over all else. The Mount Holyoke curriculum and milieu were designed to moderate these two extremes. To be taken seriously as an academic institution, the seminary had to have at its center a classical curriculum, which women "mastered" for the sake of demonstrating such mastery. But to produce women graduates who could earn a living through teaching or missionary work, the seminary had to provide an environment where service remained a top virtue, where the student's self was submerged in Christian service to others and her actions directed by the demands of the other. This tension produced a challenging rhetorical situation for women faced with writing a composition every other week for the academic purpose of demonstrating their intellectual and writing abilities.

Apparently the practical application of academic knowledge was more direct for young college men. Again, Hopkins described the distinction between men's and women's education in relation to their separate spheres outside academe: "The great motive with men in studying languages and mathematics is not, generally, to cultivate their faculties, but to prepare themselves for the attainment and practice of their professions. There evidently is not the same reason for teaching young ladies Navigating and Engineering and Hebrew, as if they were expected to take the command of our men of war, or lay out rail roads, or expound the Old Testament" (7). Because there were few careers open to them, women studied in order to cultivate their faculties. But because women's apparent point on earth was to be helpmates, they could not simply learn for themselves. Could women afford to be in a contemplative daze, self-absorbed, detached and disengaged, when their mission was to serve? Socialized to be of service, these women brought to the seminary a deep belief in and need for purpose.

Composition assignments at Mount Holyoke in the 1840s and 1850s did not always satisfy this need. As some students' compositions show, the institution failed to create a climate for expression, not just one-way personal expression but deeply social, dialogical expression. Adherence to a traditional rhetorical curriculum and pedagogy granted Mount Holyoke credibility in the eyes of an educated citizenry but limited innovative assignments that might have invited students to use their new skills in tasks they valued. By contrasting these women's compositions with those of male students who attended Harvard during the same era, I hope to illustrate the effects of gender on service, both as a concept and as an activity. For a gendered notion of service continues to inform and influence discussion of service-learning, a contemporary pedagogy that connects voluntary community service with academic study.

To understand the conditions of writing instruction for the first generation of women attending college in the United States, I read more than 300 themes written between the opening of Mount Holyoke Female Seminary in 1837 and the year 1920. From these I selected those compositions that referred directly to writing, to the conditions for composing, or to the climate of the educational institution that might affect the student's writing process. I supplemented these with other texts in which such comments occurred: school essays, letters to friends and family, diary entries, and articles in school publications such as literary magazines and newspapers. MHFS student essays open a window on nineteenth-century women's education, revealing the intellectual excitement of new activities and the personal challenge of academic expectations. The Mount Holyoke community was tightly structured and students' behavior closely monitored, conditions which affected composing, choice of topic, and perceived purposes for writing.

These students were caught between two worlds, each with a competing definition of the self. At Mount Holyoke, they were told that women were being educated to serve as teachers and as missionaries. Ten percent of all women missionaries sent out by the American Board of Commissioners for Foreign Missions in the 1800s came from MHFS (Inness 366), and 82 percent of MH graduates became teachers for some part of their lives. As Elizabeth Alden Green writes in *Mary Lyon and Mount Holyoke,* many of the early students were in their twenties, had taught for a few years, and "were motivated by high ideals of service rather than purely intellectual ambition" (182). As one student put it in a composition: "Life is real and must be active. Our service must be constant and faithful if at last we would receive the welcome plaudit 'well done good and faithful servant. Enter thou into the joys of thy Lord'" (Louise Fiske, 29 June 1867). Another student extolled the virtues of reason in order to "regulate our moral feelings, that we may be more extensively useful here and capable of enjoying a higher degree of felicity hereafter" (Martha Walker, "Use of Reason"). An ideal of service was the yardstick by which activity and thought were measured; it required a self understood necessarily in relation to others.

Many essays illustrate how these novice college writers tried to align their academic training with their desire to be of service and to fit back into their home communities. Composition was perceived as a route to developing one's reasoning abilities; connected to rhetoric, it enjoyed full academic prestige. As Laura Millett, MHFS student, perceived it, composition was "designed to strengthen our mental powers," and she tried to connect reason with typical feminine accomplishments: "Composition is fitted to improve the conversation. It teaches us to clothe our ideas in words, and to communicate with others in an easy and entertaining manner. Composition is extremely important. What is there more important for a lady than to possess a highly cultivated and rightly balanced mind?" ("Young Ladies Compositions," 1849).

In the face of competing demands on their energies, these students occasionally found themselves with nothing to say, except that their life experiences were not worthy of sharing and their opinions were too "feeble" to record. Mandana Adela Wheaton recalled her first composition, written in high school, when she was asked to describe her village. She writes that to fulfill the assignment, "I searched and searched in vain in our book case for some account of its early inhabitants . . . [for] it never once occurred to me that I could give an account of it as it seemed to me" ("A Package of Old Compositions," 22 March 1851). Of twenty-five essays in which the writer primarily discussed her schooling or writing, ten had as topic the difficulty of finding a subject to write about, a set of essays I call the "subjectless theme." Sandra Gilbert and Susan Gubar have noted the writing challenges embedded in the archetype of a "beautiful angel-woman . . . to be selfless is not only to be noble, it is to be dead. A life that has no story . . . is really a life of death, a death-in-life" (25). For these women, academic composition exercises with no apparent purpose forced them to create purposes within the text. To merely perform to dazzle an audience was anathema to those who believed life's meaning came from being of service to others.

Yet Mount Holyoke students were also socialized into a second world, an academic culture that emphasized the individual, isolated scholar. Letters and compositions indicate the isolation many of these students felt. Lucy Putnam wrote to a family friend that she was an "inmate of the Mount Holyoke convent" where she expected "to be a nun 40 long weeks!" (letter to Mr. and Mrs. Clarke, 11 October 1845). Another student wrote to a friend that "as for the villagers, we know no more of them then we do of the natives of India. We are in a sort of nunnery" (Susan Lennan, 8 January 1852). Having little or no contact with those outside Mount Holyoke Female Seminary, the students focused on studies and student life, which were well regulated. Mary Lyon's strict timetables for "silent study hours" established a model of the isolated scholar who studied in silence. Putnam complained that after three weeks at MHFS "there are not more than four young ladies out of nearly two hundred that I have ever spoken with: we have no opportunity to get acquainted if we had a disposition" (11 October 1845).

Education as Accomplishment

For those who had a disposition to socialize and to study, the cultural depiction of educated women was disheartening. Wearing one's accomplishments quietly might avoid censure, but at least one student wanted those accomplishments to be less ornamental and more a substantial part of the woman herself. In her 1846 essay "Female Education," Lucy Putnam used fictional examples to ask just how typical ideas of educating women served the woman. She contrasted the arts of "housewifery" with useless accomplishments in the moral tale of Annette P., a wealthy girl who "was sent to a fashionable boarding school, where she was taught to sing and dance, to speak and read French, to embroider muslin and work curious looking figures on cloth, to play upon the piano, and many other fashionable accomplishments of no substantial benefit to her." Because Annette's parents wanted her to be a "lady" she learned nothing of practical duties. She eventually married a fashionable gentleman, but, because theirs was an external attraction only, it cooled and they were trapped in domestic unhappiness.

Putnam used her description of Annette to critique standard definitions of education for women, anticipating perhaps her own return to a society that urged her to gain the trappings of education without providing avenues for women to use their knowledge and skills upon graduation: "The world looks upon a female possessed of a few vain and trivial accomplishments with admiration and even wonder while it regards with contempt one who is educated substantially and has none of those superficial elegances." Putnam lays the blame for this privileged definition of education on a society that treats women as ornaments:

> The existence of education which will transform woman into a mere bauble is considered by the mass as superior to that which cultivates and expands the intellectual and physical capacities. When a female can dance gracefully, sing expressly, and repeat the words of some foreign language, the world calls her an accomplished lady, finely educated, and silently adds, will be a first rate helpmate for somebody. But this very lady of whom the world says so much may be ignorant almost of the rudiments of her own language, and her moral principles are not developed, though a moping sentimentalism, taken as such, may indicate it. But popular opinion says this, and popular opinion is not the voice of one but the majority. Public sentiment in educational matters is carried to two extremes, each extreme advocated by a distinct class (for even here in the republican United States there is a nameless aristocracy) and each class avoiding, as death, the sentiments of the other. (3 April 1846)

This critique of class society is followed by two fictional caricatures that set the stage for the moderate Mount Holyoke female graduate: Mrs. Highup "will not permit her daughters to learn the arts of the housewife because she thinks them beneath their dignity" and Mrs. Lowdown has "a pious abhorrence of everything in her daughters, except cooking and baking and washing and the like." Unlike the daughters of aristocracy, who are "artificially educated that they appear well," the Mount Holyoke student had domestic duties in addition to her studies. Yet unlike the farmer's daughters, who "are fitted only for lives of drudgery," these young women were being educated for lives of service, through teaching or missionary work.

In her 1845 poem, "On Compositions," Lucy Putnam summed up the challenges of writing in a context where the ideal servant is an angel:

> Oh dear what a real vexation
> It is to write a composition;
> It fills the mind with words and phrases
> and my poor heart almost it crazes
> But for all of that, away I must write
> For this comp must be done ere Saturday night.
>
> I do not wish to puzzle my brains
> in trying to equate angelic strains
> To try to be something more than I am

is truly beyond the reach of man
But for all of that away I must write
Till the tardy strikes on Saturday night

Putnam's poem describes a rhetorical situation replete with contradictions—
trying to be "angelic" when she's only human, overcoming writing anxiety in
the face of a deadline, being creative on a timetable of "tardy" bells. The first
stanza suggests the emptiness of an assignment that fills her mind with
"words and phrases" disconnected from experiences or thoughts and
certainly removed from her poor, almost crazed heart. Putnam resists the
"angelic strains" expected from her as truly beyond any human's reach and
manages to set aside these hurdles for the seminary's rule that four hours be
devoted to writing before the bell rings. Despite the delightful humor, I hear
a writer searching for a purpose, a reason for writing other than to fulfill an
academic requirement.

The Subjectless Theme

If we assume that writing requires a certain amount of authority even to
produce text, this sub-genre in which the writer admits defeat paradoxically
offered a form of authority not available in other topics. Who could
challenge an individual's experience? Let's look closely at Laura Millett's
1850 essay, a fine specimen of this sub-genre, which more explicitly than
most catalogues the topics she could not address, and implicitly states the
qualities of a good college writer:

> "One of my Trials"
>
> A composition I must have. The circumstances of my situation are
> such, that if in a week from this time, I do not present to my teacher
> fifty lines of my own thoughts I must lay aside all my customary duties
> and employments and devote all my faculties to this object until the
> desired result is obtained. But this is not the worst. I must arise
> before all my companions, and while a profound silence pervades
> the assembly, confess to the chief magistrate of this "goodly house"
> that I, not in ignorance, but with a complete knowledge of all the
> consequences of my guilt, having witnessed its dreadful effects
> among my friends, that I, in defiance of all rules, have been delin-
> quent in composition.
>
> You may say, I see nothing so dreadful in the requirement, at which
> I seem so much disposed to murmur. Fifty lines in a week, only six
> or seven in a day, and I have spoken as though this slight effort was

entirely beyond my powers. Don't be so foolish, as to make such an ado about nothing.

But I have only eight hours in which to accomplish my task, and two of them have already slipped away in a fruitless search for a subject. The animal, vegetable, and mineral kingdoms have all of them been searched for a theme, upon which I might place my thoughts long enough to be able to write something, which if not instructive, might at least be interesting to my hearers.

If I speak of the beautiful Spring, with its buds and blossoms, its singing birds and ripply streams, I must have the pen of the enthusiastic poet to touch a chord in your breasts, which shall vibrate in unison with the beauty around us, so long have we been accustomed to witness its beauties unheeded that nothing but an eloquent tongue can move us now.

Were I to attempt to sketch for you the character and describe the life of one of the great and renowned of ancient time, I could tell you of nothing save that of which you are already better acquainted perhaps than myself. That lively imagination is not mine, which can so array its heroes in the gossamer web of fiction, as to cause one to forget the real in the ideal, so to be occupied with the embellishments of my story, as to heed but little, how far I may wander from that, which can beat the test of truth.

Of those persons who are now upon the stage of life many motives would operate, to cause me to remain silent. If I were to speak of Mr. Webster, I might be addressing both his friends and enemies and whatever view I might take of his character, I should not fail to awaken in the breasts of some dissonant emotions.

Of the many interesting subjects now before the public mind I shall also remain silent. The dissolution or nondissolution of the Union is a matter of too deep an interest to be discussed by a schoolgirl remote from the Congressional Halls.

The mysterious 'knockings' and 'throwings' upon which those whose minds are wont to be filled with the marvelous are now bestowing so much attention have been the subject of so much ridicule and again of grave debate that my feeble opinion can be of little weight in so weighty and important a decision as from whence these sounds originate.

Of subjects of a philosophical or metaphysical nature, I will not exhaust your patience, by attempting to prove my utter inability to discourse concerning them. If you are not already convinced that I cannot write a composition, no arguments of mine will be able to convince you. Does not the compelling of one to think and what is more expressing those thoughts, partake more of the barbarism of the dark ages than the refinements of this enlightened nineteenth century?

Alas for me, that I have not the 'pen of a ready writer' then would all these trials vanish away, like the mist before the rising sun. (1 June 1850)

By constructing a reader unfamiliar with the disciplinary and curricular practices at Mount Holyoke, Millett positions herself as guide to this world of student writing, authorizing herself in relationship to that subject. Yet despite Millett's authority on the topic of writing student themes, the bulk of the essay bows to her fictive (or real) reader, who knows more than the writer about history, public events, and metaphysics. Given the ways Millett disqualifies herself from addressing certain topics, we can infer the traits she thinks characteristic of a good writer or the ideals she's been taught. Millett's ideal of a lady, or at least one she describes in another composition, is "the most lovely and *useful* woman" ("A Chapter from the Journal of a Letter Box," 24 November 1849; emphasis added).

For Millett, a college composition required the writer to be knowledgeable, able to stir up controversy, naturally talented, and willing to display her abilities. To produce an effective composition, the writer must be a poet, with a "lively imagination" in order to recreate emotions and responses in the reader or to entertain. If the purpose of the essay is to address current issues, then the writer must have a deep interest in the topic and be close enough to the subject to report authoritatively. The paragraph on writing about famous people indicates that the writer must be unafraid of offending readers. Even when the writer does have a "feeble opinion" on a topic, such as the spiritualism of the day, Millett positions her views as insignificant. Finally, if the purpose of the theme is to be persuasive, then Millett's performance must be judged in that context, as artlessly, guilelessly moving the reader to recognize her conviction that she "cannot write a composition." This last move ironically places her essay's clear organization and eloquent language as a specimen of her negative abilities.

But perhaps here Millett is mocking the requirements of academic writing. Millett's comparison of the writing requirement with "barbarism of the dark ages [rather] than the refinements of this enlightened nineteenth century" may be more tongue-in-cheek than serious, or may indicate a feeling of being on trial, forced to testify to her importance and intelligence through her writing. Or she may be showing that some of the "barbarism" Mount Holyoke missionaries were trained to convert or stamp out in other people was also present in those hallowed halls.

Consistently, Millett's attention is with the reader's response, a concern necessary to anyone socialized to serve, where being attentive to the ones you serve and waiting for their summons are key. Here, Millett wants to be "at least . . . interesting to my hearers," to "move" them, and "to cause one to forget the real in the ideal." The writer is just as clear on what she hopes to avoid: "awaken[ing] . . . dissonant emotions," offering her "feeble opinion . . . of little weight in so weighty and important a decision," "exhaust[ing] your patience." Millett may have been so concerned about readers' responses because students at Mount Holyoke actually read their compositions aloud in their sections. This oral delivery of themes meant that a writer received immediate responses and that all writing was funneled through existing filters and censorious views of *women* performing, thus adding a layer of analysis (and anxiety) to the composing process. As Millett notes in her first paragraph, at Mount Holyoke, even *failure* to write was a performance.

Performance tensions for women weren't confined within college walls, however, as Theodora Martin's description of nineteenth-century women's study clubs, *The Sound of Our Own Voices,* illustrates. For white middle-class women hoping to improve their education, attending a weekly club took courage. For example, Harriet J. Robinson "attended her first meeting and noted in her diary that it was the first time in twenty years that she had spent an evening away from her husband, Tom. . . . It was not until April 1871, two years after she joined the New England Women's Club that Robinson revealed in her diary that she had spoken at a club meeting for the first time" (Martin 79). Robinson's two-year silence in her women's club suggests how powerful a fear of intellectual display or even sharing can be in the face of impending challenge or judgment. Her experience also makes the MHFS students' weekly oral and written performances seem downright courageous.

Recitation and oral delivery of compositions was standard pedagogy at colleges for men as well. Gerald Graff argues that this feature of the "old classical college" was one students found valuable: "Here the student felt that he was engaging in an activity which would be of immediate practical value in later life. A large proportion of the students would one day enter law, politics, or the ministry, callings in which oratorical powers were essential" (42). Because women did not enter these professions, though, the oratory of classical pedagogy either had to be shaped to their own ends or performed with little motivation beyond the requirements of the immediate situation.

As Millett considers the reasons she cannot participate in certain rhetorical acts, she finds her usefulness diminished for a number of reasons, not least of which is her gender. The characters from "ancient time" that Millett could discuss in her theme were most likely "great and renowned" men studied in school, whose gender might contribute to the writer's lack of "lively imagination" to discuss their lives. When dismissing "subjects now before the public mind" Millett describes herself as a "schoolgirl remote from the Congressional halls," thus highlighting and gendering the distance between public matters and academic ones. Even the province traditionally defined as woman's, the sentimental observation of nature's beauty, had been professionally treated so that an ordinary writer could not hope to move her reader.

Millett's dismissal of commonplace topics and deprecation of her own abilities (which is belied by her written performance) indicate a satiric stance all the more remarkable when situated in the context of the seminary, with its atmosphere of discipline, discipleship, and decorum. Finding a crack in a surface of deep seriousness, Millett reveals her academic acumen most in the essay's playful tone and challenging conclusion, rhetorical moves that place her on the inside of academe.

The Context of Composing

In the period between 1837, the beginning of Mount Holyoke, and 1865, the opening of Vassar College, Mount Holyoke Female Seminary occupied an important place in white women's education in the Northeast. Mount Holyoke's curriculum was similar to that of other seminaries, such as Emma Willard's in Troy, New York, and Catharine Beecher's Hartford Female Seminary, where students were also trained to be teachers, but Mary Lyon made education at Mount Holyoke affordable to women from a lower economic class, primarily by hiring no servants and having students perform all the domestic chores. To the routines and practices she had experienced at Zilpah Grant's Ipswich Female Seminary, Lyon added the requirement that all students contribute to the upkeep of the institution by working an hour a day and longer on Wednesdays, when classes were suspended so students could attend to more time-consuming tasks and recreation.

Although there is little written evidence of Mary Lyon's theory of writing or pedagogy, student reports indicate that Lyon viewed writing as a transcription of speech and urged her students to trust their own experiences and language. This pragmatic approach suited students who would graduate to serve their churches and communities. One student reported that Lyon used to say, "Commence your topic with a brief sentence. Let none of your periods be long. Avoid the use of the copulative conjunction 'and.' State your ideas and facts clearly and consecutively, not in the words of the book, but in your own best English. Aim to speak smoothly, not with hitches and jerks. Stop when you have done" (Gilchrist 379).

The actual English curriculum was traditional; in the three-year program, Samuel Newman's rhetoric was used in the middle class, Richard Whately's *Elements of Logic* and *Elements of Rhetoric* in the senior year. Yet the intended effects of studying rhetoric and composition went beyond increasing the students' literacy skills. Nan Johnson argues that the New Rhetoric of the nineteenth-century claimed that "the study and practice of rhetoric benefits the individual and society" (60), and perhaps women reading these texts could imagine such benefits. As an early catalogue suggests, the mature women MHFS targeted and attracted would benefit most from their senior studies if they studied Latin, French, Drawing, and Music first, deferring the more sober subjects, such as Whately's *Rhetoric,* as late as possible: "But let young ladies enter on their Senior year under the conviction that it is really the last year of their pupilage, and let them have the companionship of a class of as much age and maturity as such a standing in the Institution demands, and if they are not too young for sober reflection, more can be expected from its influence on their intellectual growth, on the strengthening of their moral principles, and in the cultivation of the heart, than in any ordinary circumstances" (1847–48 catalogue). Thus social effects on learning were acknowledged. Life impinged also on students who had to interrupt their program to work and earn money, to take care of sick parents, and so on. (David Allmendinger notes that one quarter of the graduates took four years to complete the three-year program, which suggests they had difficulties.) Mount Holyoke's curriculum had to suit students variously prepared, and as one woman put it, "If anyone wants to get a thorough education, come to South Hadley, I say. You cannot fail of being thorough. Every fourth lesson is a review" (Lennan, 8 January 1852).

Mary Lyon's strict disciplinary code involved self-reporting and a system of bells to indicate when it was time for the next activity. Lucy Putnam wrote in a letter, "Every day all assemble before their division teachers to tell if they have transgressed; if they have they make acknowledgment and are pardoned." She relays the rationale—"I suppose where there are so many it is necessary to keep them under some restraint"—and also critiques it—"but I think in some points they are too severe." The act of criticizing was not treated lightly, however, as Putnam adds, "Miss Lyon says we must not criticise teachers and laws: so I must be careful what I write" (11 October 1845). This comment suggests that student writing, even letters home, was carefully monitored. Another woman explained the elaborate bell system, which changed seasonally, in a letter to a friend who was thinking of applying for admission:

> The bells at first plagued me very much indeed. Would you like a
> list of them for a day? 4:45, 5:15, 5:45 rising bell. 6 tardy bell. 6:15,
> 6:25 five minutes bell. 6:30 breakfast. 7, 7:15, 7:30, 8, 8:30. 9:30
> devotions. 10, 10:30, 11, 11:30, 12, 12:15, 12:25, five min. 12:30
> dinner. 1:15, 1:45, 2:15, 2:30, 2:45, 3:15, 3:45, 4:15, 4:30, 5 exer-
> cises close and till 6 is recreation hour and then you can enter rooms
> till the supper bell. I told you wrong above, 5:30, 5:45, 5:55 five min.
> 6 supper, 7, 7:30, 8, 8:15, 8:45, 9, 9:15, 9:45 retiring bell 10 tardy
> bell. Don't you think it would somewhat puzzle a *novice* to keep the
> *run* of so many bells? We used to run at every bell, but we have got
> used to them and we know just when we ought to go to any exer-
> cise. (Susan Lennan, 8 January 1852; punctuation regularized)

The disciplinary system of Mount Holyoke Female Seminary must have
affected the students' writing processes. Being "delinquent in composition"
was one of a number of weaknesses of character that required a confession
before the assembly. Susan Lennan described the system thus: "You must not
be absent from church nor delinquent in Composition. These are called
recorded items. Every Sat. you must spend four hours on Composition. This
is as unalterable as law of Medes and Persians" (8 January 1852). And
perhaps as foreign to these women.

The significance of not meeting a teacher's expectations or fulfilling an
assignment with ease may be lost on those of us accustomed to the demands
of academic success. For these early college women, not being successful
reflected on all women as well as on their individual worth as human beings
placed on earth to serve God. One student, Lydia Baldwin, described the
hours slipping away as she attempted to find a topic that "seemed to furnish
me with that field of thought which is necessary for the commencement of
this arduous undertaking." Having missed a week already, Baldwin could not
let another week go by without producing something, in part because she
didn't want to appear before her teacher and classmates without "the
required document." But also weighing "heavily upon my spirits" was the
"consciousness of having misspent so many precious hours and thereby
incurring the righteous displeasure of Him, from whose hand I had received
every blessing." The religious discourse that infuses this essay raised the
stakes of writing block so that it not only brought personal distress and
dishonor upon the writer but reflected on her spiritual progress as well.
Baldwin used her experience as a negative example of scholarly behavior: "I
therefore determined to give a brief account of what had been my bad
experience, in hopes that it might prove a timely warning to all who might
listen to the sad tale" (4 June 1844).

This frequent conclusion from a sadder but wiser writer turned her painful experience into an object lesson that might benefit others. Caroline Field resolved "to give an account of my trials, and warn others, not to wander about with such a dissatisfied mind as I had done, lest some worse fate should overtake them" ("Unsuccessful," no date). The telling thus fulfilled three purposes: (1) it offered a subject upon which the writer could be a knowledgeable expert, a necessary quality for the academic writer; (2) it portrayed her vulnerabilities and struggles with intellectual success, thus fulfilling the culture's requirements for a "true" woman; (3) it turned a seemingly arbitrary composing exercise into something useful to someone else. The frequency and skill with which this type of essay was written also attests to women's ability to make something from what others might discard (rather like quilting).

Inventing a Proper Subject

The two worlds Mount Holyoke students negotiated honored different ways of knowing, different forms of wisdom or knowledge, and required different processes of the writers. Because invention is an act of authorization in which the writer must grant herself authority to discuss a subject in a certain manner from an accepted perspective, many of the issues of authority raised in these essays can be traced to the theory of invention prevalent in the nineteenth century. This theory offered little real instruction to students and made composition one of the most dreaded courses in the curriculum. Within a rhetorical tradition, invention has been defined as a process that helps the writer or speaker generate and then select topics and lines of argument. Aristotle, for instance, catalogued *topoi* that would help a rhetor consider any number of commonplaces to find ideas to support his argument. The emphasis in invention was on the subject matter, and the rhetor's relationship to the material and his audience was assumed to be somewhat stable, largely because this theory of invention assumed a homogeneous group of speakers and listeners whose shared values and experiences would facilitate a persuasive communicative act. Sources for the invention problems of nineteenth-century student writers centered on the two main resources they were expected to bring with them into the writing classroom: genius and knowledge. A textbook's emphasis on genius left writers with only themselves to blame if they had trouble composing.

Genius was considered not only a masculine domain, but a solitary attribute, supporting the academy's concept of the self as autonomous.

Harvard student Frederic H. Viaux states the view baldly in his theme
"Cooperative societies": "Man is naturally independent in character. It is only
the debased and degenerate in mind that lean upon the shoulders of others.
The true man takes pride in depending upon no other hands but his own for
the means of his existence" (6 November 1868).

Mount Holyoke student Lucy Flint personifies the "bright genius" of
composition as a male who has yet to make her acquaintance, despite her
attempts to find him. In one essay, she invokes genius: "Yes, come e'en now
while this sheet lies outspread before me in all its appalling whiteness"
("Composition," 12 February 1842). In another essay, her speaker goes out
on the grounds to find this genius and notices others doing the same: "As I
passed them they started and a tinge of disappointment was visible for they
were courting the genius of composition and were just ready to lay hold of
him, when they saw it was only me. Their pencil dropped and I hastened on
unwilling to witness such disappointment without the power of alleviating
it." In this instance, not only do the powers of genius elude Flint in her own
composing, but she hasn't the ability to prevent suffering in others. It would
appear from this narrative that Flint cannot turn her experience into a service
to others, and yet the extended analysis of genius might offer comfort to
readers who also feel genius has passed them by. That gender has something
to do with her relationship to genius is clear in a description of her
encounter: "He looked at me with such a playful smile I was almost ready to
extend the hand of friendship when I recollected the dignity of my sex and
was about to retire" (2 July 1842). The notion of genius as masculine and
working in solitude was emphasized in the structure of the Mount Holyoke
timetable and study suggestions, but worked against those connected
knowers who needed more collaborative invention to compose successfully.

The concept of genius implicitly carried implications of social class that
excluded these students, who were mostly from rural, farming, lower-income
backgrounds. Although enrolled students represented a range of family
wealth, most students came from families of modest means: "more than one-
third came from families whose real estate in 1850 was valued at $2,000 or
less. More than half came from families listing real estate worth $3,000 or
less; estates of this size were below the average value of estates in mature
farming areas at midcentury" (Allmendinger 30). Flint's genius informs her
that he will visit her more often "if you prove yourself worthy," but she does
not discuss the criteria for such worthiness.

And even though the other requirement of invention, knowledge, was a
more social resource that students could use in academic writing, these

writers conveyed an unease with bringing familiar metaphors and practices from the private sphere of home with them into the public sphere of schooling. In "Unsuccessful" Caroline Field begins to develop topics such as "a steamboat" or "an old shoe." but abandons them for "no particular reason." Devoting herself to the "dreaded business of composition making," Field compares her invention process to a domestic task: "I began poking over my brain something in the manner that some housewives would an everything basket but could find nothing to match the subjects on the paper." After "shaking up my nearly empty idea box," Field decides to postpone the process for another week, hoping she "can find something to read upon the subject" that will help her produce "a comp as good as will be expected from me."

Not wanting to disappoint beloved teachers, or to appear foolish or unintelligent before their peers, these writers had enormous pressure to perform well. Without more writing instruction, though, a successful performance seemed capricious, dependent upon the right topic rather than the writer's skills. Field found "no great deficiency in quantity" of topics, only in "quality." Her roommate suggested that she try "the power of a thought," but Field, sitting down to write the night before the composition was due, dismissed it, for she "should want a fortnight to think of that, and now I have not even twenty-four hours." Field blames her "dissatisfied mind" for her writing block. Similarly, Louise Fiske records that "we wish to produce something which will not be a disgrace to our mental powers, but all attempts on any subject seem to prove utterly futile and so we toil not withstanding discouragements until reminded by the bell not to be delinquent, and then hastily close, dissatisfied with composition, with ourselves, and every one else" ("A Rainy Day," 3 October 1863).

Such attention to one's intelligence seems natural enough in an environment where studies stretched the intellectual experiences and capacities of women students and gave them an opportunity to reconsider their intellects. Susan Lennan's 1853 letter to a friend thinking of applying to Mount Holyoke indicates the intellectual excitement her education offered. Lennan mentions that algebra "has done me the most good in the way of thoroughly exercising my brains, of anything I ever studied," and she explains how the grammar they used at MHFS would make the one she studied before seem like "nothing more than the Alphabet" (8 January 1852). Along with this intellectual excitement came the students' surprise at how intelligence was measured at school and doubts about their own intellectual

abilities. Martha Walker's 1841 theme, for example, personifies the faculties
of the mind, as she examines a tendency among Mount Holyoke students:

> The powers of mind exercised in writing compositions most of all
> the faculties deserve our pity and condolence. We need only to esti-
> mate their worth and be acquainted with the almost numberless
> faults of which they are unjustly accused to have our tenderest sym-
> pathy awake in their behalf. One would think from the unsparing
> abuse cast upon them that they were really undesirable occupants.
> But who would be willing to dismiss them? I often wonder that their
> patience is not quite exhausted and that they do not refuse to bring
> forth one idea, when after being taxed to the utmost and having pre-
> sented their choicest treasures, they meet with a contemptuous
> repulse, and if received at all it is but to model or rather mangle over
> an amalgamate with those of another, or if written as presented by
> them, when exposed to the criticism of others the crimson cheek and
> trembling voice convey the conviction more forcibly than words of
> an unworthy author.
>
> Were I fully persuaded that my production was inferior to all oth-
> ers it should not want the essentials of being my own and a confi-
> dence that it was worthy the hearing of others. Let us rather than
> indulge in reproving thoughts be grateful for and diligent in improv-
> ing the talents committed to us knowing that to only such is the
> promise of greater things given. (1841)

Walker appeals to traditional feminine qualities of sympathy as she turns
her theme into a teaching moment and observes the estranged relationship
between women and their minds, which are "occupants" in their heads and
not extensions of themselves. This mind/body dichotomy, while still
institutionalized today, was an explicitly gendered distinction in the
nineteenth century. Indeed, Mark Hopkins's preference for "possessed of
accomplishments" rather than "accomplished" suggests that women should
be considered separate from their intellectual gifts, rather than identified with
them and wielding their power. In the above essay, Martha Walker's opinion
that she needs no justification for writing other than that the words are hers is
unusual, and drew the approval of her teacher, who wrote in the margin
"that's right."

Lists of titles suggested for composition supplied by Mary Lyon and other
teachers show the range of subjects considered suitable for these female
student writers, but why an individual student selected certain topics over
others is more difficult to determine. Mary McLean (class of 1852) compiled
a notebook of suggested topics from her own student days, most likely when
she was preparing to teach: there were many suggestions from the Bible
("Esther," "Daughter of Herodias," "Joseph's desire for home"); possible

subjects from home ("I miss my home," "My Grandmother's Upper Drawer," "My First Companion"); philosophical choices ("Action, the law of Nature," "How little we know," "The teachings of reason"); opportunities to observe ("A rainy day," "the human voice," "a drop of water"), to reminisce ("Alas, poor Dolly!", "Memory," "My Sister's Grave"), and to imagine ("Will the dead know us?", "A visit to the planet Saturn," "Dialogue between Selfishness and Benevolence," "Thoughts of an Infant"). And among the several hundred phrases there were many titles designed to help the young women think of their place in society: "Odd minutes: some estimate as to the amount of such minutes in a given time: methods of improving them gracefully and profitably, especially for young ladies: examples of persons who have done this"; "A perfect lady"; "The Requisite Qualifications for a Good Wife"; "Young Ladies' Compositions. Why are they no better than they are at present? Why are they not equal to young gentleman's? Why do not young ladies take more pains with theirs?" (McLean, *Holyoke Scrapbook)*. That the gloss on composing was so much more detailed than that on being a good wife may indicate how new the role of student writer was for women.

Taking up the challenge of the topic "Young Ladies Compositions," Laura Millett echoes the prompting question "how do the productions of young ladies of equal attainments with young gentleman compare?" She writes:

> We are obliged to yield the palm of victory to young gentlemen. But why is this? Have not young ladies the same mental endowments or has nature bestowed her choicest gifts on the other sex? I think not. There have been gifted females enough to prove that we as a sex are not destitute of mental powers. We have only ourselves to blame, for our general inferiority. Our natural indolence, and the aversion of the human mind to prolonged mental effort is the only obstacle. This obstacle our brothers know they must overcome if they wish to possess any influence in the world. And should we not overcome them also. . . .
>
> This subject suggests to us two or three reflections. Young ladies do not write in a manner equal to their abilities. Is it not wrong for them to waste the talents, a benevolent Creator has bestowed upon them, to be used to his own glory? Are we not required to return them improved, not merely preserved? We see also if we wish to improve our talents, we must use them. We must not be content with our present attainments, but must press forward, striving every day, with increased vigor to obtain a cultivated mind. (27 October 1849)

Millett is quick to point out that this mental strength will not be selfishly used, and her appeal to the common good allows her to combine woman's traditional role of service with her new status as college student entitled to reach her intellectual potential. By placing the blame for their lack of accomplishments on women, Millett grants them agency to change that situation by locating their strength in their own abilities to persevere and study. Yet she also avoids interrogating the institutions and cultural practices that have constructed "woman" as fearful of her mind. Her concluding direct speech to those who may not fully appreciate the weekly composition warns her listeners to be aware of gaps between their performance and their ability. Here, reliance on religious discourse plays on her listeners' sense of duty to use their potential and offers a Christian path of hard work to deliver the mediocre student. How much of the expressed lack of self-confidence was simply a part of being a student and how much came from being socialized as a woman?

Invention and Male Writers

On the basis of the approximately 100 themes I examined at Harvard and Amherst written during this same period, male students seemed to write less frequently about the difficulty of finding a topic, perhaps because they were not expected to have difficulties or, if they did, not to reveal them. But occasionally themes by male students did address the difficulty of finding a subject. Lee Max Friedman, for instance, writing daily themes in a Harvard upper-level English course, describes an upcoming football game which he hopes will provide "subjects for two weeks of daily themes. Of course I shall be too much excited watching the game to get subjects during the playing, but think of my opportunity in the train. I shall get a character sketch from the man opposite me, a funny story from the man besides me, while some little incident in the train will afford a subject for 'a joke I saw a few days ago'" (21 November 1891). Reflecting the same theory of language as Mary Lyon, that in writing one transmits thoughts to paper without any translation, interpretation, or change, Friedman nonetheless seems to find the search for subjects challenging rather than demoralizing:

> The search for subjects for daily themes is interesting. If any story or anecdote is told to a crowd of fellows, some one is sure to call out 'copyright.' That gives him the exclusive right to dress up the story for a daily. Then again a fellow sets all his friends to collect suitable material for him, or he wanders around Cambridge with a hope like Mr. Micawber 'that something will turn up.' Muckers have a peculiar interest to an English 12 man. He follows them around, a listener

> to their conversations in the hope that they will say something bright.
> He looks around the town with an eagle's eye for a 'little touch of
> nature.' Truly the lot of the writer of daily themes is a happy one!
> (17 December 1891)

Overall, Friedman seems less focused on how he is perceived by the
reader than on the challenge of finding so many topics for daily themes. The
scarcity of composition subjects seems to have provided an opportunity to
compete with other men, a sentiment not expressed in the women's themes.
(What woman could follow a "mucker" around town?) Friedman's catalogue
of inventional devices also seems more social than the women's. His
conclusion may be as ironic as the women's pleas for pity, but he transforms
the student position into a challenge he can meet with the help of friends.
His instructor, Barrett Wendell, responded with the comment, "the course is
fulfilling its purpose," likely referring to the building of character as well as
writing skills.

Perhaps the most distinct difference between the men's and women's
themes lies in their treatment of genius. Recall that Millett and Flint worried
that genius would pass them by and tried to be worthy of his attentions.
Friedman, in contrast, takes the professor to task for assigning a sonnet, for
which the writer has "not a speck of inspiration." He writes:

> I think it was decidedly unfair for Mr. Wendell to demand such a
> thing. In the first place writing poetry has no place in the course. Sec-
> ondly, he has demanded something that is a gift in man. A man can-
> not acquire the art of writing poetry either by 'grinding' or practice.
> He might as well require each man to write music. Furthermore,
> granted that every man can write something that will pass amongst
> kind hearted friends for poetry, a man cannot write whenever he is
> called upon. He must be in a certain mood. This mood may not come
> for months, so to demand a poem by a certain day, no matter how
> much time for preparation be given, is unfair. And finally, why a son-
> net? Not every man who can write poetry can write a sonnet. To write
> a sonnet requires a peculiar genius. Tennyson has never written a suc-
> cessful sonnet. (26 January 1892)

Calling the assignment unfair is a very different move from sharing a
personal struggle to compose. At no point does Friedman acknowledge that
he lacks the "gift" of poetic genius. External conditions are to blame: the
assignment was unfair, composing poetry requires a mood, good sonnets
require peculiar genius. Friedman refers to "a man" and "every man" to
make his point and contextualizes his own composing difficulties by
invoking the company of Tennyson.

One man whose search for subjects seems more reminiscent of the women's searches acknowledged, "I have exceedingly hard work to select subjects for my daily themes." Cecil Herbert Burdett believed that "when you come to write, you want a subject possessing dignity or importance," and he was eager to avoid recording anything "very commonplace." This desire was complicated by his professor's remark during a lecture "that our subjects shall be commonplace, the more so the better." Further, Burdett had received that very comment on one of his themes, and he wrote to Wendell, asking if he meant his description as praise or as meaning "hackneyed and trite," in which case Burdett could see "no ground however for such a criticism." He ended his daily by asking, "which of these two interpretations is right?" (20 November 1886). There is nothing like this interaction in the women's writing, perhaps because the classes were small enough to ask the instructor face to face, or perhaps because such questioning might have been too direct an affront to their esteemed teachers.

In a later theme Burdett seems bereft of invention techniques other than to "sit and think and think" with the poor results that "the longer I think the harder it is to find anything" (15 December 1886). Burdett's resolution of this problem, however, differs from strategies employed by the women at MHFS, who sometimes chose to be delinquent in composition rather than commit something unsuitable to paper. Burdett writes:

> So I sit and think and think, and the longer I think the harder it is to find anything. If I only could keep the fact in mind that I was on the lookout for subjects and could catch the casual points on the fly and treasured them up for future use it would be all right but what with lecture, examination, reading, and the thousand and one things a man has to do, this thing is liable to escape him. But at the end of ten minutes I get disgusted and take the weather as a subject and write abominably about it or when there isn't anything in that line I fall back on the question "ever new and ever fresh" politics. (15 December 1886)

Making fun of his "ever new and ever fresh" standby, Burdett occupies the position of man about town who comments on national issues, something few women seemed willing to do. Like the women students who described the composing process as arduous, even painful, Burdett concludes that "a subject must come anyway and somebody or something has to suffer for it." Here, though, Burdett is less concerned with his reader's appraisal of him as a writer and thinker than with getting the process over.

Finding Purpose in Service-Learning

Imagine how the self-consciousness evident in many of these Mount Holyoke essays might have been relieved or eliminated had their writing filled a larger community need. In *The Call of Service,* Robert Coles celebrates the lives of people such as six-year-old Tessie, who, in integrating a New Orleans school, "connected a civic moment in her life with a larger ideal, and in so doing had learned to regard herself as a servant, as a person 'called to service'" (6). Coles argues that such a calling offers focus, courage, and purpose and allows a person to come through difficult challenges with grace and increased strength. While we may balk at MHFS's explicit emphasis on missionary work, these nineteenth-century students demonstrate how important it is that academic work be connected to a purpose. Indeed, writers who wanted their "section sisters" to learn from their invention difficulties met a need they had experienced firsthand. There was little distance between the server and the served. (Of course, writing teachers have long known that assignments with a stated audience and purpose invite better writing.)

Today's service-learning movement linking voluntary community service with academic study has grown in the past decade to cross disciplines, institutional types, geographic locations, and staff and faculty ranks. It is arguably the most important educational movement since its ancestor, the progressive education movement (Saltmarsh 13). The very name *service-learning* identifies the goal of connecting two groups, campus and community, in a reciprocally beneficial relationship. Thoughtful service-learning provides a concrete connection to community that allows students to understand theory, history, and literature in broader contexts and to use their developing academic abilities in immediate projects.

The benefits of service-learning for students' academic performance, sense of civic responsibility, and personal esteem continue to be documented. The role of writing, however, as a tool for learning and reflecting upon the service experience has been less critically examined. In "Community Service and Critical Teaching," Bruce Herzberg describes the writing course in which his privileged students tutor adults in a Boston shelter and argues that "writing personal responses to community service experiences is an important part of processing the experience, but it is not sufficient to raise critical or cultural consciousness" (309). Herzberg suggests that a broader understanding of the social issues that created the need for the volunteer experience in the first place must be systematically developed in order for students to frame their experiences critically.

When I think about the Mount Holyoke women and the experiences they went through as the first generation of American women to attend college, I wonder how their writing might have changed had their academic courses systematically studied the place of women in history, and their writing assignments invited their experiences onto the page. For even though the Mount Holyoke teachers seemed far more receptive to reading students' experiences than professors at Radcliffe College, for instance, and mundane topics seemed more welcome at MHFS than at other women's colleges, such as Wellesley, the challenges nineteenth-century women faced in moving into a traditionally masculine domain recur across institutions and decades (see my "Controlling Voices" and "Freshman [sic] English").

What if these writers had been urged to connect with their communities rather than remove themselves from South Hadley and one another? Mary Lyon wanted her students to maintain their service orientation and become strong academically, but the institution she founded was seen as less academically rigorous than later women's colleges, such as Vassar College, which explicitly refused to prepare students for practical service like teaching. The academic reputation of Mount Holyoke suffered because of the privileging of the standard of the autonomous scholar. That same valuing of individual performance over collaborative problem-solving exists today. As Edward Zlotkowski writes, "What is at stake—what must be at stake—if service-learning is to have a future, is nothing less than a transformation of contemporary academic culture: the transformation of a set of elitist, self-referential academic assumptions into what the American Association of Higher Education's 1995 national conference characterized as 'the engaged campus'" (130). Nineteenth-century Mount Holyoke writers such as Lucy Putnam and Laura Millett suggest that providing opportunities to engage in real work may be the ultimate teaching challenge. Teachers who lessen their students' performance anxieties, help them discover and then share their gifts, and honor knowledge from outside academe not only develop good writers but also help to serve a much larger community.

Works Cited

Allmendinger, David F., Jr. "Mount Holyoke Students Encounter the Need for Life-Planning, 1837–1850." *History of Education Quarterly* 19 (Spring 1979): 27–46.

Baldwin, Lydia. Papers. Mount Holyoke College Archives and Special Collections, South Hadley, MA.

Burdett, Cecil Herbert. Papers. Harvard University Archives, Cambridge, MA.

Campbell, JoAnn. "Controlling Voices: The Legacy of English A at Radcliffe College 1883–1917." *College Composition and Communication* 43 (1992): 472–85.

———. "Freshman [sic] English: A 1901 Wellesley College 'Girl' Negotiates Authority." *Rhetoric Review* 15 (Fall 1996): 110–27.

Coles, Robert. *The Call of Service, a Witness to Idealism.* Boston: Houghton Mifflin, 1993.

Conrad, Susan. *Perish the Thought: Intellectual Women in Romantic America 1830–1860.* New York: Oxford UP, 1976.

Field, Caroline. Papers. Mount Holyoke College Archives and Special Collections, South Hadley, MA.

Fiske, Louise. Papers. Mount Holyoke College Archives and Special Collections, South Hadley, MA.

Flint, Lucy. Papers. Mount Holyoke College Archives and Special Collections, South Hadley, MA.

Friedman, L. M. Papers. Harvard University Archives, Cambridge, MA.

Gilbert, Sandra M., and Susan Gubar. *The Madwoman in the Attic: The Woman Writer and the Nineteenth-Century Literary Imagination.* New Haven: Yale UP, 1979.

Gilchrist, Beth. *The Life of Mary Lyon.* Boston: Houghton Mifflin, 1910.

Graff, Gerald. *Professing Literature: An Institutional History.* Chicago: U of Chicago P, 1987.

Green, Elizabeth Alden. *Mary Lyon and Mount Holyoke: Opening the Gates.* Hanover, NH: UP of New England, 1979.

Herzberg, Bruce. "Community Service and Critical Teaching." *College Composition and Communication* 45.3 (October 1994): 307–19.

Hopkins, Mark. "An Address, delivered in South Hadley, Mass, July 30, 1840 at the third anniversary of the Mount Holyoke Female Seminary." Published by request of the Trustees, Northampton. Printed by J. Metcalf, 1840.

Inness, Sherrie A. "'Repulsive as the multitudes by whom I am surrounded': Constructing the Contact Zone in the Writings of Mount Holyoke Missionaries, 1830–1890." *Women's Studies* 23 (1994): 365–84.

Johnson, Nan. *Nineteenth-Century Rhetoric in North America.* Carbondale: Southern Illinois UP, 1991.

Lennan, Susan. Papers. Mount Holyoke College Archives and Special Collections, South Hadley, MA.

Martin, Theodora Penny. *The Sound of Our Own Voices: Women's Study Clubs 1860–1910.* Boston: Beacon P, 1987.

McLean, Mary. Papers. Mount Holyoke College Archives and Special Collections, South Hadley, MA.

Millett, Laura. Papers. Mount Holyoke College Archives and Special Collections, South Hadley, MA.

Mount Holyoke Female Seminary Catalogue. 1847–1848. Mount Holyoke College Archives and Special Collections, South Hadley, MA.

Putnam, Lucy. Papers. Mount Holyoke College Archives and Special Collections, South Hadley, MA.

Saltmarsh, John. "Education for Critical Citizenship: John Dewey's Contribution to the Pedagogy of Community Service Learning." *Michigan Journal of Community Service Learning* Fall 1996: 13–21.

Snell, Ada F. "History of English Studies in Mount Holyoke Seminary and College 1837–1937." Unpublished typescript, 1942. English Department Records. Mount Holyoke College Archives and Special Collections, South Hadley, MA.

Viaux, Frederic H. Papers. Harvard University Archives, Cambridge, MA.

Walker, Martha. Papers. Mount Holyoke College Archives and Special Collections, South Hadley, MA.

Wheaton, Mandana Adela. Papers. Mount Holyoke College Archives and Special Collections, South Hadley, MA.

Zlotkowski, Edward. "Does Service-Learning Have a Future?" *Michigan Journal of Community Service Learning* Fall 1995: 123–33.

This book was set in Optima and Trajan by
City Desktop Productions.
The typeface used on the cover was Trajan.
The book was printed by Versa Press.